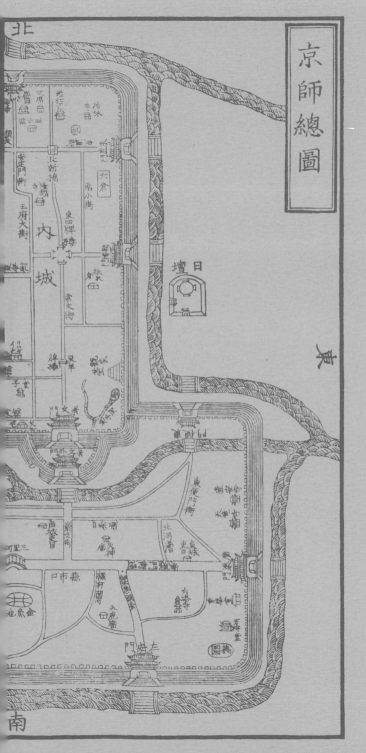

北

南

東

京師總圖

Peking

K'ang-hsi's capital, as shown in a decorative eighteenth-century woodblock map published in the Japanese compendium Tōdo meishō zue. In the center of the upper half is the imperial palace. Surrounding it is the Inner City, containing many shrines, military garrisons, and government buildings. At the bottom of the map is the Outer City, with commercial districts and residential quarters.

ALSO BY JONATHAN SPENCE:

Ts'ao Yin and the K'ang-hsi Emperor: Bondservant and Master (1966)

To Change China: Western Advisers in China, 1620 to 1960 (1969)

Emperor of China

Emperor of China

Self-portrait of K'ang-hsi
by Jonathan D. Spence

 Alfred A. Knopf   New York   1974

Copyright © 1974 by Jonathan D. Spence
All rights reserved under International and Pan-American Copyright Conventions.
Published in the United States by Alfred A. Knopf, Inc., New York, and
simultaneously in Canada by Random House of Canada Limited, Toronto.
Distributed by Random House, Inc., New York.

Library of Congress Cataloging in Publication Data:

Ch'ing Sheng-tsu, Emperor of China, 1654–1722.
  Emperor of China; self-portrait of K'ang-hsi.
  Bibliography: p.
  1. Ch'ing Sheng-tsu, Emperor of China, 1654–1722.
I. Spence, Jonathan D.   II. Title.
DS754.4.C53A33 1974   951′.03′0924 [B]   73–20743
ISBN 0–394–48835–0

Portions from The I Ching: or Book of Changes, *translated by Richard*
Wilhelm, rendered into English by Cary F. Baynes, Bollingen Series XIX,
copyright © 1950 and 1967 by Bollingen Foundation, reprinted by permission
of Princeton University Press.

Manufactured in the United States of America
Published May 30, 1974
Second Printing, August 1974

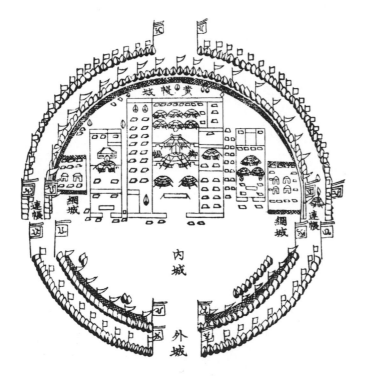

Contents

Acknowledgments   ix

K'ang-hsi's Reign   xi

  I   In Motion   3

 II Ruling   25

III Thinking   61

IV Growing Old   91

 V Sons   115

VI Valedictory   141

Appendix A. Seventeen Letters to Ku Wen-hsing,
         Chief Eunuch, Spring 1697   155

Appendix B. The "Final" Valedictory Edict   167

Notes   177

Bibliography   208

Index follows page 218

Acknowledgments

I AM especially grateful to three people for their aid and encouragement: Professor Arthur Wright, who listened patiently as I thought aloud the many variants of this book over the years, and gave valuable advice on the final drafts; Andrew C. K. Hsieh, whose ingenuity and enthusiasm as a research assistant helped to give the book the scope I had hoped for; and Jan Cochran, who transposed my convoluted longhand drafts into typescript with skill and good humor.

Many other colleagues, scholars, and students helped me with advice, criticism, translations, and references. My thanks to Beatrice S. Bartlett, Chang Wei, Chuang Chi-fa, Fang Chaoying, Joseph Fletcher, Parker Huang, Olga Lang, Anthony Marr, Susan Naquin, Jonathan Ocko, Robert Oxnam, Father Francis Rouleau, Nathan Sivin, and John Wills. Silas Hsiuliang Wu was particularly generous in sharing with me his great knowledge of early Ch'ing texts and institutions; I am also indebted to Charles Chu, who wrote the ideographs that introduce each chapter.

Drafts of this book were discussed at colloquia and seminars held at Columbia, Harvard, Princeton, the University of Vermont in Burlington, and Yale; many of those present at these gatherings gave me useful advice and cautions, for which I thank them. The leisure to think through alternative organizing structures for a study of K'ang-hsi, and to undertake the necessary basic research, was provided by the Yale Fellowship in East Asian Studies, to the donor of which I am now indebted for a second time. The final version was written on a Yale triennial leave, and speeded by additional research funds provided by a grant from the Yale Concilium on International and Area Studies.

JONATHAN D. SPENCE

Timothy Dwight College
Yale University
April 29, 1973

K'ang-hsi's Reign

THIS book is an excursion into the imperial world of K'ang-hsi, who was Emperor of China from 1661 to 1722. The purpose of the journey is to gauge the dimensions of his mind: What inner resources did he bring to the task of governing China? What did he learn from the world around him, and how did he view his subjects? What gave him joy and what made him angry, how did time pass for him, onto what did his memory fasten? How did a descendant of conquering Manchu warriors adapt to the Chinese intellectual and political environment—and how was he affected by new currents of Western scientific and religious thought that Jesuit missionaries brought to his court?

Any attempt to explore the dimensions of the Emperor's mind—if such an exploration were intended to reveal idiosyncratic and human elements—would have been viewed as both incongruous and presumptuous by K'ang-hsi's own subjects. K'ang-hsi had entered, by inheritance, into a documented sequence of emperors that stretched back for eighteen hundred years, and into a recorded history of China that reached over two millennia behind that. By acceding to office the emperor became more than human—or, conversely, if he revealed human traits, those traits must accord with the accepted historiographical patterns of imperial behavior. In becoming emperor, K'ang-hsi became the symbolic center of the known world, the mediator between heaven and earth, in Chinese terms the "Son of Heaven," who ruled "the central country." Much of his life had to be spent in ritual activity: at court audiences in the Forbidden City, offering prayers at the Temple of Heaven, attending lectures by court scholars on the Confucian *Classics*, performing sacrifices to his Manchu ancestors in the shamanic shrines. When he was not on his travels, he lived in the magnificent palaces in or near Peking, surrounded by high walls and guarded by tens of thousands of troops. Almost every detail of this life emphasized his uniqueness and superiority to lesser mortals: he alone faced the south, while his ministers faced the north; he alone wrote in red, while they wrote in black; the ideographs of his boyhood personal name (Hsüan-yeh) were taboo throughout the empire while the ideographs for "Emperor" were set apart from and above the lines of text in any document in which they occurred; his robes and hats had designs that no other person might wear; before him all subjects prostrated themselves in the ritual homage of the kowtow; and even the word which he used for "I," *chen,* could be used by no one else.

Such marks of grandeur and recognition were owed to all emperors and, since the emperor was viewed in categories that were cosmic and institutional rather than human, personal sources on emperors of China are rare. Most of them are hopelessly remote from us, hidden behind their various screens. But though K'ang-hsi was fully conscious of the inherited weight of imperial tradition, he was also, luckily, a man who expressed his private thoughts with a candor and freshness not normally found in those who govern great empires. To be sure, these personal expressions are scattered and often fragmentary, dispersed in a mass of formal edicts and utterances that were couched in stereotyped language. By searching carefully it is possible, however, to hear the unmistakably authentic voice of a man talking about his attitudes and values in his own words.

Each of the first five parts of this book constitutes one of the categories into which K'ang-hsi's thoughts—inasmuch as I was able to reconstruct them—seemed naturally to fall. Though the categories are not ones historians customarily use to organize their institutional or biographical data, it is true that the varied aspects of K'ang-hsi's public activities seem to fall naturally within a certain private and emotional framework. My belief that such is the case accounts for the structural organization of the book: by the end of it, the reader should have been introduced to K'ang-hsi's major concerns in a way that would have made logical sense to the Emperor himself.

The first part, "In Motion," is built of K'ang-hsi's ideas while in movement across the land, and of his awareness of the richness and variety of the country he ruled. In one of his letters to the eunuch Ku Wen-hsing he pointed out with pride that he had traveled over 2,000 *li* (a *li*, the basic unit of measurement in China, being about one third of a statute mile) in each of the four cardinal directions: west to the provinces of Shansi and Shensi, north across the Gobi to the Kerulen River, east through Manchuria to Ula, and south through China proper to Shao-hsing, below the Yangtze. As K'ang-hsi put it, "Rivers, lakes, mountains, deserts—I've been through them all." One of his interests in traveling was to collect and compare the different plants, birds, and animals that he encountered; and he established living collections in his various summer palaces and gardens, which, like his journey-ings, radiated to the four points of the compass within easy riding distance of Peking: the Ch'ang-ch'un Yüan to the west, the Nan-yüan to the south, the T'ang-ch'üan to the east, and—in the hills of southern Manchuria—his favorite summer palace in Jehol.

K'ang-hsi also traveled in order to hunt, and he loved ranging, with his sons and his guards officers, over the almost deserted areas of Mongolia and Manchuria, shooting with bow or gun at anything that moved or flew, and fishing for extra sport. He liked to inventory his kills, and to emphasize his robust Manchu heritage in the forested hills beyond the Great Wall. It was there that, in the early seventeenth century, K'ang-hsi's great-grandfather and grandfather had consoli-dated the various Manchu tribes, developed a centralized military organization on a settled agricultural base, conquered or allied with the neighboring Mongols, and won the alle-giance of those Chinese who lived north of the Great Wall. Thus, when a Chinese bandit army stormed into Peking in 1644 and the last Ming emperor committed suicide, the Man-chus, strong and united, were poised on the border with their tough army of mounted archers. Taking advantage of the chaos, the Manchus stormed Peking and ousted the bandits, estab-lishing the Ch'ing Dynasty with the young emperor Shun-chih (K'ang-hsi's father) as its first ruler.

If hunting meant joy and exercise to K'ang-hsi, it was also tied to the tougher realities of military preparedness, and he took thousands of troops on many of his trips, to train them in shooting, camp life, and formation riding. K'ang-hsi's reign was a time of territorial expansion and border war-fare, and his troops captured the island of Taiwan in 1683, defeated Russian forces and leveled the fortifications at Al-bazin in 1685, waged protracted campaigns against the Zun-gars in the far west and northwest during the 1690's, and were fighting in Tibet when K'ang-hsi died in 1722. In one case, that of the great Zungar warrior-leader Galdan, K'ang-hsi seems to have drawn the hunt and war together in his mind: the Galdan campaigns of 1696 and 1697 were the only times that K'ang-hsi rode out to fight in person, and he stalked Galdan as a hunter stalks his prey. He may well have been happier, during this war, than at any other period of his life, and he received the news of Galdan's suicide as a personal triumph.

Another category in which I have gauged K'ang-hsi's mind is that of the second part, "Ruling." This category is, historiographically, the one in which the overwhelming mass of sources are concentrated. Hundreds of documents were issued each week in the Emperor's name. These imperial documents are themselves only the surface of the seas of paper that flowed through the complex bureaucracy of seventeenth-century China. For the purposes of understanding this book, it is enough to be aware of the outlines of the governmental system. The central bureaucracy of K'ang-hsi's China was composed of a metropolitan division (based in Peking) and a provincial division. The metropolitan division was supervised by from four to six Grand Secretaries and directed by the presidents and vice-presidents of the Six Boards, or ministries: the Board of Civil Office, the Board of Revenue, the Board of Rites (which was in charge of the examination system, and received foreign tribute missions), and the Boards of Punishments, War, and Public Works. Bureaucratic practice was checked by officials in the Censorate. The Emperor also had a separate "imperial bureaucracy" for the administration of his palaces, bodyguards, and estates; this was composed mainly of Manchus, bondservants, and eunuchs.

The metropolitan division of the bureaucracy processed and supervised the activities of the provincial officials. During most of K'ang-hsi's reign there were eighteen provinces, each directed by a governor—the provinces being also grouped into six units each controlled by a governor-general. Each province was divided into prefectures *(fu)*, and each prefecture was subdivided into counties *(hsien)* controlled by a magistrate, of whom there were some fifteen hundred. The actual population of China at this time was about 150,000,000, so by rough average each magistrate had some 100,000 people in his charge. These magistrates, with their own sub-bureaucracies at the local level, were responsible for the collection of a total annual land tax of around 27,000,000 ounces of silver ("taels") in value; this tax was collected from 90,000,000 acres of agricultural land. The magistrates were responsible for local law and order; and they initiated that selection process of young scholars educated in the Confucian *Classics* which was a distinctive feature of the Chinese bureaucratic system: after satisfying local literary standards, students could embark on the national examination ladder. Those passing the official literary exams at the prefectural level were named "licentiates"; those passing at the provincial level were called *chü-jen;* the two hundred to three hundred *chü-jen* who passed each triennial national exam were known as *chin-shih,* and the cream of these went on to further study and literary work in the Hanlin Academy, the imperial center for Confucian scholarship. Many *chü-jen* and most *chin-shih* obtained prestigious and highly profitable office in the metropolitan or provincial bureaucracies.

Ruling, to K'ang-hsi, entailed ultimate responsibility for this entire economic and educational structure, and therefore for the life and death of all his subjects as well as for the evaluation and molding of their characters. The most important influence on his theories of ruling was undoubtedly the terrible civil war known as the "War of the Three Feudatories," or "San-fan War," which broke out in 1673 and lasted for eight years. The three feudatory princes were Wu San-kuei, Shang Chih-hsin, and Keng Ching-chung. In reward for the services they had rendered the Manchu troops at the time of the overthrow of the Ming in 1644 they had been granted immense fiefs in southern and western China, which they ran as virtually independent princedoms. In 1673, after long debates with his Council of Princes and High Officials, K'ang-hsi decided to try to make Wu San-kuei and the other two princes leave their fiefs and settle in Manchuria. This decision ran counter to the advice of the majority of his ministers and, as they had warned, precipitated a prolonged and destructive civil war which almost cost K'ang-hsi his throne.

Although the rebels were completely destroyed by 1681, K'ang-hsi continued to brood about the civil war and his responsibility for it, and he often used it as an example of the difficulty of making correct decisions. The terrible suffering of the common people swept up in the war truly moved him, just as the dilatoriness of his own armies angered him; and after the war was over he ordered harsh punishments for many of the rebel leaders. The penalties were, however, not arbitrarily imposed, but were in accordance with the Legal Code's provisions concerning treason. K'ang-hsi's general concern with evaluating all cases involving the death penalty is a further reminder that justice in China was not a matter of whim: the Code was sophisticated, and provided a common structure of interpretation and precedent for the widely scattered members of the bureaucracy. (Parallel bodies of regulations existed to give cohesion and uniformity to the vast tax-gathering apparatus, and in 1712, in announcing a freeze of the number of tax-collection units *(ting)*, K'ang-hsi sought to set a firm standard for all future time, as a proof of China's prosperity and a check on unnecessary governmental expenses.)

In the third part, "Thinking," we move away from the Emperor's worlds of action and common sense into the more amorphous realm of response to new phenomena. Successful thought, from K'ang-hsi's perspective, required openness and flexibility. This was not the same as the scholarly rigor, avoidance of idle speculation, and insistence on moral integrity which were demanded by the dominant school of Neo-Confucianism. K'ang-hsi paid regular homage to these latter approaches, and often referred to the *Confucian Classics* and quoted the dominant Sung philosopher Chu Hsi's theories concerning the "investigation of things," just as he often cited the principles of Yin and Yang and the *Book of Changes;* but he does not seem to have been a profoundly philosophical thinker. Instead, his outstanding trait was an exuberant curiosity, and he took endless delight in finding out what things were made of and how they worked. At different times in his life he was interested in geometry, mechanics, astronomy, cartography, optics, medicine, music, and algebra; he was patron to an extraordinary number of scholarly and encyclopedic projects in these and other fields. In his visit to the home and tomb of Confucius we can see how the solemnity of the occasion in no way inhibited his desire for information; and in his conversation with the papal legate we can observe him probing for precise information even as his anger mounts.

The confrontation with this legate—Maillard de Tournon—presented K'ang-hsi with a new challenge. Ever since his accession to the throne he had shown favor to the Jesuits: he had admired them for their mechanical, medical, artistic, and astronomical skills, and had employed them at his court on a number of projects. Jesuit cartographers mapped China, Jesuit physicians attended K'ang-hsi on his travels, Jesuit astronomers served as officials in the Calendrical Bureau. Jesuit fathers like Ferdinand Verbiest, Antoine Thomas, and Thomas Pereira stood high in K'ang-hsi's favor because they were unusually talented men who were willing to obey his orders. But now de Tournon brought a message that the Pope wanted to appoint his own emissary in Peking, a trusted expert from the Roman Curia, who could be relied upon to defend the interests of the Papacy, ensure that elements of Chinese "super-stition" did not creep into the local liturgy, and keep a tight rein on the Jesuit missionaries in China. K'ang-hsi's response was firm because in the realms of morality and religion he was determined to maintain the traditional authority of the Chinese throne: he wanted the Jesuits to pay allegiance to him, and to be supervised only by one of their own men whom he knew and trusted. K'ang-hsi told the Jesuits and other mission-aries that they would be allowed to stay on in China only if they signed certificates stating that they understood and agreed with the definition of Confucian and ancestral rituals which K'ang-hsi had formulated. Those refusing to sign were de-ported. And the Pope's request to have his personal emissary in Peking was denied.

K'ang-hsi viewed the past as being open to question; hence his interest in what is now called "oral history," and his in-sistence that the widest possible range of sources be consulted in composing the history of the fallen Ming Dynasty. On this project he employed a number of formerly dissident scholars who had stayed loyal to the memory of their Ming emperors and regarded the Manchus as usurpers; by recruit-ing such scholars through a special honorific examination, the *po-hsüeh hung-ju,* K'ang-hsi showed that he could combine flexibility with tact. But his tolerance did not extend to the bril-liant essayist Tai Ming-shih, whom he ordered executed for treasonous writings, despite the fact that Tai had done little more than vigorously apply principles of free historical in-quiry to the writing of Ming history. K'ang-hsi's thinking, ultimately, did not transcend politics.

But neither could politics transcend the human frame, and Part IV, on "Growing Old," shows how closely K'ang-hsi was aware of the body as fallible and how he carried this awareness into an interest in diet, illness, medicine, and memory. He was astonishingly open about physical and mental weaknesses—clearly this was partly to obtain public sympathy and to rally people to his support in times of stress, but it is also clear that such honesty was deeply important to him. Respect for the aged and filial piety were both highly ritualized in the China of his day, and certain responses and gestures were demanded for given occasions. Perhaps, however, because both his parents had died while he was a small boy, K'ang-hsi showered more than normal public affection on both his grandmother and his son Yin-jeng; and from surviving fragments of letters we can tell that this open affection was also expressed in private. K'ang-hsi was sensible about illness: he knew that admission of physical weakness was the ultimate honesty, but also that preventing weakness through medical means (and religious or magical means, if they seemed useful) was the ultimate common sense. The practice of medicine in K'ang-hsi's China was highly specialized, and was backed by an immense corpus of works on diagnosis and treatment as well as elaborate pharmacopoeias. Just as he could in other fields of natural science, so here the Emperor could indulge his whims and satisfy his curiosity—though he knew there was no escaping the specter of inevitable physical decline.

Against biological death the only bulwarks that K'ang-hsi could raise were his reputation in history and his progeny. He had fifty-six children who lived for some time after birth; one son only, however, was born to an empress, and on this boy, Yin-jeng, K'ang-hsi placed an immense burden of yearning, love, and expectation. Yin-jeng was brought up as Heir-Apparent to the throne of China. He was the center of attention and inevitably became the focus of tangled factional alignments that soured life at court and split the ranks of the hereditary Manchu nobility. The Manchu military system—built up by K'ang-hsi's great-grandfather Nurhaci in Manchuria—consisted of eight major divisions called Banners, and during

K'ang-hsi's reign the Banner system was still dominated by powerful generals from the great clans. These generals jockeyed for favors with the Heir-Apparent and their plots spread to encompass many Manchu officials and also senior Chinese bureaucrats. The theme of factional politics emerges as a dominant one in Part V, "Sons."

K'ang-hsi had broken free of his overbearing regent, Oboi, in 1669 with the help of his own uncle, the immensely wealthy and powerful Songgotu. Thirty-four years later K'ang-hsi had Songgotu put to death in jail, without trial; and, five years after that, Songgotu's six sons suffered the same fate. The Peking garrison commander Tohoci and his cronies were also put to death in 1712. The furious debates and anguished edicts of K'ang-hsi's later years take us a little way into a distorted world of love and hatred, where expectation had obviously been savagely betrayed, and an intelligent and humorous man became at times both hysterical and cruel. K'ang-hsi hints at assassination attempts on his own life. He does a little more than hint that he suspected his own beloved son Yin-jeng of indulging in homosexual activities, which K'ang-hsi himself found repugnant: he had three cooks and serving boys who had visited Yin-jeng's palace executed, he ordered secret informants to track down the "number-one man" who was connected with the purchase of small boys in the South, and he called his most trusted bodyguards to testify that he had always kept the imperial body "pure." But much else is innuendo, and in "Sons" we move beyond the historical record into a world of private despair.

It was after much stylistic and organizational experiment that I decided to present the preceding varied material by constructing an autobiographical memoir out of K'ang-hsi's own words. This seemed at once the best way to organize the many fragments I had assembled, to convey K'ang-hsi's own directness, and to catch the shifting levels of self-awareness that he showed in his public and private broodings. (There have been several fine historical-fictional studies in this vein, especially the *Memoirs of Hadrian* by Marguerite Yourcenar; but in this book I have stuck to K'ang-hsi's words as they were recorded, selecting those phrases, sentences, or paragraphs which I felt really represented his own views, without attempting to fill gaps myself. The Notes, beginning on p. 177, indicate sources.) I was immeasurably aided in this task of intellectual reconstruction by the fact that a combination of chance and the Emperor's own character has left us a group of sources that are particularly rich. As a Manchu who had learned the Chinese language in his later boyhood, K'ang-hsi wrote with a simplicity and directness rarely found among those scholars (or emperors) whose deeper knowledge of the language led them to frequent flights of literary hyperbole and allusion. His childhood difficulties under the regents brought him very close to his grandmother, to a small group of guards officers and ministers, with whom he was clearly on terms of friendship despite his imperial position, and to a few trusted eunuchs like Ku Wenhsing. K'ang-hsi was in the habit of scrawling casual notes to these people, and several hundred letters or fragments in his Chinese or Manchu calligraphy were found in the palace after the Ch'ing Dynasty's fall in 1911, among them the seventeen letters to his eunuch printed here as Appendix A (p. 155). Through these writings we get the chance to see K'ang-hsi in an informal and colloquial vein; we can catch his diction and glimpse the flow and connections of his thoughts. Here is an emperor thinking aloud in a hurry, often without secretaries to help him, letting the thoughts follow one another at random. In the normal cycle of dynastic fall and succession, these fugitive and casual materials would probably have been destroyed as soon as a properly majestic "official history" had been completed, checked, and printed. But the scholars of the new Chinese republic of the 1920's and 1930's, unawed by the historical overlays of the imperial person, collected all the random fragments they could find and published them.

The day-by-day chronological history of the governing of China—the so-called *Veritable Records*—exist for K'ang-hsi's reign as they do for the other Ch'ing emperors. Such records were often immensely lengthy and highly formalized, but K'ang-hsi encouraged brevity and directness, so we find that in his case they are manageable in size (around 16,000 pages, by Western count, for the sixty-one years of his reign) and also that they are illumined by the colloquial quality of K'ang-hsi's voice as he comments, lectures, complains, and persuades. K'ang-hsi also directed the publication of three volumes of his collected works during his own lifetime and, though many of the stylized essays may have been written by court scholars rather than by the Emperor himself, these volumes contain variant edicts not in the *Veritable Records,* as well as some engaging poems. He also developed the "palace memorial" system, a form of confidential communication in which officials wrote directly to him, rather than having their messages mediated through some branch of the bureaucracy; K'ang-hsi endorsed the memorials in his own hand and sealed them with his personal seal before returning them to the original sender. Many of these memorials, with K'ang-hsi's comments, have survived, and nine volumes of them have recently been published in photo-offset by the Palace Museum in Taiwan; there are further memorials, in Manchu, still uncollated. The memorials offer a remarkable view of an emperor at work, as do the official court diaries, several of which have been published. K'ang-hsi's views on morality, and a variety of his reminiscences, were collected by his son and successor, the Emperor Yung-cheng, and published in the 1730's. All the above

Chinese sources are supplemented by the observations of the Westerners who visited China on diplomatic missions during K'ang-hsi's reign, and of the Jesuits who served at his court.

A complex cross-check of such sources can be found in the scattered but also voluminous essays and biographies *(nien-p'u)* of scholars and officials who lived during K'ang-hsi's reign. Since K'ang-hsi was always traveling, and seems to have rarely stopped talking, he came into contact with an immense range of people, many of whom reported their reactions. Often they were dutifully awed, but in some cases—those, for example, of K'ung Shang-jen, Li Kuang-ti, Kao Shih-ch'i, and Chang Ying—their writings contain acutely observed detail that goes some way toward making up for the relative absence in China of one of the sources that is so abundant in Western historiography: namely, the well-informed, perhaps gossipy, letters, diaries, or memoirs of men and women familiar with the vagaries of court life. The power of the emperors, the organized categories of historiography, and the ever-present danger of persecution for literary indiscretion made reliable examples of such genres rather rare in China.

Implicit in my ordering of these different materials is a sense of chronological movement: from physical vigor, through forceful action and hard thinking, to histrionics and weakness. And in this sense the book approximates a biography. But at another level, the first five parts of the book are all an extended commentary on the sixth, which consists of a complete translation of K'ang-hsi's valedictory edict, as he himself drafted it in 1717. This edict constitutes K'ang-hsi's own major attempt to express his inner thoughts. He said as much, angrily, when a few months later some officials asked him if he had any other message for his people: "I began work on this account of my life ten years ago. When I told you 'I will say no more,' that was that." The valedictory edict is a confusingly short autobiography, by our standards, but then there was no tradition of imperial autobiography for K'ang-hsi to work from, and as it stands—at sixteen pages of Chinese text—it is by far the longest edict issued in his reign. If it does not seem totally coherent to us, or appears to be an odd combination of platitude and true emotion, that is more likely because we do not understand K'ang-hsi than because he did not understand himself. (This version of the valedictory may be contrasted, incidentally, with the more formal, stereotyped version issued after his death. See Appendix B, p. 167.) The first five parts of the present book thus become K'ang-hsi's explanations, in his own words, of his later shorthand.

This perspective allows the reader to assign a different temporal structure to the book. Not only do its parts span the sixty-three years K'ang-hsi had lived before delivering his valedictory edict; they can also be compressed into the single hour that passed before he delivered that edict. It was on such memories that K'ang-hsi drew as he prepared to address his officials on the twenty-first day of the eleventh month of the fifty-sixth year of his reign: December 23, 1717, in the Western calender. Events combined at this time to make him unusually conscious of both death and history: the Empress Dowager was dying; he himself was suffering from spells of dizziness, his feet were so swollen and painful that he could barely walk; and the bitter factional feuding among his sons over the succession to the throne was flaring anew. The book may, therefore, be seen as an attempt to explore the power that memory has to transcend time, an attempt to depict the events of a lifetime as they can be reborn by a few moments of mental concentration.

"An hour," Marcel Proust wrote near the end of *Remembrance of Things Past*, "is not just an hour, it is a vase full of perfume, sounds, projects, and moods." And he continued: "What we call reality is a certain rapport between our sensations and the memories that encircle us at the same moment." The passage is daunting to a historian, for he knows that he will never be able to fill that vase; and, even if he could, his randomly surviving sources would never be adequate to catch that "certain rapport."

But being daunted is not the same as being deflected, and here is K'ang-hsi inasmuch as I have been able to recapture him, across language and across time, stating his own case.

Emperor of China

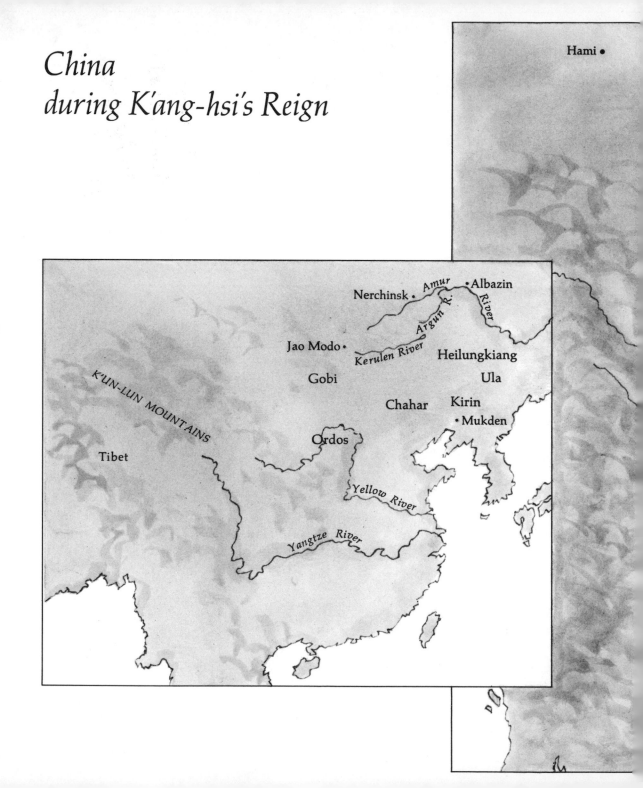

China
during K'ang-hsi's Reign

Hami •

Nerchinsk • *Amur* • Albazin

Argun R.

River

Jao Modo •

Kerulen River

Heilungkiang

Gobi

Ula

Chahar

Kirin

• Mukden

Ordos

Tibet

K'UN-LUN MOUNTAINS

Yellow River

Yangtze River

Kalgan
(Chang-chia-k'ou)

Jehol

Kuei-hua-ch'eng

Pai-t'a

Peking

Shan-hai-kuan

Ta-t'ung

CHIHLI

Ninghsia

▲Wu-t'ai-shan

Tientsin

Pao-te

Ning-wu

Te-chou

T'ai-yüan

SHANTUNG

KANSU

Yenan

SHANSI

T'ai-shan▲

SHENSI

Yellow River

Ch'ü-fu

HONAN

Chiangnan

KIANGSU

ANHWEI

Yangchow

Nanking

Hu-ch'iu

SZECHWAN

Yangtze River

HUPEH

Soochow

Ching-chou

Hangchow

KIANGSI

CHEKIANG

HUNAN

KWEICHOW

Yung-hsing

FUKIEN

KWANGSI

NNAN

KWANGTUNG

Canton

Macao

K'ang-hsi at 20

K'ang-hsi at 45

K'ang-hsi at 60

Prince Yin-chen, K'ang-hsi's Fourth Son, dressed up as a Westerner. He became Emperor Yung-cheng at K'ang-hsi's death in 1722.

I In Motion

HUNTING IN THE ORDOS, THE HARES WERE MANY

Open country, flat sand,
Sky beyond the river.
Over a thousand hares daily
Trapped in the hunters' ring.

Checking the borders,
I'm going to stretch my limbs;
And keep on shooting the carved bow,
Now with my left hand, now my right.

K'ANG-HSI, c. 1695

THERE are some wild geese that live far beyond the northern frontiers, a little-known species that leaves the north just before the first frost, and flies down into China. The border guards use their coming as a sign that the first frost is on the way. I had some caught, and caged in the Ch'ang-ch'un Garden at the water's edge, so they could drink or peck up food at will.

In springtime, near them, the crested white ducks play on the water, and in other cages are peacock and pheasant, quail and parrot, and baby cranes no larger than your fist. Deer lie on the slopes—fallow deer and roebuck—and if you poke them with a stick they stand and stare. In the gardens grow peony and white lilac, wild plum, flowering peach and magnolia, and acres of vines brought from Hami, yielding grapes of every kind—white, black, purple, and green.

Since childhood I have loved to watch the new shoots grow, and to transplant flowers and seedlings from other provinces and from foreign lands. The scented rice and water chestnuts I brought back from the Southern Tours could not withstand the Peking frosts, but with intense care the green bamboo survived and grew tall despite the cold winds. Ginseng grows in pots in the palace gardens, and the *ilha muke* from Ninguta now flourishes in Jehol, filling the air with its strange scent, its fruit as good-tasting as the lichees from Kwangtung or Fukien; while the wild barley sent by General Furdan is strong in the T'ang-ch'üan Gardens.

Even near Peking, among the hills and valleys of the palace gardens and hunting grounds at the Nan-yüan, T'angch'üan, and Ch'ang-ch'un, there is game in plenty. Wild boar are kept in the marshes, and pheasants and hare to be hunted with falcons and hounds, and caged tigers which—on release—can be baited with a blunted arrow and shot with a fowling piece or killed with spears. There are mock hunts too, by actors in the evenings, and wrestling, acrobatics, dance, and music. In the firework displays horsemen of blue fire dance in red vines, flaming lanterns tumble ever smaller, one from inside the other, while rockets burst in colored explosions. The gardens are beautiful: the springs are pure, the grasses fragrant, wooded hills rise among the lakes.

But it is when one is beyond the Great Wall that the air and soil refresh the spirit: one leaves the beaten road and strikes out into untamed country; the mountains are densely packed with woods, "green and thick as standing corn." As one moves further north the views open up, one's eyes travel hundreds of miles; instead of feeling hemmed in, there is a sense of freedom. It may be the height of summer, but there is dew on the trees, and some of the leaves are turning yellow already, as if it were late autumn; you have to wear a fur jacket in the mornings, even though in Peking it is so hot that you hesitate about having the eunuchs lead the consorts out of the palaces to greet you on your return.

There are forests of oak and poplar and beech, and wild pears and peaches, apples and apricots. Riding by, one can pick the little plums known as *ulana*, pale red like sharp cherries, and in Jehol there are cherries both white and red and the large sour cherries, perfect in color and taste; or one can eat the hazelnuts fresh fallen from the trees and mountain walnuts roasted over an open fire. There is tea, made from fresh snow on the little brazier slung between two horses. There is the perfect flavor of bream and carp from the mountain streams, caught by oneself in the early morning—you can keep something of that flavor for Peking eating if you enclose the fish in mutton fat or pickle them in brine before frying them up in sesame oil or lard. There is venison, roasted over an open fire by a tent pitched on the sunny slope of a mountain; or the liver of a newly killed stag, cooked with one's own hands (even if the rain is falling), and eaten with salt and vinegar. And in the northeast one can have bear's paw, which the imperial cooks value so highly.

Everything I know about hunting was taught to me when I was a child by my guards officer A-shu-mo-erh-ken: he always fearlessly corrected my shortcomings, holding nothing back, and I will never forget him. Since my childhood, with either gun or bow, I have killed in the wild 135 tigers and 20 bear, 25 leopards, 20 lynx, 14 tailed *mi* deer, 96 wolves, and 132 wild boar, as well as hundreds of ordinary stags and deer. How many animals I killed when we formed the hunting circles and trapped the animals within them I have no way of recalling—most ordinary people don't kill in a lifetime what I have killed in one day. One captain, born and raised in the North, said it seemed as if I were a god, to kill so many stags; but I said to him: "I often call for the stags and trap them in the ring; what is so godlike about killing a lot of them?" For I have left camp two hours before dawn to hunt stags, and returned two hours after sunset, with only a short nap at noon. I have myself killed 36 in one day, and once I and the other hunters got 154.

I have shot them, too, with blunted arrows to test the power of my bow. Riding three-oared boats on shallow lakes, I have used fowling pieces to shoot water birds. By moonlight and by torchlight I have hunted herds of wild sheep, and I have had beaters drive hare to the river bank so I could shoot them from a boat. I have used hawks to catch quail and pheasant, hit quail in flight with my arrows, gone with two hundred boats to look for sturgeon in the rivers north of Kirin, and fished in mountain streams from collapsible boats carried there on the backs of camels.

South of the Wall once, as we started home from Wu-t'ai-shan riding along the river bank, the water rushing over the rocks drowned the sound of our horses' hooves, and we surprised a tiger half hidden in the underbrush. He fled up the hillside but I pursued him, and killed him with an arrow. On another occasion, in the North, the noise of our guns startled a sleeping tiger, and I shot him on the run, across the river. Two days later I shot a leopard and two days after that my fowling piece brought down two bears. Hunting with the Khorcin, I shot clean through two mountain sheep with one arrow, and my officers were astounded; but I explained that it is all a question of using the force of the sheep's own leap to get extra penetrating power for the arrow. The crossbow may have the distance, but it lacks the penetration and the precision of the reflex bow; it makes a good plaything, but is not reliable for regular use. And though one can use a fowling piece instead of a reflex bow, one always must be careful with gunpowder and worry about it—an ounce can blow up a two-room house, and the force of a catty can hardly be described. This I know by experience, for on the northern journeys I used to order the cannon fired in deep valleys so that we could hear the reverberations from the cliffs; and in other experiments, conducted nearer Peking, I compared the cannon's roar with thunder. A thunderclap is usually not heard over 100 *li* (as the *Book of Changes* rightly says), and the rumble of thunder travels only 7 or 8 *li*. But the roar of a cannon can be heard for 200 or even 300 *li*, and those I ordered fired at Lu-kou-ch'iao were heard in Tientsin.

One day, at Lung-ch'üan Pass, I ordered the retinue to stop, and shot three arrows high over the rocks above us; and another time, riding with my sons Yin-t'i and Yin-chih toward the Hailasutai River, we passed the jutting peak called Na Hari, and I and the retinue shot our arrows at it. Besides mine, only the arrows of Sangge and Narašan reached the summit. I ordered the mountain's name changed. The Chinese declared that it was shaped like a pagoda, but the Manchus had earlier named it Na Hari, thinking it resembled a dangling bag of deer guts; so I chose the new name Ha Hada, "Crag like a hunter's net."

"Hunting's basically for exercise," I have said. "Now I see people being wounded. What kind of hunt is that?" The earlier Manchus had all practiced foot-hunting, and many men were wounded by the tigers' claws; this disturbed me, though the generals thought nothing of it. So I prohibited such hunting in the future, saying the generals were sometimes too careless with human life. If there was not a clear shot, and the tiger was concealed in the long grass, I kept the retainers back and had the dogs sent in. With their gold collars and red tassels, they would circle the tiger so we could tell his exact location, and by barking and snapping they would anger him out into the open. Of course, hunting cannot be without danger: my horse has stumbled in a pothole, and thrown me; and a retainer has fallen just as he fired at a stag, his arrow nicking my ear. Others have had bad falls while out riding: Wang Chih was so badly hurt that he begged permission to retire, and I sent guards officer Joban, who was also an excellent doctor, to attend to him.

Verbiest had a bad fall from a bolting horse, and died not long after; and the court astronomer Mucengge was killed by a fall. At T'ai-yüan, in a military inspection, a soldier's horse bolted and would have crashed into me, had not Borden rushed forward and managed to stop it.

No one not good at riding can be any good at mounted archery; you must start as a child to get the proper experience, and you must learn to have no fear. It is the boy who can gallop at ten who will handle a horse properly when he's a man. As for the horses, we have the shamans pray aloud in our presence before five pair of white horses who stand with heads turned toward the west, near the holy tree where twenty-seven paper offerings hang: "Oh Lord of Heaven, Oh Mongol leaders, Manchu princes, we pray to you for our swift horses. Through your power may their legs lift high, their manes toss; may they swallow the winds as they race, and grow ever sleeker as they drink in the mists; may they have fodder to eat, and be healthy and strong; may they have roots to nibble, and reach a great age. Guard them from ditches, from the precipices over which they might fall; keep them far from thieves. Oh gods, guard them; Oh spirits, help them!"

When Manchus and Mongols go out to hunt in the North we are dealing with a skill that eludes words. The hunters mass like storm clouds, the mounted archers are as one with their horses; they fly together and their arrows bring down the fleeing game. Heart and eye are cheered to see it. The good rider always positions himself correctly in relation to his quarry, and the well-trained horse knows his man's intent and moves accordingly, approaching or veering to get the best result. There are some fine riders who don't even care if their horse is admirable or vicious, for as soon as they mount you see only the good points. So can man bring the best out of a horse, and a horse bring the best out of man.

The hunt is also training for war, a test of discipline and

organization: the squads of hunters have to be organized on military principles, not according to convenience on the march or family preferences. In olden days, to get more practice, men used to hunt four times a year, but that was excessive—the hunters grew tired and the animals had no chance to breed. Two main expeditions a year is better: one in the spring by the rivers, to give the people practice with boats, and one in autumn, far from camp, to give practice at mounted archery. So the animals thrive and our troops are unbeatable. As the great circle of horsemen spreads out, and then begins to close around the fleeing game, none may shoot until the Emperor gives the order; even members of the Imperial Clan must stay in their squads, not breaking forward or lagging behind, left on the left, right on the right. So at the military inspections do the troops advance in order, under their signal flags: as the conches blow and the drums beat, all advance; when the golden horn sounds, all stop. Nine times thus, and on the tenth the cannons fire. And at base camps, too, we form circles and enforce discipline: in the center, my tent surrounded by its yellow hangings; then the seven-foot-high net of heavy cordage; then the massed tents of the guards; and finally the rows of tents of the retinue and the troops.

The conditions in these northern areas can be understood only if you travel through them in person; and as you move you must attend closely to details of transport and supply. You can't just make guesses about them, as they did in the Ming Dynasty—and even now, the Han Chinese officials don't know much about this region. Generals Boji and Sun Ssu-k'o thought, in the 1696 campaign against Galdan, that it was enough if they attended to military matters and left supplies to others. When I traveled from Pai-t'a northward in the following year, I saw the remains of the bodies of the troops who had died of hunger in their armies on that march, and ordered them buried by the roadside.

Water supply is another crucial area in which mistakes cannot be tolerated. When Sekse was sent to supervise digging wells for the troops in 1696, and later gave me the idiotic response that he didn't even know how many horses and men the wells he had dug would supply, I had him dismissed from his post as vice-president of the Board of Revenue and sent to serve in the ranks. The weight and purity of the water differ from area to area, but you can always find some, even in the desert. In the Gobi there were at least four types of water— one that lay two feet under the sand; one at a depth of one foot; *buri* water, which was no good; and *yen bur* water, which you can get by just scraping the sand away with your hand. By careful calculation you can also tell where a well might lie under the ice of winter, and prepare it for the troops before they arrive. So can an army march for 1,900 *li* and live, without ever seeing a river.

Usually, north of the Wall, we drink river water all the time, and it's not harmful; but in summer one has to be careful of mountain streams if no rain has fallen for some time to wash away the impurities, just as one has to watch out for dysentery if the springs have been stirred up by rain. While on the march it's dangerous to drink from the ditches at the roadside—they can give you cholera. If there's no decent water to be found, you must just distill what there is, and make tea with it.

On hunting trips or campaigns, the selection of a base camp is also of the greatest importance. Never return to an old site—that is a Manchu taboo that must be honored. And in summer and autumn be aware of the danger of flooding, and choose high dry ground; just as in winter and spring you should worry about fire and find a place without too much grass, sheltered from direct wind. If there is grass growing all around, then take the time to cut it down. One can prepare in advance against possible danger: if it's the *tung-chih* period of approaching winter, and the Yang forces are coming into the ascendant, the winds will be strong and dry and there is a great danger from fire. If there has been a prolonged drought, a sudden rainfall will lead to flooding of the mountain streams, and you must observe by what routes the water is likely to come, and avoid those places, for the flood might come at night.

There are certain recurrences that I have drawn from the annual *Records of Sunshine and Rain,* and these can be used to forecast the weather, even though each area is not exactly the same. It is likely to rain on the eighth, eighteenth, twentieth, twenty-second, and twenty-fourth days of every lunar month. Between the ninth and fifteenth days there will not be rain if you can see the moon; but if deep clouds obscure the moon, you can expect a storm of rain that will last several days. I have also observed the wind's directions: southwest winds are rare in all seasons; the northwesters—what the people call "guest winds"—will only blow three of four days before they change; northeasterly and southeasterly winds are popularly called "rain winds." Observing the clouds will only help you for about half a day ahead, and of course when it's completely overcast it's hard to tell when the skies will clear, just as in prolonged drought it's hard to know when it will rain. The day's lengths will also vary in different areas: thus in Heilung-kiang, which is in the far northeast, near the place where the sun rises and sets, the nights are short and the days long, and even at night it does not get completely dark.

I always have a little flag set up, so that I can tell the wind's exact direction, and compare my own observations with the weather reports that come in from other provinces. Once I took a gnomon and, having marked with my brush the exact point at which the sun's shadow would fall at noon, had the courtiers sit and watch till they could see that my calculations were correct. I have sat out on a clear night and told the time from the star charts that Verbiest had prepared for me. Many of the officials could not even recognize the basic twenty-eight constellations, and I showed them such things as the way the constellations *Ts'an* and *Tsui* paired together in Orion and how the principles of astronomy and geography meshed. So we could see how China's mountain ranges sprang out from the K'un-lun ranges and also how general principles regulated the rivers, those south of the forty-fifth degree of latitude flowing to the south and east while those north of this line flowed to the north.

On hunting expeditions, as on campaigns, one must look after the officials and men in the retinue. In hot weather, when possible the Board of Revenue and the Board of Works should have cold drinks ready by the roadside to refresh the marchers—iced water, or herbal wines, or plum cider. When it was snowing, I used to send guards officers over to the camel drovers' tents with food and charcoal, so that hot meals could be prepared for the carters who had not yet arrived, and they could rest up. I would even provide food for the vendors following along behind the troops, and let merchants double up with my guards officers on their horses if there was a really cold river to ford. I checked that rewards were given to the various people who helped us move across the country—the guides, scouts, grooms, and well-diggers, the herders and their womenfolk—and always insisted that the horses be lovingly tended: if there is a danger of rain, cover them up properly; if they have been ridden hard and have sweated, don't give them water right away or they'll get ill. Send people ahead to check on the grass and water supply, and if springs have to be uncovered or wells dug, do it enough in advance so that the water clears. If there is only a little grass, and the horses have to compete for it with the sheep, then go hunting on foot.

At the same time, I have had to take measures to protect

the people in the areas through which our troops passed: to stop the soldiers trampling the wheat fields or stealing grain to feed their horses; to make them sleep in camp, not in local temples; to have them keep in line and not wander around; no drinking or shouting while on the march; no taking of any object from local villagers, and no assaulting of any locals, whether male or female.

On the first Galdan campaign in 1696, I would rise before dawn in the fifth watch, break camp, and ride off while it was still cool; then I'd camp around eleven, and eat my only meal of the day. But I had to urge others to do the same—as I left, I could see the smoke rising from their cooking fires and some were even still asleep. Such laziness causes delays everywhere: the baggage doesn't arrive, the guides and camel drovers get held up, so that the troops who have arrived on time can't relax and pitch camp. While on the move, I'd live roughly and without formality—those passing in front of me didn't have to dismount, and as on the hunts we would cook fish or food we caught in a simple way, and sit sometimes in the herders' tents and eat, and drink kumiss as we talked. Once the cooks brought only the meat dishes, without any rice at all, and my sons and bodyguards wanted to have them beaten. But I said, "It wasn't intentional, they just forgot to bring it: it's a small thing, we can let it pass." And in the frontier towns I would not have the streets cleared, but would pass by particularly slowly, so that all would have a chance to see me; or I'd let the common people gather round and watch me as I ate, and give them millet and meat.

Wherever I went among the rank and file, I would call some of the soldiers forward and chat with them, for after a longish period of peace men forget about fighting, and the youngsters need to learn from the veterans. Perhaps an old veteran would volunteer to fight with my armies once again, although he was in retirement; or I'd call forward the sons of famous warriors, and offer them a drink with my own hands. In all the sessions of archery practice on the various parade grounds I would have the names of those who shot particularly well noted down; and then have them shoot once again in my presence, and ask them if they had had ancestors or relations who died in action, and if they had I promoted them on the spot. I would also think of the soldiers when I had to decide between one area where the hunting was good but fuel for cooking was scarce, and an area where the hunting was average but the fuel plentiful; and I would choose the latter, for the soldiers don't march well when hungry for good food. I would encourage the local forces by pitting their best archers against my own guards officers, all shooting especially heavy-pull bows; or else shift from bows to fowling pieces, and make them shoot in turns—riding, kneeling, lying down—and show them how I can shoot a bow with either my right hand or my left. I attended all the military examinations in person, checking out both foot and mounted archery, and selecting the very best for a brief written exam so that a fair and final listing could be made. I kept the regular troops working at drill to perfect their formation marching; had them innoculated against smallpox as I did my own children; and had them taught to swim—or at least got them used to the water—before they were sent to climb on the rocks and go fishing.

The frontier areas can be cold and damp and remote, with deserts that seem to stretch forever, with a few wild sheep and asses but no people, no houses, and no birds flying. I have seen, with my own eyes, men having to boil up a few nuts and eat them to keep alive, with no knowledge of how they might get through the winter; and cattle so thin that, though living, they soon must starve to death. So planning and attention to details are essential, and the advice of the veteran commanders should always be considered. Before we moved against Galdan in 1696 I told the senior officers—Manchu, Mongol, and Chinese—to meet together by Banner and discuss how we might anticipate Galdan's movements and how we should deploy our own troops. Even the most casual suggestions were to be collected and reported to me. After the basic strategy of a western strike from Ninghsia and a central strike from Peking across the Gobi was agreed upon, the Council of Princes and High Officials worked out the details of rations for soldiers and servants, fodder for camels, the number of carts, and so on, basing their figures on an estimated 10,790 troops in the western army, and 8,130 in the center—with four horses, one servant, eighty days' basic rations, and an extra two pecks of rice per month for each active combatant soldier (with the exception of the gunners, two of whom could share one servant).

For my part, I reviewed the campaign instructions of my ancestors' victories and combined them with the demands of this new campaign, in the form of seventeen basic route orders. Each soldier was to write his name on the shaft of each of his war arrows, and on his helmet and armor; each horse was to be branded, and to each horse's tail a wooden slip was to be affixed, listing the Banner and the company commander's name. All stragglers, brawlers, deserters, drinkers, or those who pilfered the horses' accouterments would be instantly disciplined. All tents were to be pitched in neat rows, a moderate distance apart. Soldiers on guard duty were to keep their horses saddled and ready, to use no fires or tents at night, and at all times to have boots on, bow strung, armor fastened, water bottle full. They were to challenge anyone with strange clothes or equipment. For neglecting to report an enemy approach, or for falsely reporting an enemy approach when there was not one, the penalty was to be execution in front of the army. Good grazing terrain for all camels and horses had to be selected, and special detachments appointed to round up stray animals and, after identifying them by brand and name, return them to their rightful owners. Sick or exhausted animals

were to be left in local villages or in Mongol camps to be looked after—not abandoned or killed off. After battles, captured weapons were never to be sold or allowed to fall into the Mongols' hands. And there was to be no idleness in camp: when there was some spare time, soldiers could practice shooting or repair and sharpen weapons.

After leaving Peking in the spring of 1696, we were committed—by statements to the suffering Khalkas, by our sacrifices to the gods and the ancestors, by the tenacity of the troops and even their servants—to finish off Galdan. But again, the exact procedure was a fit subject for debate, and I asked for the views of some generals, and sent guards officers Mau and Lasi to sound out others, thus obtaining seven different alternatives on how to proceed. I finally combined three separate tactics as suggested by Oja, Tunju, and Songgotu, and envoys were sent to Galdan on the Kerulen River in order to panic him and make him flee west, which would lead him straight into Fiyanggu's army marching from Ninghsia. This seemed the best plan, based on what I had learned about Galdan's character. Twenty years before, General Chang Yung had made secret inquiries about Galdan, and assessed his impetuous yet indecisive character, his age and family situation, his problems with the Moslems, and his love of wine and women. Since then I had observed Galdan's cunning and delight in feinting, his overconfidence, his gullibility and inability to think far ahead. After we sent the envoys, our scouts watched for the smoke of his campfires and assessed his army's movements on the evidence of hoofprints and horse dung. And as Galdan began to flee we moved into pursuit, first strengthening a base camp in which to leave the sick horses and the servants who had been marching on foot, then leaving behind the slower Green Standard Infantry, then abandoning the cannon, and finally sending Maska on ahead as commander of a flying column.

As I waited on the shores of the Kerulen River for news from Maska, I wrote to the Empress Dowager: "Our troops have chased the Ölöds now for five days. I have seen their abandoned Buddhist scriptures and tents, the women and children and the sick whom they slew themselves, their fish kettles and their brewing apparatus, their hunting nets and their armor, their saddles and bridles and clothes, their food, the wooden spoons still standing in the bowls of soup, their leather skins filled with kumiss—all these poor items of their daily life, all thrown away."

Galdan fled into our trap, and was met by Fiyanggu at Jao Modo. They fought there for four hours over a distance of 30 *li*. But though over two thousand Ölöds were killed, Galdan himself escaped. Then from prisoners we learned the strange story of how the Dalai Lama had in truth been dead for over nine years, and how the Tipa had covered this up and forced the Panchen Lama to go along with him, and how they had issued a false prophecy in the dead Dalai Lama's name: "Galdan will be successful if he goes to the east." And so I took another army that autumn, and marched west to Kuei-hua-ch'eng, conferring with the Khalka princes and also with the leading lamas, whose temples I visited in person.

Again Galdan eluded us, and the following spring I pursued him for a third time, marching west to Ninghsia. The Shansi censor Chou Shih-huang tried to dissuade me, saying, "The despicable wretch is in desperate straits, and will be dead in a few days. I beg the Emperor not to travel out into the deserts again." But I said that Galdan had to be finished off like Wu San-kuei, and that our troops, though exhausted by continuing campaigns, were longing for a chance to show their valor, and that I had written poems on this theme to make our intentions known. Then General Wang Hua-hsing also tried to divert me, suggesting that we all ride up to the Lake Hua-ma hunting grounds, and I told him: "Galdan is not yet destroyed, and the question of horses is a crucial one. If the Ninghsia troops go to Lake Hua-ma—seven or eight days there and back—the horses will be tired out. Hunting is a small matter, it's the catching of Galdan that's urgent. Now, let's cancel the hunt and rest the horses, and then go hunting Galdan. How about that?"

For in war it's experience of action that matters. The so-called *Seven Military Classics* are full of nonsense about water and fire, lucky omens and advice on the weather, all at random and contradicting each other. I told my officials once that if you followed these books, you'd never win a battle. Li Kuang-ti said that in that case, at least, you should study classical texts like the *Tso-chuan,* but I told him no, that too is high-flown but empty. All one needs is an inflexible will and care-ful planning. And so it was that, in the far northwest on the bend of the Yellow River in the early summer of 1697, I heard the news that Galdan, abandoned by nearly all his followers, had committed suicide. As I wrote to my eunuch Ku Wen-hsing: "Now Galdan is dead, and his followers have come back to their allegiance. My great task is done. In two years I made three journeys, across deserts combed by wind and bathed with rain, eating every other day, in the barren and uninhab-ited deserts—one could have called it a hardship but I never called it that; people all shun such things but I didn't shun them. The constant journeying and hardship has led to this great achievement. I would never have said such a thing had it not been for Galdan.

"Heaven, earth, and ancestors have protected me and brought me this achievement. As for my own life, one can say it is happy. One can say it's fulfilled. One can say I've got what I wanted."

Five years before, on one of my hunts, in the autumn of 1692 just as I was finishing dinner, came news that a bear had been cornered among some rocks in a small wood. I rode out immediately, reaching the wood just before sunset. At first neither shouting, nor beating on trees, nor cracking our whips would dislodge that bear, but finally he roared and came out into the open country. My huntsmen rode along beside him, at a distance of fifteen or twenty paces, and steered him to a defile between two hills. There I shot an arrow at him, which hit him in the side and pierced his stomach. He tore at the arrow, breaking it in pieces, ran a few paces and stopped. I dismounted and took a pike in my hands and, with four hunters at my side, carefully approached the bear and speared him, killing him outright. Never, I told my retinue, had I enjoyed a hunt so much.

治

II   Ruling

EULOGY FOR GOVERNOR-GENERAL CHAO HUNG-HSIEH

For forty years you served around Peking;
Soldiers and people praised your measured goodness.
I protected and favored you all the way
And all now weep that you have died.

You didn't fear the thugs, you kept the laws,
While you guarded the money, honesty reigned.
Now you are in the underworld but your office remains.
Riding past I think of your insignia—hanging there.

K'ANG-HSI, 1722

Giving life to people and killing people—those are the powers that the emperor has. He knows that administrative errors in government bureaus can be rectified, but that a criminal who has been executed cannot be brought back to life any more than a chopped string can be joined together again. He knows, too, that sometimes people have to be persuaded into morality by the example of an execution. In 1683, after Taiwan had been captured, the court lecturers and I discussed the image of the fifty-sixth hexagram in the *Book of Changes*, "Fire on the Mountain": the calm of the mountain signifies the care that must be used in imposing penalties; the fire moves rapidly on, burning up the grass, like lawsuits that should be settled speedily. My reading of this was that the ruler needs both clarity and care in punishing: his intent must be to punish in order to avoid the need for further punishing.

Hu Chien-ching was a subdirector of the Court of Sacrificial Worship whose family terrorized their native area in Kiangsu, seizing people's lands and wives and daughters, and murdering people after falsely accusing them of being thieves. When a commoner finally managed to impeach him, the Governor was slow to hear the case, and the Board of Punishments recommended that Hu be dismissed and sent into exile for three years. I ordered instead that he be executed with his family, and in his native place, so that all the local gentry might learn how I regarded such behavior. Corporal Yambu was sentenced to death for gross corruption in the shipyards; I not only agreed to the penalty but sent guards officer Uge to supervise the beheading, and ordered that all shipyard personnel from generals down to private soldiers kneel down in full armor, and listen to my warning that execution would be their fate as well unless they ended their evil ways.

In times of war there must be executions for cowardice or disobedience. When the city of K'u-ch'eng-hsien fell to the rebels in the Hupeh campaign of 1675, the commander-in-chief reported that Colonel Malangga had fled; and after Prince Cani verified this in his secret report, I had Malangga beheaded. A few months later two more senior officers fled in the face of the enemy in Shensi, and I had them beheaded in front of their troops. Sekse was beheaded in 1697 for openly disobeying the imperial order that he inform Danjin Ombu of Galdan's death (though I did not order his head exposed as the judges had recommended).

The final penalty of lingering death must be given in cases of treason, as the Legal Code requires. Chu Yung-tso was arrested, and condemned for following the treacherous monk I-nien, for writing wild poems and deceiving the people, and for adopting false Ming reign-titles. The Board of Punishments recommended that he be beheaded, but I ordered that the death be lingering. I had awarded the same punishment to the rebel Wang Shih-yüan, who had claimed to be Chu San T'ai-tzu, the

surviving Ming claimant to the throne, so that the Ming prince's name should be invoked no more as a rallying point for rebels, as had been done too many times before. When Ilaguksan Khutuktu, who had had his spies in the lamas' residences so that they would welcome Galdan's army into China, and had plotted with Galdan and encouraged him in his rebellion, was finally caught, I had him brought to Peking and cut to death in the Yellow Temple, in the presence of all the Manchu and Mongol princes, and the senior officials, both civil and military. All that was left of Galdan were the ashes, but these we exposed to the public outside the Forbidden City. The corpse of Wu San-kuei I ordered scattered across the provinces of China and decreed the lingering death for Keng Ching-chung and ten other generals who had fought for him or Wu San-kuei.

But apart from such treason cases, when there are men who have to be executed immediately (even if it's spring, when executions should not be carried out), or when one is dealing with men like those who plotted against me in the Heir-Apparent crisis and had to be killed immediately and secretly without trial, I have been merciful where possible. For the ruler must always check carefully before executions, and leave room for the hope that men will get better if they are given the time. In the hunt one can kill all the animals caught inside the circle, but one can't always bear to shoot them as they stand there, trapped and exhausted.

As the "San-fan War" began in the South, Yang Ch'i-lung and his men rose in Peking, and the Manchu troops were so stern in reprisal that the people fled in panic to the hills outside the walls. I not only ordered the city gates closed, to stop the city emptying, but promised amnesty to all save the ringleaders, since Yang had misled so many of the common people that we would never be able to clean up all those involved in the case. As the war spread, and reports came in of over one hundred alleged "bandits" beheaded after a single engagement, I sent an edict to the Board of War ordering commanders to use more compassion:

"I feel that when ignorant country folk are forced [by the rebels] to cut off their queues, it's in the special situation of their having a natural desire to hang on to life and avoid being killed. If my armies arrive and execute them all, this contradicts my desire to save the people, and denies them any chance to reform. Also, cunning bandits can take advantage of this to arouse them. In future, when our troops enter an area, if the locals use armed resistance, or skulk behind their moats or in their mountain hideouts, and refuse to surrender immediately, then let them be killed. But spare the others. When bandits have been killed in a campaign, their children must be made captive. But the women in the bandits' camps were often initially taken there by force—so after the bandits themselves have been destroyed, let the other local people have a chance to identify and reclaim the refugees and their children—don't just arrest everyone indiscriminately." Only when the war was over did I learn of another group of victims: because I had said that the troops at the beginning of the war should "travel fast by day and night," my orders had been literally obeyed and a great many of the barge pullers had died.

Of all the things that I find distasteful, none is more so than giving a final verdict on the death sentences that are sent to me for ratification after the autumn assizes. The trial reports should all have been checked through by the Board of Punishments and reviewed by the Grand Secretaries during the autumn months, yet still one finds errors of calligraphy—and even whole passages miswritten. This is inexcusable when we are dealing with life and death. Though naturally I could not go through every case in detail, I nevertheless got in the habit of reading through the lists in the palace each year, checking the name and registration and status of each man condemned to death, and the reason for which the death penalty had been given. Then I would check through the list again with the Grand Secretaries and their staff in the audience hall, and we would decide who might be spared.

The point is not to abandon the category of "Definitely guilty" and have the judges give all kinds of murderers a suspended sentence; it is rather to review those found "Definitely guilty" of murder and check the motives and circumstances. Nor is that simply a question of the weapon used: Ch'en Ju-hsien tried to interest me in the categories employed in the coroners' handbook, *Hsi-yüan Lu,* which suggested that we distinguish between obvious "murder weapons" made of metal, such as daggers and arrowheads, and other, wooden implements that might lead to death. I said, "Death can be caused by striking with fists, or kicking, or beating with wooden clubs; if we calculate the weight of the guilt on the basis of the weight of the murder weapon, that's bound to lead to errors being made. Take a needle: it's a tiny object, but you can kill someone with it—how can you say that there is less involved because a needle is not a murder weapon?" Each year we went through the lists, sparing sixteen out of sixty-three at one session, eighteen out of fifty-seven at another, thirty-three out of eighty-three at another. For example, it was clear to me that the three cases of husbands killing wives that came up in 1699 were all quite different. The husband who hit his wife with an ax because she nagged at him for drinking, and then murdered her after another domestic quarrel—how could any extenuating circumstances be found? But Pao-erh, who killed his wife for swearing at his parents; and Meng, whose wife failed to serve him properly and used foul language so that he killed her—they could have their sentences reduced. Sometimes the crime seemed unpardonable—like Chu Shang-wen killing his cousin over a small argument—yet I had the death sentence remitted out of compassion, since the murderer was already sixty-seven years of age. At other times what looked like a lighter crime proved to be serious: thus Liu-ta had killed Ma-erh with a stone, but as the Grand Secretaries explained, the victim had been struck twelve times in all, and his brains had burst out onto the ground. Liu-ta was obviously an experienced killer and should be executed. Sudden murders without a cause could sometimes be forgiven—deaths resulting from drunken brawls, for example, or a lover killing his mistress in anger when her husband tried to dun him. Or a certain crime could be pardoned in peacetime: the Board of Punishments wanted the bandit Fan Sung beheaded for stealing horses from the imperial retinue, but I changed it to exile, since the nation was at peace and horse theft was therefore not so serious as it would have been in time of war.

It's a good principle to look for the good points in a person, and to ignore the bad. If you are always suspicious of people they will suspect you too; that was why, when Dantsila was brought to my tent, although he was Galdan's nephew and had been fleeing to Tibet with the ashes of Galdan's body before he despaired and surrendered, I showed my trust by having him sit near me, and offered him a knife with which to cut his meat. Later I gave him a prince's title, and he served me faithfully. Though the Russians had been killing our people on the northern frontier, I ordered that the Russian prisoners should be given new suits of clothes and be released just as we began the siege of Albazin, and after the second siege in 1687 I ordered that the sick Russians be treated personally by my own doctors and sent home. So thirty years later the Uriang-hai people submitted to us without a battle, because they remembered our clemency to the Russians long before. Three thousand Miao troops who had been fighting for Wu San-kuei's armies in Szechwan were captured by our forces there, and I ordered them sent home to Yunnan, not punished; later Wu San-kuei's grandson tried to enlist their support, but they refused to fight for him. Thus even Miao can be controlled through compassion. When the Governor-General requested that the Miao be prevented from having weapons, and that Chinese merchants be forbidden to trade with them in such items as lead, saltpeter, and sulphur, I did not grant his request. It was not only that the Miao depended for their livelihood on the game they could kill by hunting with crossbow and fowling piece—it was also that effective control of them had to depend on the sensitivity of the local officials. Besides which, of course, there was the question of how you can get the common people to hand over their weapons to the government officials at all—as I pointed out to the Board of Works vice-president Muhelun when he presented his crazy scheme for disarming the people of Shantung province.

Again, I was warned not to appoint Admiral Shih Lang to lead the campaign against Taiwan, because he had once served under the Ming Dynasty and under the rebel Coxinga, and might rebel, himself, if I gave him ships and troops. But since the other Chinese admirals had said Taiwan would never be taken, I summoned Shih Lang to audience and said to him in person: "People at court all say you are bound to rebel when you reach Taiwan. It's my opinion that unless you are sent to Taiwan it will never be pacified. You won't rebel, I guarantee it." Shih Lang captured Taiwan speedily, and proved a loyal official. Even if he was uneducated and arrogant, he made up for it by his rough and ready military abilities; and his two sons have served me with distinction.

In pacifying southern China after the "San-fan War," I first chose six former subordinates of Wu San-kuei, promoted them, and sent them on ahead of the main armies with copies of the pacification edict, offering amnesty to those who surrendered, lodged information leading to the capture of bandit troops, or came over with troops of their own. Rebel generals surrendering to us were kept on full pay, and Icangga was told

to find two articulate defectors who understood the rebels' situation, and ride fast with them to Peking so I could consult with them. At the same time we began to review each case of officials who had had households in rebel areas: some had been involved, some forced to join the rebels because of family pressures, some had resisted and suffered for it; those rebel generals who dared not defect openly because their wives and children were still in Yunnan were urged to declare their loyalty secretly to us, and then pull back into Yunnan so that they would work for us from within the enemy's base area.

Although Keng Ching-chung had surrendered in November 1676, while Shang Chih-hsin surrendered in January 1677 and Wu San-kuei died in October 1678, there were still others fighting, and the war was by no means over. Wu's troops, led by his grandson, battled on, and Keng and Shang might well rebel again. So when, in the spring of 1680, Prince Giyešu suggested that he have Keng killed, I forbade it, telling him: "It is my belief that when something is to be put into operation, the sequence must be carefully calculated; when there will be benefit to the country, then is the time to initiate action. Lightly embarking on a dangerous course inevitably leads to trouble. Kwangsi, Hunan, Han-chung, and Hsing-an have already been pacified. The remaining rebel groups are stretching out their necks in their desire to return to their allegiance—and not just by the hundred or the thousand. If we now kill Keng Ching-chung, then not only will those who have surrendered to us expect to receive the same punishment at a later date, but also those who have not yet surrendered will note this example and grow cold at heart—with unknown consequences."

So I told Giyešu to work on trying to get Keng Ching-chung to come to Peking, while I sent Icangga to go to Kwangtung as an alleged "Sea-Defense Inspector," to keep an eye on Shang Chih-hsin. It was only in December 1681, when the final victory memorial came from Jangtai, commanding general in the southwest, that the severe punishments began: with Yun-nan-fu fallen, Wu San-kuei's grandson Wu Shih-fan committed suicide, Kuo Chiang-t'u and his son cut their throats, Hu Kuo-chu strangled himself, Wang and Li burned themselves to death, Wu San-kuei's "Grand Secretary," Fang Kuang-chen, and his son and nephew were chopped to death before our troops, and the other rebel generals were beheaded, except for Wu San-kuei's son-in-law, who was sent to Peking along with Wu Shih-fan's head. The war being over, I ordered Keng and his family killed, together with the other rebel leaders whose guilt was truly inexcusable.

But as the impeachments poured in, I reiterated that I would not execute all those who had been involved in the war, and that they were free to return to their homes. I firmly rejected the suggestion that all those who had served as officials in the rebel areas be sent to Peking, or that their descendants should be barred from future official employment; and I even gave permission for certain officers who had served Shang Chih-hsin and Keng Ching-chung to be re-enrolled in the regular Banners when vacancies occurred.

There had been eight years of bitter war and, though peace had come, the scars were not yet healed. I refused, and continued to refuse, all requests that I be granted new honorific titles as a victor, because this war had resulted from my miscalculations, and the responsibility for it—for all of it—was mine. I had not expected Wu San-kuei to revolt in 1673 when I accepted his retirement pleas. I had not expected so many to follow Wu when he did revolt. And this I wrote out and gave to the Grand Secretary Ledehun to read to all my officials before the Ch'ien-ch'ing Gate that victory winter. They would have to see that I couldn't claim the name of victor in good heart, since the victory sprang from so much error. Nor would I have them evade this issue by finding other scapegoats for the errors and leaving me the role of blameless victor. This, too, I had Ledehun

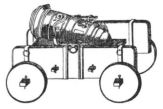

tell them: that in the summer of 1673 only Molo, Mishan, Mingju, Sekde, and Subai had backed my decision to accept Wu's retirement, and in so doing had reinforced my previous convictions, not misled me. Once rebellion broke out, many had sought the deaths of those five advisers, but I had not executed them then nor would I now. I would allow no complacency, after the event, to the rest of my wavering councilors, most of whom were still alive to kneel before Ledehun that morning. They had read the future no more clearly than myself.

Though the Council of Princes and High Officials had not agreed with me in 1673, I had pushed ahead. It seemed possible that, if we were thorough enough and showed that we were in earnest about the transfers of the three southern princes, then they would have no choice but to follow through. So I had briefed Jerken and Fudari, and sent them off from Peking to Yunnan to discuss the details of the move with Wu; I sent other commissioners to Shang and Keng; I told the Boards of War and Civil Office to start selecting potential appointees for the new vacancies that would be opening up in the South; and I set the Board of Revenue to estimating the land and building needs for the princes and their retinues in Manchuria. I have said that even then I did not anticipate a war, but it would have been folly not to take certain precautions: I started Mingju standardizing each Banner company at around 130 men, to make rapid mobilization of our troops simpler; with a few close advisers I made certain contingency plans on defensive zones and staging areas; and I sent a four-man team of Manchus —all skilled horsemen—to keep an eye on Jerken and Fudari, and their reception by Wu.

Then Samha and Dangguri galloped across China with the news of Wu's revolt, and the solution seemed clear: send a hero, send Šodai—who had slain the murderous Suning in my father's own entourage—to hold the Yangtze at Ching-chou. Choose princes as generals, men with the founding emperor's blood in their veins, men of courage above the squabbles of this ordinary world, who would win a speedy victory. Give them robes and sables, gold and armor, pray with them in the shamanic temple, and see them off with majesty from outside the city gates. But then, year after year, I had to watch them blunder and fail, hesitate to advance, stay snug in their base camps; and had to rely—even as rebellious Chinese generals cut the Manchus back—on other Chinese generals to turn the tide.

Throughout, I tried to appear calm to those around me. Each day as usual I rode to Ching-shan, for archery practice. Because most of the troops were at the front, this was resented, and someone illegally posted a placard beside the road, reading: "Now the three rebels have risen, and there is a revolt in Cha-har and campaigns on all fronts; in these times of danger, how do you have the heart to relax in Ching-shan?" I tried not to respond or show fear, lest others' hearts be shaken, though when Yung-hsing was besieged, and communications were cut off, my anxiety showed—and I was rebuked in my ancestors' name by General Biliktu; also in late 1679, when the war threatened to go badly again, when my friend Lasari died, the palace burned, and earthquakes shook the city, I fell sick with exhaustion and was unable to eat, and my grandmother sent me off to rest in the Nan-yüan Gardens.

At the war's beginning I had not followed Songgotu's suggestion that I should execute those whose advice had led to war; so, near the war's end, I would not countenance Wei Hsiang-shu's request that Songgotu be executed, even though Songgotu and his family, besides having given bad advice, were abusing their high position in the arrogance of their great wealth. Wei was a fine official and censor, but as I said to him: You are always talking of morality and following the Tao. How can you be affected by your personal quarrels with Songgotu, and harbor so much hate? And the other leading exponents of morality in behavior—Li Kuang-ti, T'ang Pin, Hsiung Tz'u-li—they always talked of the Tao but could never get on with each other.

There are too many men who claim to be *ju*—pure scholars—and yet are stupid and arrogant; we'd be better off with less talk of moral principle and more practice of it. Even in those who have been the best officials in my reign there are obvious failings. Li Kuang-ti only backed Chinese civil officials, and constantly impeached Chinese Bannermen, though obviously they couldn't *all* be bad; and he was always being cheated by his own disciples, believing anyone who talked about the Tao. P'eng P'eng was always honest and courageous—when robbers were in his district he simply put on his armor, rode out, and routed them—but when angry he was wild and vulgar in his speech, and showed real disrespect. Chao Shen-ch'iao was completely honest, traveled with only thirteen servants and no personal secretaries at all, but was too fond of litigation and was constantly getting the common people involved in complex cases. Shih Shih-lun was an official of complete integrity, but he swung too much in favor of the poor—in any lawsuit when a commoner was involved with a junior degree holder he'd favor the commoner, and when a junior degree holder was involved with a member of the upper gentry he'd favor the junior degree holder. In the same way Yang Ming-shih kept insisting on failing the rich examination candidates and passing the poor, even if they were really crude at letters. And Chang P'eng-ko, whom I praised so often and kept in the highest offices, could write a memorial so stupid that I ordered it printed up and posted in major cities so that everyone could read it—for he claimed that the drop in the river's level was due to a miracle performed by the spirit of the waters, when the real reason was that no rain had fallen for six months in the upper reaches of the Yellow River.

Furthermore, when I accused Chang P'eng-ko of always

backing Chinese over Bannermen he had nothing to say. This is one of the worst habits of the great officials, that if they are not recommending their teachers or their friends for high office then they recommend their relations. This evil practice used to be restricted to the Chinese: they've always formed cliques and then used their recommendations to advance the other members of the clique. Now the practice has spread to the Chinese Bannermen like Yü Ch'eng-lung; and even the Manchus, who used to be so loyal, recommend men from their own Banners, knowing them to have a foul reputation, and will refuse to help the Chinese. When a bad fire broke out in the Chinese quarter of Peking, the senior Manchu officials stood with their hands folded in their sleeves and took no notice, even though I had gone to the scene of the fire in person, and had ordered them to check that it was extinguished.

Therefore, one has to read the impeachment memorials carefully—behind the accusation might lie the fact that one party is Chinese and one a Chinese Bannerman, or one a Chinese and one a Manchu. A good soldier is suddenly impeached for cowardice and having no armor, and one can guess that he is being impeached in order to strike at someone else—a superior, perhaps, or a relative. Or the governor-general of one province impeaches someone's favorite, and suddenly all the officials in his own province are impeached—obviously there is an act of vengeance here.

There is no way the emperor can know every official in the country, so he has to rely on the officials themselves for evaluations, or on censors to impeach the wicked. But when they are in cliques, he has to make his own inquiries as well; for no censor impeached the corrupt army officers Cho-ts'e and Hsü-sheng until I heard how they were hated by their troops and people and had them dismissed. And in Shensi and Shansi there were officials whom I hated even worse than Galdan: for example, Governor Wen-pao, who reported that he was so virtuous that the people had begged to be allowed to erect honorary tablets in his name. But I made inquiries and found that most of them were murmuring in fury and would much rather have eaten him. Partly the trouble lies in failure of contact between top and bottom—after I began to make regular tours through Shantung, Chekiang, and Chiangnan, then things got better there.

The emperor can get extra information in audience, on tours, and in palace memorials. From the beginning of my reign, I sought ways to guarantee that discussion among great officials be kept confidential. The palace memorials were read by me in person, and I wrote the rescripts on them myself, with my left hand if my right was paining me too much. And I checked to see if the senders were writing their memorials in person, even if, like the Kweichow governor, Liu Yin-shu, their sight was so bad that they could hardly write properly. Or else I ordered them to write in Manchu, though military governor Li Lin-sheng claimed that his eyes were too dim to write in Manchu, and that if someone wrote for him in Manchu "because he was poor at Manchu grammar, his deepest sentiments would not shine through and he deeply feared there might be some improprieties of diction." As I told him, "This Chinese certainly can't have been written out by you either!" Of course there were always some who wanted to abuse this right of secrecy, like Molo and Ya-ch'i-na, who insisted on presenting palace memorials on completely unimportant matters. So I simply told them to come in and talk openly about what concerned them in front of the court diarists—after that the two of them presented no more such memorials.

A court audience has the important function of reducing arrogance. Naturally one can't summon all military governors for audiences at the same time, but regular audiences are crucial with military men, especially when they have held power a long time. There might have been no rebellion if Wu San-kuei, Keng Ching-chung, and Shang Chih-hsin had been summoned for regular audiences and made properly fearful. And army officers on the frontiers tend to obey only their own commander, acknowledging him as the ruler. Once, when I sent an edict to General Ma Ch'eng-yin, and he obediently knelt to receive it, his subordinate officers all said, "Does our general kneel to others?" After hearing this, I resolved never to allow too long a tenure of military power. And even in the audience one can attain a level of secrecy. I would let trusted officials sit close beside me, and also those who were a little deaf, so they could speak quietly to me and I could write out my replies; I would ask direct questions that might reveal a whole complex of fraud and misunderstanding, and sometimes I would take my own private notes for later reference.

On tours I learned about the common people's grievances by talking with them, or by accepting their petitions. In northern China I asked peasants about their officials, looked at their houses, and discussed their crops. In the South I heard pleas from a woman whose husband had been wrongfully enslaved, from a traveling trader complaining of high customs dues, from a monk whose temple was falling down, and from a man who was robbed on his way to town of 200 taels of someone else's money that he had promised to invest—a complex predicament, and I had him given 40 taels in partial compensation. But if someone was attacked in an anonymous message, then I refused to take action, for we should always confront a witness directly; and if someone exaggerated too stupidly, then too I would not listen. A man swam toward my boat in Hangchow with a petition tied around his neck, shouting out that he had a certain enemy who was the number-one man in the world for committing evil acts—and I simply had my retainers ask him, "Who then is number two?"

I've tried to be impartial between Manchus and Chinese, and not to separate one from the other in judgments: neither to

have the ministers sit in silence like wooden puppets, nor to let them write out enormous memorials on some subject like the granting of an honorary sage's title to a Sung scholar. There are certainly differences in their characters: the Manchus are direct and open, whereas the Chinese think it better not to let any joy or anger show in their faces. And the Manchus are often tougher and braver than Chinese Bannermen, and treat both slaves and horses better. But the Manchus' scholarship is often in no ways inferior to that of the Chinese and, even if they commit some abuses—riding their horses into the civil officials' yamens or disrupting proceedings in the courts—there is no need for a senior official like Shao-kan to plead that people are bound to be fearful of him since he is a Manchu. And though the Manchu vice-president Šalai had to be demoted for drinking too heavily and playing the dice—and drinking and gambling were prevalent in the army, and even among the Manchu nobles—Han T'an too drank heavily as Chancellor of the Hanlin Academy and continued to do so as president of the Board of Rites, while many of the Hanlin scholars drank also or wasted their time playing chess. Drinking and gambling are curses that lessen any man's mind and strength and waste his substance, ruining rich and poor alike. As Shao Yung once said, Yang numbers are even, Yin numbers are odd, the Yang are the smaller, and the Yin the larger, so in all things there are less of the good and more of the bad, and people find it hard to follow the good and easy to follow the bad.

For his part, the emperor has to withstand the praise that showers upon him and fills his ears, for it is of no more use to him than so-called "restorative medicine"; these banalities and evasions have all the sustenance of dainty pastries, and one grows sick of them. In 1680 I had begun a preliminary reading of the *Book of Changes* with K'u-le-na, Yeh Fang-ai, and Chang Yü-shu, taking three days over each hexagram. Four years later we began to go through it again, and I became aware of the lecturers' category of "things there was no need to discuss," in which they had placed the sixth line of *Ch'ien*, the first hexagram: "Arrogant dragon will have cause to repent." The Commentary said, "Arrogance means that one knows how to press forward but not how to draw back, that one knows existence but not annihilation, knows something about winning but nothing about losing"; and I told the lecturers: "In heaven, as among men, everything follows this principle as it is expressed in the *Book of Changes*, that arrogance will lead to sorrow. We should by rights take this as a warning; it's not something we should shy away from. In the future, as we discuss the sections of the Commentary, make no divisions between what should and what should not be discussed. Discuss each section as it appears, in sequence." For we had already discussed, in the hexagram *Feng*, how "When the sun stands at midday, it begins to set; when the moon is full, it begins to wane. The fullness and emptiness of heaven and earth wane and wax in the course of time. How much truer is this of men, or of spirits and gods."

The third line of the same hexagram talks of the mean men who push themselves forward and prevent the able men from undertaking major work. You have to define and reward people in accordance with their status in life. If too much grace is shown to inferiors they become lazy and uppity and will be sure to stir up trouble—and if you neglect them they will abuse you behind your back. That was why I insisted on such strictness when the eunuch Ch'ien Wen-ts'ai beat a commoner to death, saying strangulation was not enough. For eunuchs are basically Yin in nature. They are quite different from ordinary people; when weak with age they babble like babies. In my court I never let them get involved with government—even the few eunuchs-of-the-presence with whom I might chatter or exchange family jokes were never allowed to discuss politics. I only have about four hundred, as opposed to the immense numbers there were in the Ming, and I keep them working at menial jobs, I ignore their frowns and smiles and make sure that they stay poor. Whereas in the later Ming Dynasty, besides being so extravagant and reckless, they obtained the power to write endorsements on the emperors' memorials, for the emperors were unable to read the one- or two-thousand-character memorials that flowed in; and the eunuchs in turn passed the memorials on to *their* subordinates to handle.

Admittedly there has to be a limit to the work that any one person can do, and when the P'ing-yang prefect, Ch'in, boasted that he could handle seven or eight hundred items of business in one day, I demoted him, saying: "I've been ruling for forty years, and only during the Wu San-kuei rebellion did I handle five hundred items of business in one day. Nor did I myself hold the brush and write the documents, and even so I could not get to bed until midnight. You may fool other people but you can't fool me." In other military campaigns there were sometimes up to four hundred memorials, but usually there are about fifty a day and it's not too hard to read them, and even to correct the mistakes in them. What those memorials must contain is specific and detailed information on matters that the emperor cannot check for himself. I told General Fulata, when he reported in 1675 that "the bandits' supplies are low and they are ready to surrender," that such a rough sketch gives no clarification at all. I want to know about the bandits' defenses both on land and water, I want to know the names of the bandit leaders, and the condition of our troops, and whether or not they can take the offensive. Only then did Fulata reply that there were two senior bandit generals and eight junior generals, commanding six thousand cavalry, extended in twenty-five linked camps on a north–south axis from Ch'ang-shih-ling to San-chiang, and three naval commanders with about ten thousand men and three hundred vessels.

In river conservancy work also, though there are only two broad choices—should one speed the flow of water to the sea, or should one heighten the dikes?—it's the constant attention to details that is of the greatest importance. There are the related problems of grain transport on the Grand Canal and what that does to the comparative prices of grain, as well as the rivers' backing up and flooding the lands and farms. So I not only dismissed incompetent directors-general, but also supervised the able ones like Yü Ch'eng-lung and Chang P'eng-ko in person. In addition, I made regular tours of inspection and had river maps drawn for me by my own trusted staff.

Later, when the palace memorial system was well established, Governor Chang Po-hsing reported that his troops had arrested the pirate Ts'ai Shun, and confiscated both ginseng and gunpowder from his boat. I had to remind him that "you must report things clearly in your palace memorials. I don't know [from your report] where in the South this 'big bird boat' of the arrested Ts'ai Shun came from, nor where it was going in the North, nor is there any evidence about these people. Make further investigations." By this time I had known for a decade that these "bird boats" were made in Fukien and Chekiang, that they followed the trade routes by moving north up the coast to Tientsin in the sixth month, and then sailed back in the tenth month when the winds blew from the north. To learn about pirates you need more than official reports—you can question pirate leaders in person, as I did Ch'en Shang-i, and learn how to cut down their fleets, how to stop them landing, and how to cut off their supplies of gunpowder. You can map the islands they use as bases, and restrict them to rocky islands where no crops or trees will grow, and where there is no good drinking water. So the robbers on the sea are made no different from the robbers on the land, and in the winter months they will be forced to come ashore. Or you can let trusted officials recruit their own special forces, like Shih

Shih-p'iao and his force of one hundred Fukienese, which was so effective in patrolling the coast. Or you can let the local generals make better models of firearms—even if not as good as the ones made in the palace, they are still better than the old "horse-hoof" cannon, which were only good for the noise they made. You can employ captured pirates themselves as advisers, or use them to take messages to their fellows and induce them to surrender, or send agents to travel on merchant ships and trace the pirates' routes. But it is not a good method to disguise troops as merchants and send them out as decoys to catch the pirates—when that was tried in Kwangtung, the disguised "merchants" attacked "pirate" boats that were in fact genuine merchant boats, and caused much hardship.

Much of the advice I received for controlling pirates was simply stupid: that all merchant vessels should be flat-bottomed, for instance, and limited to one mast, or that merchants should carry arms and gunpowder. Such advice came from people who did not understand that a merchant vessel carries its cargo below the level of the waterline so as to ride the waves properly, and that even when they are armed, merchants will still not fight. Though certainly if the arms were good enough the pirates would stay away; Ch'en Shang-i said that his band never used to attack Western ships, out of fear of their cannon. One needs, too, to examine the type of person who is a pirate— some are not experienced robbers at all, but simply merchants who lost their capital and had no recourse but to turn to crime; and some, as Shih Shih-p'iao observed, are local no-goods who stole a fisherman's boat and went to sea, then captured a merchant vessel—but they remain independent stars and never form a united fleet. What one must do is check constantly, even if everything seems peaceful.

Similar problems occur with salt smugglers: the unemployed vagrants from Honan or Shantung come into the Lianghuai area and meet up with local smuggling gangs—perhaps as few as sixty or as many as two hundred, armed and reckless men with their own boats—and load up their shoulder packs (or even whole carts) with illegal salt. Here at least one can assemble fleets of river patrol boats, give them identification markers, and assign them a specific terrain; but with the miners in the South, supervision is even harder. Many were driven out of work when the mines were closed, and either continued to mine illegally or robbed those who lived nearby. They hid out in the mine shafts and tunnels, or even forced local merchants to shelter them. Some robbers were local men, some were outsiders, known as "galloping horses." The two groups would work together—the locals gave help with topography, the "galloping horses" gave the locals extra strength. When troops approached, the "galloping horses" would flee swiftly, or else be hidden in the locals' houses. There's no way to catch them unless you buy the information, and the only long-range solution is to forbid new mines being opened so that no miners will have to be disposed of afterward.

Sometimes I have stated that the people of a certain province have certain bad characteristics: thus the men of Fukien are turbulent and love acts of daring—even their scholars use shield and sword; while the people of Shensi are tough and cruel, they love feuding and killing, their practices are truly repugnant. Shantung men are stubborn in a bad way; they always have to be first, they nurse their hatreds, they seem to value life lightly, and a lot of them become robbers. Khalka Mongols are moody and never know when they have enough—you'll never be able to please them by giving them things; no one would ever be able to satisfy their desires. Whereas the people of Shansi are so stingy that they won't even care for the aged in their own families; if a stranger comes to them they won't give him a meal, but they'll encourage him to drink and gamble and lead him into wild expenditures. And since the Kiangsu people are both prosperous and immoral—there's no need to blow their feathers to look for faults—I was not surprised to learn that the "rich merchants" I'd heard about in Kiangsu were mostly from Shansi.

But we can't go on from this to say a whole area is worthless, as Governor-General Chu Hung-tso branded Fukien in his triennial assessment, or insist there are no good scholars in the whole Yenan border region, or claim every Southerner is frivolous and worthless. Talent does not depend on geographical location. Even in the mountain wildernesses how can there be no one with ability? Have the talented ever chosen where they were to be born?

In 1694 I noted that we were losing talent because of the way the exams were being conducted: even in the military *chin-shih* exams most of the successful candidates were from Chekiang and Chiangnan, while there was only one from Honan and one from Shansi. The successful ones had often done no more than memorize old examination answer books, whereas the best *should* be selected on the basis of riding and archery. Yet it is always the strong men from the western provinces who are eager to serve in the army, while not only are troops from Chekiang and Chiangnan among the weakest, they also pass on their posts to their relatives who are also weak.

Even among the examiners there are those who are corrupt, those who do not understand basic works, those who ask detailed questions about practical matters of which they know nothing, those who insist entirely on memorization of the *Classics* and refuse to set essays, those who put candidates from their own geographical area at the top of the list, or those who make false claims about their abilities to select the impoverished and deserving. One can sometimes tell stylistically if a candidate is a Northerner or a Southerner, but how can one tell from a *chü-jen* exam paper, with the name sealed over, whether the candidate is rich or poor? As to the candidates, not only are there few in the Hanlin Academy who can write a proper eulogy, there are many whose calligraphy is bad and who can't even punctuate the basic history books. When I had the Chinese Bannermen who'd bought their ranks given a special examination, many either brought in books to copy, or handed in blank sheets. Other candidates hire people to sit the exams for them, or else pretend to be from a province that has a more liberal quota than their own. It's usually easy enough to check the latter, since I've learnt to recognize the accents from thirteen provinces, and if you watch the person and study his voice you can tell where he is really from. As to the other problems, one can overcome some of them by holding the exams under rigorous armed supervision and then reading the exam papers oneself—in a boat while inspecting the river works, if necessary, as I did with the 183 re-examined *chü-jen* candidates in 1700, grading their papers by four ranks in different categories, and letting the best sit for the *chin-shih* exams in Peking—or in a tent at Pa-chou, as I had done with the *po-hsüeh* exams twenty-two years before. And with the smaller number of scholars in the Hanlin Academy I could scrutinize them in batches of ten before the exam, write out the questions myself in vermilion, and have the candidates take the exam in the Ch'ang-ch'un Palace under the eyes of senior officials. So I could tell if they knew Manchu or not, and if their poems were their own, and speak to them personally after the written exam was over.

When a person is truly good, then one should use him and promote him—even into the Hanlin—regardless of whether he has advanced degrees: mathematicians like Mei Ku-ch'eng and Minggantu; Wang Lan-sheng in phonology; Kao Shih-ch'i in classical scholarship; and Li Tu-no in calligraphy. And on occasion I have chosen those who had made their reputations in the Hanlin Academy or in scholarship, and sent them off to be provincial governors, as with Wang Tu-chao, Chang

Po-hsing, and Ch'en Yüan-lung, all from the *chin-shih* class
of 1685.

On appointing Ch'en in 1711, I told him: "When you get
to Kwangsi you must ensure harmony between civil and military, and keep troops and commoners at peace. The governor
is responsible for the troops, and must drill them constantly.
You've been in the Hanlin Academy for many years, so I am
going to make a special experiment of appointing you to a
senior provincial post, and see how you are able to manage
things." At first his memorials were too long and in the wrong
format, and he passed on a report that magical *chih* fungus had
been found on a mountaintop under a fragrant cloud, sure
proof of the Emperor's virtue and promise of long life to come;
and even though he knew I did not value such auspicious
omens, he was duty-bound to send it in to the palace, so I
could examine it or use it for medicine. I replied that the *Histories* are full of these strange omens, but they are of no help in
governing the country, and that the best omens were good har-
vests and contented people. Later his memorials were shorter,
there was no more *chih* fungus, and he became a sensible governor.

In 1711, too, I made Wang Tu-chao Governor of Chekiang,
and despite his lack of experience he was good from the first,
ably discussing problems of high prices in Hangchow because
of the size of the population there, and tracing a drop in customs yields at Nan-hsin to the absence of timber shipments
due to intensive tree felling. When he attacked a powerful chief
clerk, and was in turn slandered for being involved with a
troupe of actors, I was conscious of the complexities of the case,
and handled it without bringing in the other senior officials,
and even made him Acting-Governor of Kiangsu during Chang
Po-hsing's trial. But his memorials began to show less and less
concern for the people, and finally I dismissed him from the
governorship and made him a vice-president of the Board of

Works. (So, when a Board vice-president turns out to be dishonest, do we sometimes transfer him to be a military general.) As for Chang Po-hsing himself, I had to transfer him in 1716 from being Governor of Kiangsu and make him a superintendent of granaries in Peking. In 1707, hearing of his reputation on the Southern Tour, I had asked the senior provincial officials if there was anyone as good as him, and they all said there wasn't. So I said, "Why, then, did none of you recommend him? I'll recommend him myself. If he turns out to be a good official, then the people can say I'm a perspicacious ruler. If he turns out to be corrupt, and breaks the law, then the people can laugh and say that I am no judge of men." I appointed him Governor of Fukien, and then of Kiangsu, but he got involved in the impeachment case with Gali and was finally condemned to death by the Board of Punishments for panicking about pirates and unlawfully killing several innocent people in jail. I refused to punish him, but did tell the Grand Secretaries: "He is truly not a man fit to be a governor. Yet he can prevent bribery, and has great integrity. Let him be put in charge of some financial post where there's not too much going on."

Ever since the "San-fan War" had ended, and the ravaged provinces of Yunnan, Kweichow, Kwangsi, and Szechwan had returned to their former prosperity, I had sought some way of both leveling off taxes and getting accurate assessments of the population increase. Wang Tu-chao had pointed out skillfully, in a palace memorial of 1711, the fact that the canceling of taxes might *not* in fact bring benefits to an area like Chekiang. For among the great variety of taxes there, priority had to be given to the grain-transport system, and only after that had all been collected did people concentrate on raising money for the basic *ting* land-tax assessments. Furthermore, in the fourth month people were busy with silk production, and in the fifth month busy in the fields, and their livelihood depended on the state of the weather—yet these honest farmers paid up their taxes

before the deadline, whereas scoundrels or corrupt clerks delayed their payments year after year and piled up millions of taels, so that when an exemption was granted it benefited these bad people and not the good ones who had already paid. His suggestion was to combine the current 1711 exemptions with a thorough attempt to clear up all the 1710 unpaid *ting* taxes, and stop the scoundrels profiting from the system. I concurred, adding that many of these local scoundrels were actually provincial officials, and telling Wang to rephrase a few sentences of his palace memorial and resubmit it as an open memorial, for discussion by the Boards.

For, whenever I had gone on tours, I had made a point of trying to find out what was the status of the local *ting* unit. One household might be listed as having five or six *ting* but have only one person paying any taxes; another might have nine or ten *ting* but only two or three taxpayers. Obviously the population was increasing; but, at the same time, the amount of land was not increasing—even rocky and sandy soil, even the mountainous areas, were fully cultivated. So it would not be right to increase *ting* assessments in accordance with the population increase—yet for fear that I would do this, the provincial officials were not accurately reporting the increases in their localities when they sent in their census reports. So I resolved to make a perpetual quota of the current *ting* figures for tax purposes, at a little over 24,620,000, and list the population increases above that number in a census category of "Increased population never to be subject to increased taxation." I acknowledged the fear of local officials that if they reported increased population, they would be assessed for increased taxes, and tried to end that fear: "How could you have known that I would not increase taxes, but wanted only to know the exact figures? If the senior provincial officials do not henceforth report exact figures, I'll start with Chihli and send men to make a check, household by household, so that I can find out the truth. What will you all have to say then?"

Hu Tso-mei, a vice-president of the Board of Rites, pointed out a number of problems, particularly those that would arise from deciding who should be on the taxpaying quotas. For there would be no advantage to those currently listed on the *ting* registers—all the benefits would go to the newly registered people (except for those of them who were chosen to maintain the old quotas at their old levels). If five men die, and there are ten new ones, which men shall be chosen to pay taxes? Surely there would be corrupt clerks who would leave out the strong and include the weak, not list the rich but charge the poor? The more the population increased, the more extortion there would be. His suggestion was that in each census year the tax quotas should be redivided among the entire surviving population, so that all would pay the same, and each year the tax burden could get lighter. But I decided to go along with the original plan, after first giving massive rebates of over 32,000,000 taels, to enable all arrears to be made up.

I reminded the provincial officials that I really was concerned about the people's livelihood, and warned them to permit no fraud or concealment which might prevent my favors from reaching the common people, and not to use these changes to exact new payments. And I ordered them, on the very day they received the edict, to display it in every city and its schools, and in every village and hamlet.

In the winter of 1672, when I was young, I had told the lecturers in the Mao-ch'in Palace that good government seemed to depend on letting the people live at rest, that the way of good government was in not hurting them: having a whole lot of trouble was not as good as stopping trouble from occurring. Likewise I rejected the suggestion that I might let the censors report to me on the basis of hearsay, because dishonest people might use this means to harm the worthy and stir up trouble. Thirty-two years later, when Ts'ao Yin suggested rooting out all excess fees in the salt monopoly, working down from the governor-general to the local magistrates, I combined these phrases from the past in my warning to him: "Stirring up trouble is not as good as preventing trouble occurring. If you just concentrate on matters of immediate concern, I'm afraid that you'll get more than you bargained for." And I used the same caution to others, to military governor Shih I-te in 1710 and to General Chang Ku-chen in 1711.

When Governor Marsai was impeached for extreme corruption in Shansi, I said to Korkon, the president of the Board of Revenue: "You told me, before, that Marsai was a straightforward man who did not stir up trouble. Who first said this?" Korkon replied that everyone knew that Marsai was honest, but it was censor Ch'en T'ing-ching, a Shansi man, who had first said Marsai did not stir up trouble. Ch'en, however, said that in discussion with the other ministers he had said that Marsai was "average," not that he did not stir up trouble. So I asked Korkon again, and this time he said it was vice-president Chiang Hung-tao who had used the phrase. Chiang replied that he'd been away from home a long time and had no idea what Marsai's behavior was like. So after criticizing them for making feeble excuses, I gave them this warning: "Among current officials are there others who are as avaricious as Marsai? If you say that such men as these 'don't stir up trouble,' what credibility will my senior officials have for me hereafter?" As I wrote to Governor Lang T'ing-chi, when he first reported on the military officials in Kiangsi, and on the prevalence there of padded rolls that inflated the real number of active soldiers on duty: "There's an old saying that if the civilian officials don't seek money and the military officials aren't afraid of death, we need never fear that the country won't have Great Peace." How true that is! And again I told him: "The Tao of being an official lies in nothing else than this: Be sincere in your heart, and sincere in your administration, don't stir up too much trouble, and have officials and people love you as a mother. That is being a good official."

The *Doctrine of the Mean* says: "The superior man does what is proper to the station in which he is; he does not desire to go beyond this. In a high situation, he does not treat with contempt his inferiors. In a low situation, he does not court the favor of his superiors. He rectifies himself, and seeks for nothing from others, so that he has no dissatisfactions. He does not murmur against Heaven nor grumble against man. Thus it is that the superior man is quiet and calm, waiting for the appointments of Heaven, while the mean man walks in dangerous paths, looking for lucky occurrences." These are truly wise words, clear as sun or stars.

This is what we have to do: apply ourselves to human affairs to the utmost, while remaining responsive to the dictates of Heaven. In agriculture one must work hard in the fields *and* hope for fair weather. In bad droughts I have spent three days praying in a simple hut of mats, not even taking a bite of salted or pickled vegetables, and then—after the fast—walked to the Temple of Heaven; and in the spring drought of 1688 I ordered the *Book of Changes* consulted, and the diviners drew the hexagram *Kuai*, "Breakthrough," which meant that rain would fall only after some of the great had been humbled:

> The superior man is firmly resolved.
> He walks alone and is caught in the rain.
> He is bespattered,
> And people murmur against him.
> No blame.

And again:

> In dealing with weeds,
> Firm resolution is necessary.

That same month I removed from office all the senior members of Grand Secretary Mingju's clique.

My diviners have often been tempted to pass over bad auguries, but I have double-checked their calculations and warned them not to distort the truth: the Bureau of Astronomy once reported that a benevolent southeast wind was blowing, but I myself calculated the wind's direction with the palace instruments and found it to be, in fact, an inauspicious northeast wind; I told the Bureau to remember that ours was not a dynasty that shunned bad omens; I also warned the Bureau not to guess or exaggerate in interpreting the omens that they observed, but simply to state their findings. Human affairs are involved in the phenomenon of eclipses, and it makes no difference that we can now calculate them with absolute precision; we must still make the reforms necessary to avoid trouble and obtain peace. Just as human affairs are involved in the problem of locusts: it makes no sense to say, with the common people, that locusts just cannot be prevented; if their eggs have hatched before the cold weather comes, people can still save themselves from calamity by plowing the eggs under and so saving the next year's harvest. Things may seem determined in our lives, but there are these and other ways in which man's power can develop Heaven's work: with something as small as the burning-glass [a lens] and the south-pointing compass we can penetrate the shaping forces. And being precise about forecasting the motions of sun, moon, and planets, the winter and summer festivals, the eclipses of sun and moon—all that is relevant to regulating spring planting, summer weeding, and autumn harvest. We must urge on Heaven in its work, not just rely upon it.

Similarly, in our own lives: though fixed by fate, yet that fate comes from our own minds, and our happiness is sought for in ourselves. Thus predictions are made from the planets' courses about marriage and fortune, children, career, and the passing years—but these predictions are often not fulfilled in later experience. That's because if you do not perform your human part you cannot comprehend Heaven's way. If the fortune-teller says you will be successful, can you then say, "I'm bound to do well and needn't study properly"? If he says you'll be rich, can you sit still and let the wealth come? If he offers you a life without misfortune, can you be reckless without fear? Or be debauched without harm because he says you'll live long without illness? When a soothsayer is crazy and heterodox like Chu Fang-tan, and able to mislead the governor of a province or the senior military commanders with his wild remarks and seditious books, then he must be beheaded. But when a man casts a horoscope as well as blindman Lo, then even the most senior generals should be sent to consult with him.

Once as a youth I was in the mountains, among deep woods, when suddenly there were crashes of thunder and I fled. Moments later the trees among which I had been walking were struck. So we see that though it is hard to fathom Heaven's signs, if you approach them openly you can attain a kind of foreknowledge. I have never tired of the *Book of Changes,* and have used it in fortune-telling and as a source of moral principles; the only thing you must not do, I told my court lecturers, is to make this book appear simple, for there are meanings here that lie beyond words. The written word has its limits and its challenges, for the primal sound in the whole world is that made by the human voice, and the likeness of this human voice must be rendered in dots and strokes. Therefore, I have practiced my Chinese calligraphy regularly, often writing more than a thousand characters a day; I use my own hand to write my edicts, I copy ancient calligraphic styles in my old age (as I used to when I was a boy, studying with my eunuchs in the palace), and I also practice my Manchu writing, to keep it clear and fast. Yet I never forget that the voice, too, is important: when my name appears in the invocations to the gods, I tell my ritual officials: Don't mumble or hesitate. Speak it in a loud voice, clearly, and without fear.

思

III   Thinking

LINES IN PRAISE OF A SELF-CHIMING CLOCK

The skill originated in the West,
But, by learning, we can achieve the artifice:
Wheels move and time turns round,
Hands show the minutes as they change.

Red-capped watchmen, there's no need to announce dawn's
    coming.
My golden clock has warned me of the time.
By first light I am hard at work,
And keep on asking, "Why are the memorials late?"

K'ANG-HSI, c. 1705

Too many people claim to know things when, in fact, they know nothing about them. Since my childhood I have always tried to find things out for myself and not to pretend to have knowledge when I was ignorant. Whenever I met older people I would ask them about the experiences they had had, and remember what they said. Keep an open mind, and you'll learn things; you will miss other people's good qualities if you just concentrate on your own abilities. It's my nature to enjoy asking questions, and the crudest or simplest people have something of value to say, something one can check through to the source and remember.

Most good artisans have some special skills that they want to keep secret, and they don't want to reveal them to anyone else. I make it a condition that I won't tell anyone if they tell me, and so they do. Their concentration on one specialty, their refusal to dissipate their mental energy, seems to give strength to their bodies: calligraphers born as long ago as the late Ming, painters, artisans who make various utensils—they often live to be seventy or eighty, healthy and skillful as in their youth, like old Chou, the Soochow instrument maker, or the palace music instructor Chu Ssu-mei, who at eighty still knew so well the *p'i-p'a* lute and its tones.

If you want to really know something you have to observe or experience it in person; if you claim to know something on the basis of hearsay, or on happening to see it in a book, you'll be a laughingstock to those who really know. For instance the Ancients used to talk of *lu* and *mi* deer as two species, taking the shedding of their horns as evidence, though they didn't understand the sequences by which horns grew. In fact there are a great many species of *lu* deer—in mountains, marshes, on rivers, near the seashore—and the Ancients didn't know the difference. Or take the two musical instruments called the *hsün* and the *ch'ih*. The *Book of Poetry* says:

> The elder blew the porcelain *hsün*,
> The younger blew the bamboo *ch'ih*.
> It was as if I was strung on the same string
>   with you.

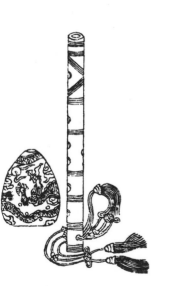

Scholars in their poems are always using *hsün* and *ch'ih* to refer to the affection between two brothers. But when I asked them if they'd ever seen a *hsün* or a *ch'ih*, they all said no. So one New Year's Eve I told the eunuchs to take a *hsün* and a *ch'ih* out of the musical-instrument collection in the Ch'ien-ch'ing Palace, and show them to the scholars in the Hanlin and the Southern Library, who then realized what these instruments were really like. Similarly with the music itself—the pitches and the principles are the same in all countries and across all time, but the instruments must be manufactured and kept in tune, and the harmonies properly studied.

Sometimes an exact answer is hard to find, as with the morning and evening tides. Whenever I was on the seashore—

whether in Shan-hai-kuan, or Tientsin, or near the mouth of the Yangtze River—I would observe when the tides rose and fell. But when I would question the locals they generally all gave different answers, and the records of the times kept in different places were also different. Later I found that even water in springs and wells fluctuates slightly in level, though again one can't be precise about the time. I questioned Westerners and ocean sailors; they all disagreed. Clearly Chu Hsi was right that there is a relationship between tides and the moon's waxing and waning, but it's hard to get clearer than that.

So we draw our idea of "principle" from experience rather than from study, though we need to keep aware of both. Many people, after all, call old porcelain vessels "antiques"; but if we think of vessels from the view of principle, then we know that once they were meant to be used. Only now are they grubby-looking and unsuitable for us to drink from, so we end up putting them on our desks or on bookshelves, and look at them once in a while. On the other hand, we can change the function of a given object and thus change its nature, as I did by converting a rustless sword that the Dutch once gave me into a measuring stick that I kept on my desk. As the Jesuit Antoine Thomas observed, this was converting something that gave fear into something that gave pleasure. The rare can become common, as with the lions and other animals that foreign ambassadors like to give us and my children are now accustomed to; though when something new appears, I always take a close look at it, as with the sea lion that the Korean king gave me once on a Northern Tour. I immediately sent riders back to Peking for a copy of the book in which the Westerners said this creature could be identified.

Western skills are a case in point: in the late Ming Dynasty, when the Westerners first brought the gnomon, the Chinese thought it a rare treasure until they understood its use. And when the Emperor Shun-chih got a small chiming clock in 1653, he kept it always near him; but now we have learned to balance the springs and to adjust the chimes and finally to make the whole clock, so that my children can have ten chiming clocks each to play with, if they want them. Similarly, we learned in a short time to make glassware that is superior to that made in the West, and our lacquer would be better than theirs, too, were it not that their wet sea climate gives a better sheen than the dry and dusty Chinese climate ever could.

Ask questions about everything and investigate everything; things will start to go well when you are not fooled by books—how can you believe Tung Chung-shu's statement that "Peace comes upon the world when the wind does not make the branches sing nor the rain break up the clods of earth"? Unless the wind moves in the branches how will things be stirred up into life? Unless the rain breaks up the clods how can the land be plowed and seeds sown? On investigation we see that his words are gloss and nonsense, not to be believed. Pereira could explain, when I asked him, why it was that stags might set fire to a tree when they rubbed their horns against it, and why rotting trees gave off a kind of light in the darkness. Ancient books also recorded that students could study at night by the light of fireflies placed in a bag—but I had my retainers in Jehol collect hundreds of fireflies and place them in a big bag, and they didn't give out enough light to read a single character. Yet in the case of the Han author Tung-fan So, who recorded that in the north there was ice hundreds of feet thick that never melted, and rats weighing thousands of pounds that lived underground, the Russians have recently reported that there is indeed a region of ice, and that rats as big as elephants [i.e., mammoths] have been found there with bones of ivory from which utensils can be made. These utensils I have seen for myself. Other strange things I have only read about but have had corroborated by those I trust: Lasi and Cangšeo said that they knew that in the lands to the west of China, though there was no drought such as we have, yet hardship came in other ways. Sometimes the grains turned into insects and flew away, and at other times when the grain was ripening the kernels filled with blood.

I told Chang Ying once, on a Southern Tour, that there is no need to visit a temple again if you've already been there several times, and I myself like to go to different shrines, whether to the temples in the South, to Wu-t'ai-shan (where I wrote a eulogy in Manchu and had it carved on stone), or to the top of Mount T'ai (where Confucius once stood and surveyed the world below). On that journey, in 1684, I refused my retainers' requests that we visit the precipices where people sometimes killed themselves, hoping that by offering up their own lives they might save those of their dying parents. I refused to condone such acts by visiting the place where they occurred; for even if the suicide was committed in the name of filial piety, by killing himself the victim cut off forever all chances of helping his parents. Instead, I proceeded to Confucius' home at Ch'ü-fu, made the ritual prostrations and offerings, heard the ritual music, and listened to the ritual lectures on the *Great Learning* and the *Book of Changes.* Then I told Confucius' descendant, the Yen-sheng duke, K'ung Yü-ch'i, and his clansman K'ung Shang-jen to show me around.

The guards officers removed the protective screens and brushed off the dust from the precious objects, and I asked for details about them, one by one. "Tell me about this." "A statue of Confucius made by Governor Li T'ing during the Eastern Wei Dynasty [in A.D. 541]." "And these sacrificial vessels, of what date?" "Left here by Han Chang-ti when he worshipped here [in A.D. 85]." "Which of these portraits is the most authentic?" "One claimed to be drawn by Confucius' disciple Tzu Kung, as copied by Ku K'ai-chih [fourth century A.D.]." "And this calligraphy?" "'Flying White' style by Emperor Sung Hui-tsung."

And to K'ung Shang-jen: "How old are you?" "Thirty-seven." "What generation descendant of the Sage?" "Sixty-fourth." "What generation is K'ung Yü-ch'i?" "Sixty-seventh." "You who are aged thirty-seven have how many sons?" "Two." "You're not more than thirty-seven?" "No, thirty-seven." "Can you compose poetry?" "I've made some study of it."

There was a tree that Confucius planted with his own hands. I asked, "This tree is not rotten, why doesn't it have any branches?" "Because the leaves and branches were burned off in a Ming Dynasty fire [in 1499] and only the bare trunk remained; for two hundred years now it has neither decayed nor bloomed, it is as hard as iron, and known as 'Iron Tree.'" I ordered my retainers to touch it, for this was a strange thing. "And where are the Han Dynasty tablets?" "In the K'uei-wen Hall, where the books of the past are stored. To the right of the gateway is the one now called the 'Hundred Family Tablet,' dating from the Han Yüan-chia period [A.D. 153]." "Why is it called the 'Hundred Family Tablet'?" "After a Han Dynasty ritual office that had its incumbents nominated by the Sage's descendants."

I asked, "Are there any other antiquities beyond this doorway?" Yes, they said, there was the "Wall Stream," but since it had no spring it dried up easily; one had to deflect a spring from the east to make the water flow into the temple, then the "Wall Stream" filled up, but they didn't dare to do this without authority, unless there was an edict.

The temple grounds were so extensive: where was the Sage's own dwelling? Behind the hall where I heard the lectures were the Lu wall ruins, where Confucius had his home. So I leaned over the railings of Confucius' well and, admiring, drew some water and tasted it. I asked about the ruins, and they said it was in this wall that the ninth-generation descendant of Confucius hid the *Classics* when the Emperor Ch'in Shih-huang burned the books. They were rediscovered when Emperor Han Ching-ti's fifth son started to pull down the buildings to make way for his own palace [*c.* A.D. 150]. I had them point out the actual places, and looked them over carefully.

Trees and grasses grew on Confucius' tomb, and I faced north and kowtowed before it, offering three libations from the golden bowl of wine that Mingju held. "What are those trees and grasses growing on the tomb? What are the *k'ai* trees used for? Isn't there any *chih* grass? Bring me some to look at. If fifty blades are growing in one clump of *chih* grass, the divinations you make with it will be fulfilled. Is there any of that kind here or not?" Not at present, they said, but some would surely grow in honor of the Emperor's visit. So I had them hunt for what there was, and when they found some I took a double handful and inhaled its strange fragrance.

Finally, when I had looked around at everything, I sat in the Hall, facing south, and asked them:

"How big is the estate around this wood?"

"The area covers 18 *ch'ing*. For two thousand years now the clan has been growing, so there's no room left in the burial ground."

"What are you going to do about it?"

"That the Emperor should ask such a question is truly a blessing for a thousand generations. But beyond our woods the land is all registered as people's fields; we absolutely cannot expand it. We just hope for special favors from the Emperor."

I laughed with my retainers and said, "Send in your memorial."

To K'ung Yü-ch'i I gave a ceremonial robe trimmed with fox fur, and a black sable jacket; to K'ung Shang-jen and his brother I gave stipends as students in the Imperial Academy.

Earlier on that tour I had ridden in a junk across the Yang-

tze and it had moved swiftly enough over the calm waters; but neither that nor the other boats I tried seemed really safe. So later I visited the Soochow shipyards and investigated the construction of vessels, and I personally supervised the design of a "Yellow Boat," which was both beautiful and sturdy. Even in high winds there was no need to worry in this boat—that was another case of studying the root of a problem, discussing it with ordinary people, and then having it solved.

I realized, too, that Western mathematics has its uses. I first grew interested in this subject shortly after I came to the throne, during the confrontations between the Jesuit Adam Schall and his Chinese critic, Yang Kuang-hsien, when the two men argued the merits of their respective techniques by the Wu-men Gate and none of the great officials there knew what was going on. Schall died in prison, but after I had learned something about astronomy I pardoned his friend Verbiest in 1669 and gave him an official position, promoting him in 1682. In 1687 I let the newly arrived Jesuit Fontaney and the others come to Peking, although they had come to China illegally on a Chinese merchant vessel and the Board of Rites had recommended their deportation; and throughout the 1680's I discussed Western skills in Manchu with Verbiest, and I made Grimaldi and Pereira learn the language as well, so they could converse with me.

After the Treaty of Nerchinsk had been signed with the Russians, I ordered the Jesuits Thomas, Gerbillon, and Bouvet to study Manchu also, and to compose treatises in that language on Western arithmetic and the geometry of Euclid. In the early 1690's I often worked several hours a day with them. With Verbiest I had examined each stage of the forging of cannons, and made him build a water fountain that operated in conjunction with an organ, and erect a windmill in the court; with the new group—who were later joined by Brocard and Jartoux, and worked in the Yang-hsin Palace under the gen-

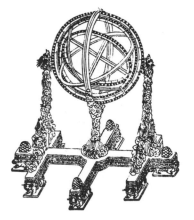

eral direction of my Eldest Son Yin-t'i—I worked on clocks and mechanics. Pereira taught me to play the tune *"P'u-yen-chou"* on the harpsichord and the structure of the eight-note scale, Pedrini taught my sons musical theory, and Gherardini painted portraits at the Court. I also learned to calculate the weight and volume of spheres, cubes, and cones, and to measure distances and the angle of river banks. On inspection tours later I used these Western methods to show my officials how to make more accurate calculations when planning their river works. I myself planted the measuring device in the ground, and got my sons and bodyguards to use their spears and stakes to mark the various distances. I held the calculating tray on my knee, wrote down the figures with a stylus, then transposed them with a brush. I showed them how to calculate circumferences and assess the area of a plot of land, even if its borders were as jagged as dogs' teeth, drawing diagrams for them on the ground with an arrow; and calculated the flow of river water through a lock gate by multiplying the volume that flowed in a few seconds to get a figure for the whole day.

Initially, when Jartoux presented his tables to analyze the different phases of the sun's movements, I thought them not worth accepting. But I changed my mind—for I've always been willing to admit I made a mistake, be it over a trifle or some serious matter—and I ordered him to bring the tables to me once again. I was able to calculate why, because of the horizon and the roundness of the earth, an eclipse of the moon visible in Peking might not be visible in the western provinces of Szechwan or Yunnan, and I corrected the provincial eclipse reports accordingly; I was able to follow the passage of a solar eclipse and calculate its duration more precisely than the staff in the Bureau of Astronomy; and I taught my Third Son Yin-chih how to calculate the latitude of the Ch'ang-chün Palace— he fixed it at 39 degrees 59 minutes and 30 seconds. And because the existing maps for the land and cities of China were sketchy, and had distances that were inaccurately calculated, I sent the Westerners to map the empire from the far south to Russia and from the far east to Tibet, using their methods of calculating the degrees in the heavens to obtain precise distances on earth.

But I was careful not to refer to these Westerners as "Great Officials," and corrected Governor Liu Yin-shu when he referred to the Jesuits Régis and Fridelli—whom I had dispatched to make a geographical survey of his province—as if they were honored imperial commissioners. For even though some of the Western methods are different from our own, and may even be an improvement, there is little about them that is new. The principles of mathematics all derive from the *Book of Changes,* and the Western methods are Chinese in origin: this algebra— "A-erh-chu-pa-erh"—springs from an Eastern word. And though it was indeed the Westerners who showed us something our ancient calendar experts did not know—namely how to calculate the angles of the northern pole—this but shows the truth of what Chu Hsi arrived at through his investigation of things: the earth is like the yolk within an egg. The Westerners seem to have principles found in the *Book of Changes,* echoing that book with four axes and four points; and they have magic squares like those in the *Ho-t'u lo-shu,* a sequence of the numbers one, three, nine, seven moving around from the left, and the number five stationary in the center, representing the sum of three for heaven and two for earth—the harmony of mankind.

4	9	2
3	5	7
8	1	6

I did praise their work, saying "the 'new methods' of calculating make basic errors impossible" and "the general principles of Western calendrical science are without error." But I added that they still cannot prevent small errors from occurring, and that over the decades these small errors mount up.

After all, they know only a fraction of what I know, and none of the Westerners is really conversant with Chinese literature—except perhaps for the Jesuit Bouvet, who has read a great deal, and developed the ability to undertake serious study of the *Book of Changes*. Often one can't keep from smiling when they start off on a discussion. How can they presume to talk about "the great principles of China"? Sometimes they act wrongly because they are not used to our ways, sometimes they are misled by ignorant Chinese fellows—the papal legate de Tournon used wrongly elevated characters on his memorials, employed improper phrases, implied that the word "emperor" [*huang*] was also used among his own people, wrote his memorials on paper decorated with five-clawed dragons, and so on.

De Tournon was ill when he reached the court in 1705, so I treated him generously, allowing him to be carried to the very door of the audience hall, letting him bend the knees and incline the body forward instead of performing the full prostration; and because he could neither squat cross-legged nor sit in Chinese fashion I had eunuchs pile up for him a couch out of cushions. When his paralysis grew worse I sent him to the T'ang-shan hot springs. In audience I gave him tea and meat, fruits, and offered my golden wine cup to him with my own hands, telling him I favored him so because he had been sent by the Pope and was one who cultivated the Tao.

But he was a biased and unreliable person, who muddled right with wrong. In a summary of his first memorial he mentioned three goals of his mission: the Pope's desire to see to his flock, to express his esteem for the Emperor, and to thank the Emperor for protecting those who taught the faith in China. This much he had said before, and I told my servant Henkama to tell the legate that it seemed a small reason to undertake the perils of a journey round the world; so de Tournon added that the Pope also wanted a prudent and learned person to reside in Peking, act as "superior" of all the missionaries, and keep in touch with Rome. These requests, too, I found trivial, and noted that the legate's business would be over in no time if that was all he wanted. I added, after strolling by and seeing the Chinese translation of the legate's message that was being prepared by the Peking Jesuits Gerbillon, Pereira, and Grimaldi, that the "superior" should be someone whom I knew to be experienced in Chinese life, language, and customs, who had been a resident for ten years or more. Otherwise multiple mistakes and confusions would arise. I would not, after all, send Henkama to take up a similar office in Europe. To this de Tournon responded by telling Henkama that I must have yielded to the pressure of the Peking Jesuits—so I asked my courtiers which of them would like this pointless "superior's" job, and told the Jesuits to report to de Tournon that they would never accept it. Gerbillon and Pereira, in turn, informed me that it was a mutual exchange of correspondence between Peking and Rome that was the legate's dearest goal.

So I summoned de Tournon to an audience, and spoke to him:

"Is the Pope in good health?"

"In good health, that will be increased when he hears the number and nature of the honors that have been heaped upon his emissary by the Emperor."

"You are right to say that I have been generous to the Westerners. It is fitting for a ruler to be generous if he combines that with justice. Generosity should be born of justice, though justice can stand by itself, tending to fulfill its own reason for being. So far I have treated the Westerners with generosity because they have behaved well, and done nothing deserving of punishment. But if they start acting contrary to our laws they

must experience the full penalties that our laws prescribe—
even if I personally might wish to pardon them." I told the interpreter Gerbillon to emphasize how seriously I meant this,
and added, "The Pope and yourself must sympathize with
those Europeans who have been away from their homelands
for so many years, and have endured so much in a strange
land."

The legate said, "No one could sympathize more than I,
who have learned by experience the fatigues they suffered on
their journeyings."

Said I, "We are now dealing informally, both in time and
place. You can speak more freely, even with a smile."

"The Emperor is playful in dealing with serious matters.
He governs this vast empire playfully."

"Perhaps your strength is not up to talking further?"

"My strength and spirits are quite restored by the kind-
ness and generosity of the Emperor's speech."

At this point, I gave refreshments to the legate, the in-
terpreters, and the entourage and continued: "Exactly why
have you come here? I have asked you this several times already through intermediaries, and have not forgotten your
replies. But now that you are here in person, you may have
something in your heart to say that goes beyond those earlier
replies. Don't worry about your eloquence—speak and act
freely, keep nothing back."

De Tournon said that he had come to repay debts of grati-
tude, and also to institute reciprocal contacts between the Emperor and the Pope—such contacts were valued, he said, by
the rulers in the West.

"To handle such matters," I said, "choose whom you
like."

And the legate replied: "The responsible party for the
proper handling of such an interrelationship must be one who
is in the confidence of the Pope, and deeply versed in the ways

of the courts of Western rulers, and especially in the ways of the Roman Curia.''

I raised my brows and told him, ''China has no matters of common concern with the West. For the sake of religion I put up with you—while you in turn should have no concerns beyond your minds and your doctrine. Although your group came here from different countries, you all have the same religion, and for that reason any one of the Westerners here is capable of writing and receiving papal correspondence of the kind you've been talking about. I don't know what you mean about a man in the Pope's confidence. We make no such distinctions in choosing persons in China. Some are closer to my throne, some in the middle range, some further off. But to which of these would I entrust any business if there were any lack of due loyalty? Who among you would dare to deceive the Pope? Your religion forbids you to lie; he who lies offends God.''

The legate answered: ''The missionaries dwelling here are honest men, but they lack inside knowledge of the Papal Court. Many envoys from other countries converge in Rome—and they are experienced in negotiation, and so are to be preferred to those who are here.''

So I told him, ''If the Pope would send a man of impeccable conduct and spiritual gifts as good as those Westerners here now, a man who won't interfere with others or dominate them, he'll be received as warmly as the rest. But if we give such a man power over the others, as you requested, there will be many and serious difficulties. You have seen here Westerners who have stayed forty years with us, and if they are still somewhat lacking in knowledge of imperial affairs, how could someone just transplanted from the West do better? I would not be able to get along with him as I do with these. We would need an interpreter, which means distrust and awkwardness. Such a man would never be free from error, and if he were appointed the leader of all he would have to carry any blame earned by the others and pay the penalties according to our usage."

The legate suggested he had a candidate, nevertheless; but I said: "Enough of this. From the days of Matteo Ricci to the present we have had Westerners in this court, and we've never had any reason to blame them. I wish this my testimony to be made known in the West." De Tournon said that only good missionaries had been sent; he begged my protection for them, and praised my person. "Your business is over," I said. "Give a full account to the Pope." And on the threshold I paused and added, "I have your meaning." When he had gone I said to Thomas, Pereira, and Gerbillon: "I spread myself in praises of you, but could not make him utter a word expressive of good will. Clearly he does not like you; he distrusts you and suspects the worst."

On the question of the Chinese Rites that might be practiced by the Western missionaries, de Tournon would not speak, though I sent messages to him repeatedly. I had agreed with the formulation the Peking fathers had drawn up in 1700: that Confucius was honored by the Chinese as a master, but his name was not invoked in prayer for the purpose of gaining happiness, rank, or wealth; that worship of ancestors was an expression of love and filial remembrance, not intended to bring protection to the worshiper; and that there was no idea, when an ancestral tablet was erected, that the soul of the ancestor dwelt in that tablet. And when sacrifices were offered to Heaven it was not the blue existent sky that was addressed, but the lord and creator of all things. If the ruler Shang-ti was sometimes called Heaven, *T'ien*, that had no more significance than giving honorific names to the emperor.

If de Tournon didn't reply, the Catholic Bishop Maigrot did, coming to Jehol and telling me that Heaven is a material thing and should not be worshiped, and that one should invoke only the name "Lord of Heaven" to show the proper reverence.

Maigrot wasn't merely ignorant of Chinese literature, he couldn't even recognize the simplest Chinese characters; yet he chose to discuss the falsity of the Chinese moral system. Sometimes, as I pointed out, the emperor is addressed honorifically as "under the steps of the throne"; would Maigrot say this was reverence to a set of steps made by some artisan? I am addressed as "Wan-sui, Ten Thousand Years"; obviously that too is not literal—since from the beginnings of history to the present day only 7,600 years have passed. Even little animals mourn their dead mothers for many days; these Westerners who want to treat their dead with indifference are not even equal to animals. How could they be compared with Chinese? We venerate Confucius because of his doctrines of respect for virtue, his system of education, his inculcation of love for superiors and ancestors. Westerners venerate their own saints because of their actions. They paint pictures of men with wings and say, "These represent heavenly spirits, swift as if they had wings, though in reality there are no men with wings." I do not find it appropriate to dispute this doctrine, yet with superficial knowledge Maigrot discussed Chinese sanctity. He talked for days, with his perverse reason, his poorly concealed anger, and fled the country when he could not get his way, a sinner against the Catholic teaching and a rebel to China. As my son Yin-jeng said to Bouvet on another occasion, "If Buddha and other idols are shown in clothes does that prevent you from wearing clothes? They have temples, yet you build them also to your god. One doesn't blame your attachment to your religion, but one does blame—and rightly—your obstinacy on matters of which you know nothing."

Every country must have some spirits that it reveres. This is true for our dynasty, as for Mongols or Mohammedans, Miao or Lolo, or other foreigners. Just as everyone fears something, some snakes but not toads, some toads but not snakes; and as all countries have different pronunciations and different alphabets. But in this Catholic religion, the Society of Peter quarrels with the Jesuits, Bouvet quarrels with Mariani, and among the Jesuits the Portuguese want only their own nationals in their church while the French want only French in theirs. This violates the principles of religion. Such dissension cannot be inspired by the Lord of Heaven but by the Devil, who, I have heard the Westerners say, leads men to do evil since he can't do otherwise.

I finally told the Westerners that they must follow Ricci's interpretations of the Chinese Rites; and if, because they followed these interpretations, the Pope were to order them to return to Europe, then I would say to the Jesuits: "You've been here many years, you're used to our climate, you're like the Chinese now, I'm not willing to send you back." If the Pope thereupon insisted that the Westerners were guilty and must return, I would write to him and say: "Pereira and the rest of them in China are used to our climate and have worked hard for me many years. You insist they be sent back, but I refuse to send them back alive. I'll cut off these Westerners' heads and send those back." In this way the Pope could be content that he had "re-formed" them all. Or, I suggested, since the Catholic Church was so strict about heresy and Bouvet studied Chinese books and was therefore clearly a heretic, why did not Bouvet's superiors take him into their church and in front of the assembled company have him burned to death and purify him of his apostasy, and then pull down the church?

Since I discovered on the Southern Tour of 1703 that there were missionaries wandering at will over China, I had grown cautious and determined to control them more tightly: to bunch them in the larger cities and in groups that included men from several different countries, to catalogue their names and residences, and to permit no new establishments without my express permission. For with so many Westerners coming to China it has been hard to distinguish the real missionaries from other white men pretending to be missionaries. As I clarified it for de Tournon: "Hereafter we will permit residence in China to all those who come from the West and will not return there. Residence permission will not be granted to those who come one year expecting to go home the next—because such people are like those who stand outside the main gate and discuss what people are doing inside the house. Besides these meddlers there are also those out for profit, greedy traders, who should not be allowed to live here." After the arguments with de Tournon and Maigrot I made all missionaries who wanted to stay on in China sign a certificate, stating that they would remain here for life and follow Ricci on the Rites. Forty or fifty who refused were exiled to Canton; de Tournon was sent to Macao, his secretary, Appiani, we kept in prison in Peking.

Despite these sterner restrictions, the Westerners continued to cause me anxiety. Our ships were being sold overseas; reports came of ironwood for keel blocks being shipped out of Kwangtung; Luzon and Batavia became havens for Chinese outlaws; and the Dutch were strong in the Southern Seas. I ordered a general inquiry among residents of Peking who had once lived on the coast, and called a conference of the coastal governors-general. "I fear that some time in the future China is going to get into difficulties with these various Western countries," I said. "That is my prediction." Similarly I had warned earlier that China must be strong to forestall a possible threat from Russia. General Ch'en Mao insisted even more strongly on the dangers from Holland and France, Spain and England, and of missionaries and merchants conniving together. I did not agree with him that we should disarm all their ships, but I did agree to reiterate the 1669 edict that banned Westerners from preaching in the provinces.

Three of the Peking Jesuits—Suares, Parrenin, and Mourao —came to protest: "We learn that the Boards have pronounced a strict sentence and the Christian religion is proscribed."

I reassured them: "No. The sentence is not strict, and the Christian religion is not proscribed. Only Westerners without the certificate are forbidden to preach. This prohibition does not affect those who have the certificate."

"This distinction as made by the Emperor is not clearly expressed in the sentence."

"It is clearly expressed. I have read the sentence with care. If you were hoping that those without certificates might be permitted to preach your laws, then that hope is no longer possible."

"But at the beginning of the sentence the 1669 edict is cited."

"That is true, but the point of it is to prevent those without certificates from preaching."

"We are just afraid that the provincial officials will treat us all alike, and that they will not permit even those of us who have certificates to preach the holy law."

"If that occurs, those who have certificates have only to produce them. The officials will see that permission to preach your laws is granted. You can preach the law, and it's up to the Chinese to listen—if they so choose. As for those without a certificate, let them come here, and I will give them one." (I smiled during these last words.) "Anyway, even those with the certificate are only being permitted to preach for a time. Later on we'll see what decision to take in their case."

"But if they cause trouble to those with certificates, we will come to the Emperor for help."

"Take care to inform me if such is the case."

"There is one thing that causes us particular anguish—namely, that the Boards treat us as rebels."

"Don't worry about that. It's just a conventional formula that the Boards use."

"As soon as this edict is published, the officials will search out the missionaries and Christians and stir up trouble."

"As far as this searching out goes, it's essential. When I sent Li Ping-chung to Canton I gave him an order for the Governor-General, telling him to search out and to assemble in one place all those without certificates. And I've just given similar orders to Governor-General Yang Lin on his return to Canton, and am awaiting his reply."

The Westerners in China were only as drops of rain in the immensity of the ocean, said de Tournon in our audience, and I had to laugh. Yet some of their words were no different from the wild or improper teachings of Buddhists and Taoists, and why should they be treated differently? One of my censors wrote that the Western god fashioned a man with a human soul from the blood of a virgin, Mary; and they claimed that Jesus was born in the reign of Han Ai-ti [reigned 6 B.C.–A.D. 1], that he was killed on a cross for man's sins, and that they had meetings in which slaves and masters, men and women, mixed together and drank some holy substance. I had asked Verbiest why God had not forgiven his son without making him die, but though he had tried to answer I had not understood him. Also, though in China there had been a flood at about the same time as that reported for Noah, those on the Chinese plains had been drowned, while those who escaped to the mountains were saved. And I told Fontaney that I would gladly witness some of the miracles they talked about, but none was forthcoming.

In the past, both Buddhists and Taoists had been made to fill out certificates, and the superiors in the various temples have to register their monks—they are not allowed to chant or beg for alms or set out their sacred images in the streets of Peking, and may not act as exorcists for patients suffering from seizures without getting official permission. Certainly there are more Buddhists and Taoists—the census of 1667 listed 140,193 monks divided among 79,622 temples of various sizes—but there were many Christians also. When I asked Verbiest for exact figures in 1688 he said there were 15,758 Christians just

in Peking. Even though I realized it was quite impractical to close down temples, and order people to return to secular life, there was no harm in following the principle of "preparing for trouble before trouble comes." So I strictly banned all the sects such as the "non-action," "white lotus," "incense smelling," "origin of the dragon," and "all-submerging Yang," and stiffened the penalties for all officials who failed to report heterodox teachers in their localities. Also I banned the so-called "incense associations," where men and women mixed together and sold erotic works and special medicines; I ordered the printing blocks of certain mystical and magical books burned; and I continued to enforce the prohibitions against the private ownership of forbidden books—though I allowed exceptions for those working at home in astronomy and mathematics.

Yet in all my reign I only executed one scholar for treasonous writings, and that was Tai Ming-shih. Not only had he written and published wild and reckless works while a student, but he had connections with that Fang family which once had worked for the rebel Wu San-kuei; and after he entered the Hanlin Academy he had failed to burn the blocks of his early works. In his book *Nan-shan-chi,* Tai Ming-shih printed the reign-titles of the three Ming claimants who had continued to fight after the Manchus had founded the new dynasty. He claimed that, if we followed Confucian historiographical principles, Kung-kuang's reign in Nanking and Lung-wu's reign in Fukien, and Yung-li's reign, first in Kwangtung and later in Yunnan and Kweichow, must all be properly recorded. He said that our government had imposed a censorship, that people still avoided the subject of the Ming fall as a taboo, that the evidence about the conquest was gradually being destroyed and covered up. He said there were all sorts of books he knew of which had not been handed in to the Court—even titles that the Bureau of History had openly said it wished to buy—and that he knew of works by scholars in retirement which had been kept secret.

He dared to share the ambitions of Ssu-ma Ch'ien and Pan Ku, to pick up and piece together the myriad fragments, as he said, before they were destroyed by the clear wind and transformed into cold ash. The Board of Punishments recommended that Tai Ming-shih be put to the lingering death, that all his male relations over sixteen be executed, and all female relatives and children be enslaved. But I was merciful and lowered his sentence to beheading, while sparing the relatives.

History may be written by officials, but it is the emperor in whose reign the history is written who is finally responsible, and it is he who will be blamed by posterity if there are distortions and errors, as there were in both the *Sung History* and the *Yüan History*. Not only that, but in their histories the Yüan writers ridiculed the Sung, and the Ming writers ridiculed the Yüan. I refused to allow that.

Of course, absurd things had happened during the Ming: when Emperor Ch'ung-chen learned to ride at the end of the dynasty he had two men to hold the horse's bit, two to hold the stirrups, and two to hold the crupper—yet even so he fell off, and had the horse given forty lashes and sent off to do hard labor at a military post-station. Similarly, when a huge stone to be used in palace construction couldn't be moved through the Wu-men Gate, Ch'ung-chen had it given sixty lashes. In the early years of my reign I used to learn about Ming history by questioning eunuchs like Yüan Pen-ch'ing who had served in the Ming court and were still living. Similarly, I asked officials like Chang P'eng-ko, who came from Szechwan, to question their fathers about the bandit Chang Hsien-chung—and I myself saw the adopted sons of Chang Hsien-chung, who had been captured, and verified that they had indeed had their noses and ears cut off.

Most histories contain some material that cannot be believed: even in the *Shih-chi* and the *Han-shu* one finds stories such as Hsiang Yü burying two hundred thousand Ch'in Dynasty troops. But how could such a thing be possible? Would the soldiers have stood quietly with their hands folded in their sleeves waiting to be buried? So in the Ming *Veritable Records* there were certain things that could not be accepted: for instance, that the officials had objected when the Empress summoned one of the princes to court—although according to the *Book of History* there is precedent for such action; or that many officials died because they were made to kneel outside the palace in the heat—when I had seen that soldiers can fight for hours in the sun in full equipment without suffering; or that the fall of the Ming was caused by eunuchs. In this last case, though we do know that there were indeed evil eunuchs, it is completely incorrect to say it was the eunuchs' power that caused the dynasty's fall. It was, rather, a problem of factionalism, in which the Ming officials were fighting for power at court, competing with each other, and ignoring the needs of the country. Here again, interviews with eunuchs revealed to me extra details about what had really happened: that Yang Lien and Tso Kuang-tou were beaten to death in front of the Wu-men Gate and not in prison; that the Emperor T'ien-ch'i called the eunuch Wei Chung-hsien his *lao-pan,* "old companion," and put him in charge of everything; that Emperor Ch'ung-chen could read fairly well, but none of the later Ming emperors was knowledgeable about the *Classics* and several were in fact illiterate. Others described the death of the last Ming emperor: how, when the bandits entered Peking, he disguised himself as a commoner and went with some eunuchs to his uncle's house, but the uncle had locked the gates in order to watch theatricals and the Emperor couldn't get in. And then, though the Emperor wanted to flee, the eunuch Wang Ch'eng-en said that that could only lead to further humiliations, and so the Emperor committed suicide. It was this same eunuch, Wang Ch'eng-en, who committed suicide to accompany his emperor, not Wang Chih-hsin, as the books usually record. I

know the true facts because my father wrote a eulogy for Wang Ch'eng-en.

Compiling the *Ming History* was difficult, because of the random nature of the sources. Parts of the *Veritable Records* for the T'ien-ch'i reign were missing, and there were none at all for the Ch'ung-chen reign, so they had to be reconstructed by using the transcripts of documents in the *Peking Gazette,* or else by relying on private, unofficial histories, which were themselves crammed with mistakes. On the other hand, the editors complained that there was almost too much material on the Wan-li reign, and at other times there was so much action that it was hard to grasp the main thread. Besides which, there were many distortions in the *Veritable Records,* particularly for those after the Hsüan-te reign.

Furthermore, the time of the Ming Dynasty was still near to us and it was easy to have bias. I read the drafts of each biography and chronological section as it was completed, and warned the editors not to criticize the rulers of the past too lightly—as a ruler myself, I wanted to see their good points as well as their shortcomings. And I warned them not to feel they were above criticism as writers, for there is no word or sentence that is not capable of being corrected, regardless of what the prouder Hanlin scholars might say. As I myself worked through the condensed dynastic histories in the *Tzu-chih t'ung-chien*— on a schedule to punctuate it, section by section, over a three-year period—I always had scholars check over what I had done, and corrected it where necessary. (T'ang T'ai-tsung was an emperor who got on so well with his subjects mainly because he was willing to listen to criticism.) And I told the editors that, even after they had finished their final version of the *Ming History,* they should make sure the original *Veritable Records* were preserved, so that later generations could study them— for it is easy enough to discuss others but hard to criticize yourself, and if you only discuss the past superficially, even though what you write is easy to read it will not be of value. Hung-wu and Yung-lo were greater emperors than their successors, and many of our precedents were drawn from them, while Hsüan-te was good too, because he was a preserver of the dynasty—none of these men should be lightly criticized. But neither could one ignorantly blame Ch'ung-chen as an "emperor who destroyed his country"—he had at least tried to govern, but there was nothing that he could do about the state of the country. It was his three predecessors, Wan-li, T'ai-ch'ang, and T'ien-ch'i, who had ruined the kingdom—none of those three should even have offerings made to him in the temples.

In history one needs the facts, not hollow words or literary elegance; and one must not work so fast that one leaves out important things. As I told the Grand Secretaries who submitted the official account of the suppression of the "San-fan War": "The country itself has a shared opinion about truth and falsity, gain and loss. How do you increase the value of something by praising it, or damage it further by not praising it? In general, when recording something, we should desire to get the facts—that's all."

Ch'i-shih-wu, while governor of Kansu, forced the local people to erect tablets praising his virtuous administration. I learned of this and demoted him five grades, and warned him: "If an official is really good, even if he wants to prevent the common people from erecting tablets to him he won't be able to; but if it's clear that he has a bad reputation, then even if he forces people to put up tablets they are sure to be smashed up later on. I have heard that when Ch'ü Chin-mei returned to Peking after being governor of Kwangsi, the common people hated him so much that they came with their spades and hoes to root out the hoofprints of his horse. How can you force the people to grant you their affections?"

IV   *Growing Old*

GIFT FOR AN OLD OFFICIAL

How many now are left
Of my old court lecturers?
I can only grieve as the decays of age
Reach ruler and minister.
Once I had great ambitions—
But they've grown so weak;
Being disillusioned by everything,
I don't bother to seek the truth.
Shrinking back I look for simple answers,
But everything seems blurred.
Complexities bring me to a halt,
Exhausting my energies.
For years past, now,
I've neglected my poetry
And, shamed as I grope for apt phrases,
Find dust on my writing brush.

K'ANG-HSI, c. 1720

IT was *i-yüan* powder we gave to Kao Shih-ch'i to stem his nosebleeds and diarrhea on the Northern Tour; licorice root, grated soapstone, and scallion hearts, dissolved in iced water, which also cut the fever and made the urine flow.

Wang Chih credited *ts'ui-hsien* pills for his liveliness at eighty, saying he'd been taking them for fifty years. I asked him for the exact formula and the Court Medical Department made it up: the ingredients included two tenths of an ounce of ginseng, lotus root mixed with milk and steamed, oxlip and raspberries fried in wine, scallions, dried buds of the white lotus, dog rose, knotgrass steamed and sun-dried, and peach pits. Wang said he's found it particularly valuable in Szechwan, where the weather is dank and muggy by turns, and as a protection against malaria. He had been given the prescription by Ch'en Tiao-yüan (who had children at eighty and lived to be ninety-six). Doctor Chang Lu picked up the formula, and included it in the medical treatise his son gave to me in the South. He added dogwood and left out the scallions and peach pits; used white honey to bind the mixture into pills. Take on an empty stomach, in lightly salted water.

When Wei Hsiang-shu fainted, first at Pao-ting and again after the imperial lectures, I had him given *liu chün-tzu t'ang*— ginseng blended with licorice root, orange peel, raw ginger, and other agents, to bind the stomach, stop the vomiting, and cut the phlegm. We gave the same to old Chang Yü-shu, after Doctor Li Te-ts'ung had made his diagnosis: Li said that since the disordered pulses had slowed, the swelling of the limbs subsided, and the blocked pneuma no longer harmed the intestines, therefore modulated doses were now in order. To other old folk with upset stomachs I usually gave the steamed ginseng plasters called "spring snow," though we also tested out eunuch Ho Shang's own prescription for cutting the flow of dysentery.

There are many different types of drugs—those from new shoots, those dried in the sun, those picked by hand or gnawed with the teeth. They must by blended together with precision, and a prescription only works when applied to an illness the origins of which have been carefully evaluated; and though they be no bigger than a tiny grain they can have great strength —as they draw on the forces of metals or stones, or on the heart of grasses and wood. When the Ancients said, "One gets to the heart of medicine without drugs," they didn't mean you should never take drugs when you were ill; but rather that you shouldn't abuse them, and should check the pulses with care. I myself gave the Grand Empress Dowager restoratives in 1673 when I was young, but after taking them myself in 1710 I realized that they could be terribly bad for ordinary people, unless carefully administered by a doctor, and I warned Li Kuang-ti against them. A certain medicine might be of a nature to stimulate the heart, yet be bad for the stomach; or good for the lungs and bad for the kidneys. Our Manchu ancestors took few restoratives and yet they were strong, so I too take as little as possible—just as I stay away from massages, which can cause serious damage.

The best thing for health is to eat and drink carefully and rise and retire at regular hours. When sick, keep away from cold and rough foods, and avoid goose and fish. Fowl, mutton, and pork should be boiled or stewed, but not roasted. Ch'a Shenhsing had bad stomach trouble, so I sent him some of my Western medicine and told him: "The most important thing is to regulate what you drink and eat. The medical texts say: 'If it's not hot and humid, you won't get dysentery. If you don't stop eating, you won't have pain.' They also say: 'Clear yourself out and there will be no pain. If there's pain it's because you are not cleared out.' Everyone knows that he ought to be regular, but when it comes time to drink and eat then he can't do it." General Yang Chieh, who had suffered so badly from the damp and sea air on the Fukien campaign (and yet at seventy-three was still regularly practicing his archery), combined a diet of one pint of millet a day and a half pound of meat with simple strengthening prescriptions.

As Lao-tzu says: "Know your limits and you'll suffer no disgrace, know when to stop and you'll be in no danger; so you will live long." Each man should eat and drink the things that suit him—and they will be different, even for the members within a single family. Let no man take too much of the things he likes the most, nor force his favorite things on others who may not like them. Peasants make strong old men because their food is plain; on all my travels I've eaten the local vegetables, and felt the better for it. In old age, they do even more good, and if I sometimes make only the motions of tasting the fruit that people offer me along the way on my journeys, that is not because I don't like fruit. It's because people compete to be the first to bring me things, and the first of any crop is never fully

ripe. Fruit and vegetables are most luscious at the peak of ripeness, and it's then that I love to eat them.

The people of the North are strong; they must not copy the fancy diets of the Southerners, who are physically frail, live in a different environment, and have different stomachs and bowels. So when I first saw how ill Wang Chih seemed to be looking, thin and white-haired (this being five years before I realized his real strength and got the formula for his *ts'ui-hsien* pills), I recommended him the simple foods that I took regularly—among them unrefined milk, pickled deer tongues and tails, dried apples, and cakes of cream cheese.

Some diseases respond quicker than others, and there's no sense in changing doctors every time you don't have a quick cure. Also you must be frank with a doctor once you've got him—it's ridiculous to conceal some of your symptoms or lie about the origins of your disease. One can have specialists, too, as we do at court—over one hundred doctors divided among eleven fields, each one properly trained and examined: for men, children, women; typhoid and smallpox; ulcers and broken bones; eyes, teeth, throat; and acupuncture and cauterization. When a specialist was exceptionally good—for example the eye doctor Min T'i-chien—I would send him to treat my favored officials with his special prescriptions and acupuncture of the eye. And I allowed any retired officials who were ill to request the Drug Section of the Court Medical Department for whatever they needed—there was no need for them to memorialize and seek my permission first—if they took the time to memorialize my answer might come too late.

At the court I take every precaution, making a doctor and a eunuch sign a prescription analysis for each disease treated, and making each taste the medicine before it's brought to me. In the same way I had the quinine that the Westerners brought tested on outsiders and then on members of the Imperial clan before I took it for myself. Western doctors have their own special lore and skills: their wine is a tonic, Rhodes' brandy and cinnamon stopped my heart palpitations as his scapel removed the growth on my lip. I keep him nearby and take him on my tours, together with Baudino the botanist and Viera the pharmacist, to complement Doctors Ma Chih-chün and T'ang Yü-chi. It's extraordinary what Western doctors can do, sewing up Lan Li after a cannon shot went straight through his stomach in the P'eng-hu phase of the Taiwan campaign, spilling out his intestines. The "Ripped-Belly General" he was called. When we met on the southern tour I made him loosen his clothes so that I could see the scar myself and touch it with my own hands.

What we need is a harmony between the treatment and the disease. Thus the Mongols gather the roots of the plant they call *jorhai*, gather it secretly, and use it successfully to cure aching joints—I checked this out and found it similar to the Chinese *hsü-tuan*. When Ch'a-sheng fell off his horse on a northern hunting tour and his hands swelled so that the fingers would not bend, and the pain was acute, I had a sheep cut open and ordered him to hold his hands in the hot stomach. The pain went away. Or take the "blood-stopping stone" which I obtained in the desert on the Galdan campaign; although we don't know exactly how, it helps those who spit blood, or have nose bleeds or bloody stool. There's also a kind of stone that can prevent colds, which works so well that I used to give it away as a present. For stomach and bowels the Manchus and Mongols use the *yengge* fruit, dried in the sun. I prefer it fresh, and had it transplanted to the Jehol palace. It's nature is hot, and two or three spoonfuls is all you need. And for congested heads you can always use *t'ung-kuan* powder: blown into the nose it'll make the patient sneeze and bring out half the bad pneuma. Then you can soothe him with the fragrance of *chiu-ho* incense.

The trouble with so many of today's doctors is that they claim to have various marvellous prescriptions that have been handed down in the family, that'll cure all sorts of sickness, and they dispense them at random. Yet you can see that even they have their doubts as to their efficacy, since they will give one prescription and then follow it with a whole lot of others—but if the first was any good why do they need these extra ones? Few of them have the intelligence or the critical skills shown in the Yellow Emperor's *Classic of Internal Medicine.* Also their teaching is shallow, and I've read enough in the medical literature to know when their claims to true antiquity are spurious. They don't keep up their studies of the pulses, they ignore relevant case histories, they distinguish between their rich and poor patients, and they concentrate on the hunt for fame and money. Often they don't know the basic principles of medicine, they tend to ask wild questions and make wild statements, sometimes even inventing prescriptions that really harm people. I know this well, and it makes me sad, but I can't prevent it. One can't prosecute all the doctors who have a little business and wander from place to place, just managing to stay alive.

When my eunuch Ku Wen-hsing started to study medicine, I told him that there's no need to fear not having the right spirit as a doctor, if that's what you are really reaching for; but those who just talk about it will never have the opportunity to get it. Though medicine has no sage's classics behind it, nor the subtleties of metaphysics, its principles are deep enough: in discussing the pulses there are the three divisions, five viscera, seven externals, and eight internals, the nine ways and so on, which are all quite different. On medical principles, there are thousands of volumes, and on different illnesses too many books to name. And so finally I discouraged him, saying: "If you study hard in order to understand the origins and the details, you'll probably be successful, but all your friends will be worried about you, fearing you'll get sick from overwork. If you exert yourself and don't succeed, the years will have passed by, and before having cured anyone else you'll have been unable to cure yourself! That'll be sad! You should be persuaded to stop. And it would be better to do nothing at all than to learn common and vulgar medical practices."

There are Taoists, too, who speak grandly of revitalizing and gaining special powers; they have no shame—but I have observed them over the years and I have seen them age like other men. These adepts are boasters—if they were immortal why should they bother to descend to our humble world? The falseness of their claims usually becomes obvious after a short time. When Hsieh Wan-ch'eng and Wang Chia-ying tried to convince me with their "external alchemy," their message was unintelligible. They were like drunkards or idiots. I told them: "The early immortals had more than one skill, broad was the gate and the way. If I take you Taoists' words on trust, it would lead to trouble. I've had experience of hundreds of you; although all your techniques are different they share the same origins, and as time goes by they often can't preserve themselves and even die suddenly." The meaning of the Great Way is not lightly to be explained. Some of these adepts' words are even harder to believe, they chill the heart and make me shiver —claims to "arrogate to oneself the cosmic creativity and rival the shaping forces," to "bring together the Five Phases and reconcile the Eight Trigrams," or to "never grow old,"or "become like Buddha or the Jade Emperor."

Hsieh Wan-ch'eng initially said that in the seventh month it would be possible to expel the fragrant pneuma and the external pneuma would not enter in, but only a short two months later he changed his mind. I noted, too, that he and Wang carried themselves no differently than other old people: their eyes were blurred, teeth fallen, hair white, legs unsteady, energy low; after speaking for any length of time they couldn't support themselves.

I said to them: "If I exert myself and my skills to enter into

your Way, how can it profit me? But if there is a core without deceit, truly it is the Great Way, which one dare not deceive. All I can do is let the months and years stretch out, and see if 'the waters recede and the rocks appear.' If there is truly a pneuma of the Immortals, even if I do not believe the evidence, I will have to submit internally. What's the point of pushing things forward in this urgent way?"

There are so many uncanny practices, like a diet of avoiding the grains, or internalizing the pneuma and other breath techniques, or sexual regimens, as well as internal and external alchemy—I can't calculate how many of these I've seen personally, and how could I lightly believe a word of them? But I like to treat people with trust, and I have the potential of all kinds of things completely checked out: I take a look at those that seem possible and reject those that are not. The external alchemy of Hsieh and Wang, I concluded, was not to be believed. Truly we had seen "the waters recede and the rocks appear." It was like others I had heard of who claimed to stand on one spot for decades or sit for years in a small room—even if they could sit so long, they couldn't stand up long, and those who could stand couldn't sit. What's demonic about skills at such a level? Because I examined them with care I know their absurdity. So when a commoner in Chiangnan offered me a book of his that claimed to contain secrets of immortality through alchemy, I ordered it thrown back at him.

As for the marks of age, our Manchu shamans pray the gods to bring them to us: "Oh go before us to lead us, march beside us, protect us to the fore and protect us to the rear, grant our desires in fullest measure, whiten our heads and yellow our teeth, that our years may be many, our lives long, our foundation strong. With the spirits as guardians and the household gods to help us, stretch out the line of our years."

When the wobbling teeth cause pain, and those that have fallen out pain you no more, why seek further for toothache prescriptions? Rejoice, instead, with your descendants that you have lived so long. Those close to me since childhood cannot make peace with their own natures, and grieve that they cannot eat the choicest flavored food; half my upper teeth have gone, and I cannot chew—so I have the food I want cooked till soggy, or pickle it to help it down.

With care in our daily habits we strengthen the body and control the mind. To look after yourself in ordinary circumstances, be both cowardly and cunning: put on warmer clothes before cold weather comes, and in the chill of winter don't bank the stoves and huddle close; by keeping back from the fire not only don't I catch colds, I can go out to hunt in the bitterest weather with hat flaps raised and ears unfrozen. Similarly, because I rein myself in I can bear the high summer's heat without using a fan or removing my hat. Even in the fiercest heat I don't open the windows to let cool breezes in, for I contain true coolness within myself; those who ignore this principle grow sick in the autumn from the heat they have shut inside themselves.

Where there are taboos we observe them. Where there is filth we keep away; there are unlucky or dirty things we hide from or shun. There are smells so vile that they must be worse than the foul vapors of Kwangsi; they hurt our very brain. So at home or on your travels, keep clean and the pure air will suffuse your body; if you stay near filth you'll be stained by its foulness and that purity will be slowly clouded over. But do not get obsessed with cleanliness, so that you end up throwing away your clothes when they are barely soiled, and forbidding your servants to wear shoes, and having your room swept several times a day, and not touching the food that others offer you.

Never mock those with physical defects, or sneer at those who stumble and fall; if you do, as our forefathers warned us, you or your children will suffer what you have mocked and lose the use of your own legs even as you laugh at the stum-

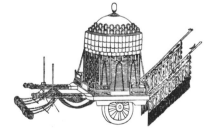

blers. One of the greatest Manchu taboos is against letting people hold you up under the armpits; and even when my feet
swelled so that I could barely move—to touch them even lightly
was an agony and I had to have them bound in a kerchief and
supported on a padded chair—I would allow only a little help to
get me up from my chair to stand erect. Then none was allowed
to hold me and I leaned on no stick; only when I had to stand
for long periods at the rituals did I let people support me a little
on each side. But today's youth have themselves held up with
two hands under each arm for no reason—it's disgusting, uncanny. We who are placed over other men, and have people
around to serve us, must bear our pain calmly and not shout
and rage. Unless we are calm in this situation, what will the
eunuchs and the poor—who have no one to help them—do
when they are ill?

When there is no treatment that can work, then we pray,
and hope Heaven hears, as I did for my grandmother: "Oh
Great God of Heaven, I am grateful for Your protection, in that
You let me serve my grandmother, the Grand Empress Dowager,
and granted her long life, and let her gain in health and strength;
but now the scarlet fever is come to her and in ten days grown
so severe that we no longer know if she can live the day. At
night I cannot rest, I neither eat nor sleep, I prepare her medicines myself, I call on the doctors but without avail, my whole
body burns with my trouble, I know not where to turn." Four
years before, I had urged her to come to the shrines at Wu-t'ai-
shan; it had been so beautiful with the mountains glistening
under new snow, waterfalls drifting in the gusty winds, and
the pine trees pressed over the winding roads. But she never
did get to see the view, or the Wu-t'ai-shan shrines. I had recon-
noitered the route the previous spring, and this time had ridden
on ahead with her chief eunuch to supervise the local laborers
as they broke up rocks to smooth the track, and to train a team
of bearers so that they knew how to keep their balance on the

steeply snaking mountain tracks. I saw them teeter as they practiced, teeter on the edge of gorges that I could not bear to look down into; for I myself have never had a head for heights, could never climb walls as a child, nor look over a sharp drop without growing dizzy, nor even bear to see others scale a wall. I warned her of the dangers by letter, and sent her eunuch to tell her what his own eyes had seen, but she had to see for herself. She was soon persuaded: "The mountain road is truly dangerous; I have managed to get this far but now must stop, I can do no more. Let the Emperor carry out the Wu-t'ai-shan ceremonies on my behalf and, as if he were I, pray before each of the Buddhas in person."

Now, as she lay in her coma, I had every kind of food prepared though she could eat none, every medicine ready, and I lay on a mat beside the bed listening for the slightest sound from her. When she died I had been near her side for thirty-five days and nights, never undressing, almost never sleeping, preparing her medicines, trying to anticipate her needs—so that whether she wanted to lie or sit, eat or drink, nothing would be lacking. I had thirty kinds of rice gruel prepared, in the hopes of rousing her failing appetite. She patted my back, and cried.

It's really unbearable not to look after the old when they grow ill; as well as money for their support, and doctors, we should send their old friends to talk with them, no matter whether the sick person is an old and loyal official, or one of my brothers' slaves, or the Jesuit Dolzé bloated with dropsy north of the Wall, or an old princess in her palace. Like my aunt, the Barin Princess Shu-hui, daughter of Abahai: I visited her regularly as she was dying in Peking, and gave her all she needed; and she *did* die with a smile on her face. As I said in my commemorative edict for her, "I have seen a great many dangerously ill people; but never have I seen someone smile like this and then die."

We can cheer old people up with presents, too. Every year

Princess Shu-hui used to send cakes of fat, and dried mutton, to my grandmother and me, and we would send her sable, black fox, and satin. I would always try to make my presents something needed, or something that I knew would bring pleasure, for if you just give an object at random it might just as easily be given back—then all you have is an exchange of items, something with no real feeling behind it. So I gave the Empress Dowager cherries that I had tasted in the South, and to my grandmother gave the flesh of a tiger that I had shot in the North (boxed and wrapped in grasses), a chiming clock, and a foreign mirror. And to my son Yin-jeng I gave a clock to which was attached a bobbing bird, to Songgotu a telescope, to Chang Po-hsing a pair of spectacles, to Kao Shih-ch'i my personal snuff bottle and snuff, and to Li Kuang-ti—when his stomach was sick from the bad water of southern Peking—I simply gave fresh water from one of the pure springs in the palace grounds. The affections and filial piety are a matter of spontaneity and naturalness, not of fixed rules and formal visits.

Incised on the inkstone I gave to P'eng Ting-ch'iu when he was almost seventy were the words "Make a practice of quietness, and so lengthen the days of your life." I myself have made a practice of sitting quietly for lengthy periods and concentrating even when others laugh and converse around me, and daily practice has made this a habit. If one can get even two or three hours of quiet relaxation it makes up for days of hardship. I don't agree with people who say it's difficult to relax, but it is true that though I have practiced relaxation for many years I have never attained to "true quietness." That is my fault and no one else's.

The adept Wang Chen followed past teachers in his study of naturalness and non-action, and seemed truly sincere in his cultivation of the self. He claimed that a man of talent and intelligence could get results within ten days, while even the stupid would have benefits within a month. I sent Fan Hungssu to check out his method of "straight-sitting." Fan sat as long as he could in tranquillity, then ate and strolled around a little, and sat once more. He saw before his eyes an expanse of empty brightness, which then changed into great expanses of yellowness and blackness warring together, while the warm pneuma rose within him. Later there was only yellowness, and the warm air still ceaselessly rising. After two hours body and spirit grew overcast; it was like being asleep and yet not sleeping. Then things grew clear as before. This is what the Taoists call "entering the darkness." You might enter this darkness for one period in each hour, but only for about the space of time needed to drink a cup of tea. After Fan came out of the state of meditation he asked Wang Chen about it, and Wang said, "It's symbolic of coming-togetherness." The eunuchs Li and Feng sat even longer, and were in a state of deepest calm. But they told me Wang was not willing to give a full explanation of his techniques.

I thought about Wang Chen carefully, and my doubts rose from this: if I was to practice his techniques it would lead to delays in the business of government, and after I had embarked in this Way I feared there might be no turning back. As it is, we know the stages necessary for learning and growth from Confucius, and the stages of the body from the Yellow Emperor: there is full potency at sixteen; firmness, strength, and full height at twenty-four; healthy flesh, bone and muscle, and great fertility at thirty-two. Then at forty the teeth decay, and there are fewer sexual emanations; at forty-eight vigor drops, face wrinkles, temples whiten; by fifty-six physical strength is gone and the semen exhausted; at sixty-four teeth and hair fall. Some will keep their vigor long past these stages, but even so they will not pass this extra vigor on to their sons and daughters.

The father I had almost never seen was twenty-three when he died, and I was eight when they cut my hair and dressed me in full white mourning, and laid my father's corpse behind nine-dragon curtains of yellow silk in the Ch'ien-ch'ing Palace while the bells boomed out across the winter city. My mother, Empress Hsiao-k'ang, who had borne me when she was fifteen, died soon after my father; and she was buried in the Hsiao-ling mausolea in the summer of 1663, together with the ashes of my father and his concubine Donggo, whom he had named Empress Hsiao-hsien in grief at her death. At the time, my grandmother would not allow me to go to the mausolea. Now many of my own sons lie nearby, and my grandmother herself; and my three dead empresses are in another mausoleum, awaiting me. The geomancers Yang Hung-liang and Tu Ju-yü chose the sites, as they did for my ancestors' tombs. Ranges of hills protect them on all sides, and the vital pulses flow into the area from the T'ai-hang Mountains to the west. The formation of the local hills links soaring phoenix and writhing dragon, and rivers sprung from the distant watershed flow one on either side to meet at last in the "dragon and tiger valley."

As for age itself, it can either help or hinder government. It's good to have some old officials around the Court. They are hard to replace; one should preserve them and try to keep them alive. If a Grand Secretary was over sixty I suggested he only come to work once every two or three days—if some crucial memorial arrived in his absence, then I could always send him a special edict. And I told Huang Tsung-hsi that he could serve as an adviser and needn't take a post at all, as he was over eighty; but he didn't come. Shih Lang requested retirement because he was old and weak, but I said it was his knowledge I wanted, not his strength, and that he should stay on in office. Grand Secretary Feng P'u started asking to retire when he was sixty-two, and I asked him in return if he was unwilling to help me, for he might be old but he certainly couldn't be classified as "old and weak." I kept him on until he was seventy-five, though at the end I absolved him from all formal responsibilities, and said he should just come to court now and again.

One should make concessions to the fat, the old, and the ill: they have to move more slowly and avoid the heat of the day. Some very old men I reappointed, and let them come to court just on the days they could walk; others I excused from the dawn audience, and told them to stay at home and have a dish of rice gruel before coming to the office, so they could preserve their bodies and serve me longer. I advised against the overhasty impeachment of the aged—if they did not break the law, and stayed uncorrupt, that should be regarded as satisfactory. Again, one could distinguish between different offices on the basis of age—in metropolitan posts, or provincial posts above the rank of intendant, old officials could sit down peacefully to work—whereas at the *chou* and *hsien* levels, where the county magistrates work, it was quite different, one needed movement and energy. And men transferred to a new part of the country might have serious problems—like Shih I-te, a Kansu man who suffered terribly as military governor in the steamy Chiangnan climate from suppurating boils, dysentery, loss of appetite, and numbness of his left arm and leg; to him I granted a special vacation for rest and recuperation.

But old officials who cling to office when incompetent must be removed; when they get so muddled that they make serious mistakes; or when like Chin Fu as director of River Conservancy, they lose the special expertise they once had. Others must be transferred if they look too ill—like the Anhwei governor Li Ping, with face yellow and emaciated, the corners of his mouth pulled down, almost unable to walk—while some who are really lazy and speak gibberish must be retired so that it doesn't look as if I am giving them some sort of honorary title. And some must be removed (even if they refuse to request retirement) so as to make way for younger men, lest their subordinate officials in turn grow old and feeble.

These officials can always use the fact that they are old and muddled as a reason for retiring, but what can the emperor use as an excuse? As we live longer our minds grow lazy. Happiness goes and troubles mount. We leave the world of the hexagram *T'ai,* where

> . . . The ruler
> Divides and completes the course of heaven and earth;
> He furthers and regulates the gifts of heaven and earth;
> And so aids the people.

And we enter the hexagram *P'i's* world of stagnation and declining powers:

> Evil people of the time of standstill do not further the perseverance of the superior man. The great departs; the small approaches.
>
> Thus heaven and earth do not unite, and all beings fail to achieve union.
>
> Upper and lower do not unite, and in the world, states go down to ruin.
>
> The shadowy is within, the light without; weakness is within, firmness without; the inferior is within, the superior without. The way of the inferior is waxing, the way of the superior is waning.

On the 1684 Southern Tour, sailing east out of Nanking down the Yangtze, a squall blew up and everyone wanted the sails furled; but I ordered them left up, and as they bellied out and we rushed along before the wind I stood at the prow and fired my arrows at the fish, quite carefree. Yet only a few years later I had palpitations of the heart while crossing the same river. And now I tremble at the sight of other people crossing the river.

Age, too, changes our tolerances. As a young man I never understood why old people said they could not bear the heat;

then suddenly, when I was in my forties, I started to find summer unbearable; it made me listless and dull. I realized that this must be because in the days of our youth our constitutions flourished and water and fire were in balance; but as our constitutions weaken with age the water can no longer overcome the fire.

In 1689 I first realized that I had been overworked for too long, that what my mind could now attain was no longer what it had been. My eyes were no longer good enough to write small letters, and I constantly had to have moxa cauterization treatment—until the very smell of it came to give me a splitting headache. I was only thirty-five then. By 1708, at fifty-four, I began to have spells of dizziness, and after my troubles with the Heir-Apparent, Yin-jeng, I grew thin and weak. By 1717 I had to realize that, had I still been young and strong, I would long since have wrapped up the matter of Tsewang Araptan's rebellion, which had dragged on from year to year. But now my voice was hoarse, legs and knees pained me, my cough was bad.

When Alantai and Icangga begged to retire because they were so old that their memories were beginning to fail, I said to them that their duty was to be circumspect and dignified—as to memory, their junior secretaries could divide that up between them. But it did seem to become true that even the memories of these secretaries were less good than they once had been, and that there were few who could apply their memories strongly enough to a given problem to brief me really thoroughly, so that I in turn could be aware of all the aspects that had to be considered before making a decision.

In my old age, I myself could still remember unusual details—that a certain E-te-le-hu involved in a particular law case, for instance, had been a bow maker of mine forty years before—but it became increasingly easy to forget things, especially when I was depressed or having spells of dizziness. Though I would still clearly remember details of administration, and could carry the contents of memorials in my head, I began to forget the books I had read; after a month or so I'd only retain part of their contents, though I could still remember in which chapter the passage I wanted was located, or where the book itself could be found. As I told Maci, "What I have relied on throughout my life has been the quality of my memory."

When you are young your mind is sharp and penetrating—after you grow up the thoughts scatter and gallop away. So you must not lose the chance to study while you are still young. The books I read when I was seven or eight were not forgotten after fifty or sixty years; those read after I was twenty are forgotten unless I review them after a few months. If you had no chance to study when young, then certainly you should still do so when you are grown-up—but things you studied as a child are the light of the rising sun; the studies in your maturity, a candle.

V   Sons

RESTING AT NANKING ON A TOUR, I RECEIVED
A GREETINGS MEMORIAL FROM THE HEIR-
APPARENT, REPORTING THAT HE HAD JUST FINISHED
READING THE FOUR BOOKS

The Books of Songs *and* Rites
Contain the Sages;
Countries differ from families
But learning is one.

I am on the lower Yangtze,
You are a thousand li *away*
Under distant Peking clouds,
Yet my thoughts never leave you.

At dawn I opened the folder;
Under the flap, your writing covered the page.
In natural simplicity you told me word by word
How you had finished the Four Books.

A child making such progress—
That you desire this makes me happy indeed.

Strive on day by day,
Brook no interruptions.

As Yü the Great treasured each moment,
So must you value time in its passing.
Learn from the Ancients in each book you open,
Seek inner meanings of every occurrence.
Slowly your heart will grow joyful,
And the beauty of sacrificial foods be yours.

K'ANG-HSI, 1684

K'ang-hsi was born in May 1654.

Shortly after the beginning of his reign, in 1661, the daughter of Ayusi, a Mongol of the Borjigin clan, was appointed to serve him in the palace.

In 1665 he was married to the daughter of Gabula of the Heseri clan; she was named the Empress Hsiao-ch'eng.

In 1667 the concubine Magiya (who was later named the consort Jung-fei) bore him a son, who died aged three.

In 1668 the concubine Chang bore him a daughter, who died aged three.

In 1669 the Empress Hsiao-ch'eng bore him a son, who died aged three.

In 1670 the consort Hui-fei of the Nara clan bore him a son, who died aged one.

In 1671 the consort Tuan-pin of the Tung clan bore him a daughter, who died aged two. And Jung-fei bore him her second child, a son, who died aged two.

In 1672 Hui-fei bore him her second child, a son, who survived. He was named Yin-t'i, First Son.

In 1673 Jung-fei bore him her third child, a daughter, who survived, and was named Princess Jung-hsien.

In 1674 the concubine Chang bore him her second child, a daughter, who died aged four. And Jung-fei bore him her fourth child, a son, who died in infancy. And the Empress Hsiao-ch'eng died bearing her second son, who survived. He was named Yin-jeng, Second Son, and was later appointed Heir-Apparent to the throne. Three days later the concubine Joogiya bore a daughter, who survived, and was named Princess Tuan-ching.

In 1675 Jung-fei bore her fifth child, a son, who died aged two. And the consort T'ung-pin of the Nara clan bore a son, who died aged five.

In 1677 Jung-fei bore her sixth child, a son, who survived. He was named Yin-chih, Third Son.

In 1678 Te-fei of the Uya clan, being then a palace attendant, bore a son, who survived. He was named Yin-chen, Fourth Son.

In 1679 T'ung-pin bore her second child, a son, who died aged one. And the concubine Gorolo bore a daughter, who survived, and was named Princess K'o-ching. And the concubine Gorolo's sister, I-fei, bore a son, who survived. He was named Yin-ch'i, Fifth Son.

In 1680 Te-fei bore her second child, a son, who was named Yin-tso, Sixth Son, but died aged five. And the consort Ch'eng-fei of the Daigiya clan bore a son, who survived. He was named Yin-yu, Seventh Son.

In 1681 Liang-fei of the Wei family, being then a palace attendant, bore a son, who survived. He was named Yin-ssu, Eighth Son.

In 1682 Te-fei bore her third child, a daughter, who died aged two months.

In 1683 the Imperial Consort Tunggiya, who was later for one day before her death the Empress Hsiao-i, bore a daughter, who *died in infancy. And the concubine Gorolo bore her second child, a son, who died aged one. And the concubine Gorolo's sister, I-fei, bore her second child, a son, who survived. He was named Yin-t'ang, Ninth Son. And Te-fei bore her fourth child, a daughter, who survived, and was named Wen-hsien. And the Imperial Consort Wen-hsi Kuei-fei of the Niohuru clan bore a son, who survived. He was named Yin-e, Tenth Son.*

In 1685 T'ung-pin bore her third child, a daughter, who survived, and was named Princess Ch'un-k'o. And I-fei bore her third child, a son, who was named Yin-tzu, Eleventh Son, but died aged eleven. And Wen-hsi Kuei-fei bore her second child, a daughter, who died aged one. And the consort Ting-pin of the Waliuha clan bore a son, who survived. He was named Yin-t'ao, Twelfth Son.

In 1686 Te-fei bore her fifth child, a daughter, who died aged eleven. And the consort Min-fei of the Janggiya clan bore a son, who survived. He was named Yin-hsiang, Thirteenth Son.

In 1687 this same Min-fei bore her second child, a daughter, who survived, and was named Princess Wen-k'o.

In 1688 Te-fei bore her sixth child, a son, who survived. He was named Yin-t'i, Fourteenth Son.

In 1689 the concubine Yüan bore a daughter, who survived, and was named Princess Ch'üeh-ching.

In 1691 Min-fei bore her third child, a daughter, who survived, and was named Princess Tun-k'o. And the consort P'ing-fei of the Heseri clan, sister to the former Empress Hsiao-ch'eng, bore a son, who died aged two months.

In 1693 the consort Mi-pin of the Wang family bore a son, who survived. He was named Yin-wu, Fifteenth Son.

In 1695 this same Mi-pin bore her second child, a son, who survived. He was named Yin-lu, Sixteenth Son. And another concubine, also born Wang, bore a daughter, who died aged twelve.

In 1697 the consort Ch'in-pin, born Ch'en, bore a son, who survived. He was named Yin-li, Seventeenth Son.

In 1698 the concubine Liu bore a daughter, who died aged two.

In 1701 Mi-pin bore her third child, who was named Yin-chieh, Eighteenth Son, but died aged seven. And the consort Ho-fei of the Guwalgiya clan bore a daughter, who died in infancy.

In 1702 the concubine Kao bore a son, who died aged two. In 1703 the same concubine Kao bore a daughter, who died age two. In 1706 she also bore a son, who survived. He was named Yin-i, Twentieth Son.

In 1708 the concubine Niohuru bore a daughter, who died aged one month.

In 1711 a second concubine born Ch'en bore a son, who survived. He was named Yin-hsi, Twenty-First Son. And the concubine Sehotu bore a son, who survived. He was named Yin-hu, Twenty-Second Son.

In 1713 a third concubine born Ch'en bore a son, who died in infancy. And the concubine Shih bore a son, who survived. He was named Yin-ch'i, Twenty-Third Son.

In 1716 a fourth concubine born Ch'en bore a son, who survived. He was named Yin-pi, Twenty-Fourth Son.

In 1718 a concubine whose name is not recorded bore a son, who died on the day of his birth.

The Emperor K'ang-hsi having, in all, 56 children who lived for some while after birth, borne by 30 consorts of varying ranks: 20 daughters, of whom 8 grew to maturity, and married; and 36 sons, of whom 20 grew to maturity, and 18 had sons—the number of the sons of those 18 being 123.

I USED to say to my sons: "In spring and summer the little ones should play outside in the garden. There's no need to stop them. Don't keep them sitting around on the verandah."

I used to say to them, don't swear like the rabble do, try to control your anger and your desires, avoid too much sex when you are young and too much fighting when you are strong. I keep only three hundred women around the palace, and those who have not served me personally I release when they are thirty years old and send them home to be married. You sons should do the same. Don't waste money on cosmetics for the women, and be content to keep the same old fur rugs on the palace floor. Don't bother with thousand-tael fur coats— they are not necessary, besides which fashions change: sable yields to fox, and fox to ermine. How the crowds pressed around my son-in-law Keng Chü-chung when he first wore his ermine coat, but now ermine is not so expensive.

I used to say to them, "Birthdays are times of joy."

I told them how, when I was a child, everyone praised my archery except for one old teacher; he said I was not good, and it was because of him, the critical one, that I now shoot and ride so well. And I led my sons almost daily to shoot at targets with my personal guards. I told them not to lose their Manchu traditions even in such things as dress, food, utensils, not to get too dyed in Chinese ways like the later rulers of Chin and Yüan. I told them to get their pleasures from living in wide spaces, not to close themselves in with screens and connecting rooms the way the Chinese consider clever.

I told them there are three kinds of students: those who are diligent, those who are vacant, those who are doltish. The doltish may, with care, be rendered diligent, but the vacant are the most difficult to handle, they are unable to learn from their mistakes, are sloppy and inconsistent. So I would try to make them learn things slowly, in order to master the material, and then gradually increase the difficulty of the things studied, moving step by step.

From infancy until around ten the child may move according to natural principles, but for the rest of his life it is training and habit that direct him, once he is taught to discriminate between alternatives; he must balance innate knowledge, study, and the knowledge gained through hard experience—there can be no shortcuts.

We hurt the children we spoil, for those who have been overindulged grow up to be either dim-witted, or sickly—with imbalanced appetites and intolerance for extremes of weather. It's better to be strict from the start than to offer such "love."

Some of my sons I entrusted to others. Yin-t'i, the Eldest Son, was raised in the house of Garu, director of the Imperial Household; Yin-chih, Third Son, was raised in the house of Ch'o-erh-chi, chamberlain of the Imperial Bodyguard; Yin-ch'i, Fifth Son, was raised in the Empress Dowager's palace. But Yin-jeng, Second Son, and my only son born to an empress,

I named as Heir-Apparent at two, and raised myself in the Eastern Palace. When he was four and survived the smallpox, I
sacrificed to Heaven and rewarded his doctors; I, the Emperor,
was his warm old nurse. I taught him to read myself, and entrusted his education to Chang Ying and Hsiung Tz'u-li, and
had the wisest Hanlin scholars instruct him in morality. He
excelled in study and in mounted archery; he studied the
Book of History with Weng Shu-yüan and watched Wang Yüan-
ch'i paint landscapes. I instructed him in the principles of government, together we discussed all problems of internal rebellion, and when I was away campaigning against Galdan I
appointed Yin-jeng my regent.

But when the campaigns were over, and I was back in
Peking, I learned that four persons had been engaging in illicit
behavior within Yin-jeng's palace: two of my palace cooks, a
boy called Deju, and a man called Yato from the tea store. They
had been so utterly perverse and unruly that I ordered that
Deju, Yato, and one of the cooks be executed; the other cook I
put under house arrest in his father's care. I had had troubles
with some of my other sons: my Third Son Yin-chih disobeyed
the mourning laws when the consort Min-fei died, and had to
be demoted; Yin-t'i, the Eldest Son, quarreled with my brother
on the 1690 campaign and had to be ordered back to Peking;
my Fourth Son Yin-chen was extremely moody, and for a time
I had to look after him myself. Yet none of them showed the perversity and brutality of Yin-jeng and his followers, or made me
so ashamed: he intercepted the tribute gifts sent to me, taking
even the imperial horses without permission, so that the Mongols were angered. Loving luxury, he made his wet-nurse's
husband, Ling-p'u, a director of the Imperial Household, so
that he could take whatever he wanted from there. He had no
compassion for my other sons or for me when we were sick. He
even came by night to my tent and slit open the inner curtains
so he could see inside.

When he fell ill at Te-chou on the 1702 tour, I sent his great-uncle Songgotu to look after him. But not only was Songgotu himself intensely arrogant, riding up to the central gate on his horse, and terrifying everyone around him; I also heard that he was talking a lot about killing. So in 1703, acting on information supplied by one of his slaves, I had Songgotu arrested, and told the chamberlains of the Imperial Bodyguard: "There was absolutely no way of calculating, when it was time for this 'killing,' whether it was Songgotu who was going to kill someone, or Songgotu who was going to be killed. If there is this talk of killing, who is the intended victim?" It was my feeling that if I did not take the initiative, then it would be Songgotu who took it. So I searched the homes of his retinue, and confiscated the letters that were found there, and then had Songgotu put to death.

I began to suspect that Yin-jeng planned to avenge that death. I couldn't tell if I would be poisoned one night or killed the next morning; I was never at rest. How was I to let Yin-jeng take up his imperial inheritance, he who killed his mother at his birth, he who was so extravagant, so demanding, so interfering?

Then, in 1705, I heard that numbers of children were being illegally purchased in the Soochow area. I made inquiries among my own family, and ordered Wang Hung-hsü to investigate the matter carefully and report back to me in secret. Wang's investigation showed that there were, indeed, a large number of people being bought up in the South. Some were sold locally, to officials, merchants, or merchants' associations; others were shipped to Peking and sold through various intermediaries. My guards officer Uge bought three from a Mrs. Fang, at prices ranging from 70 to 450 taels, and Mai-tzu and Decengge bought several others.

Many of these dealers were legitimate, but Fan P'u was different. For services rendered he had been granted an imperial arrow, and he used this arrow as a symbol of authority to bring all sorts of prostitutes to Peking and to make contacts there among the guards officers and in the princely households. He abused his authority further by forcing local officials to connive at his purchases of young boys. He made one of Chao Lang-yü's servants sell his son for 500 taels, although this boy was not registered as an actor, and had the purchase warrant enforced by the Soochow assistant prefect. When the boy's mother went to the prefect to lodge a complaint, the prefect mistakenly thought she was accusing a local official, and had her locked up. Her deposition was never taken. Fan P'u forcibly bought other boys and girls from the common people, claiming that he was acting as the Emperor's agent, though we couldn't find out what had happened to many of these children. On the purchase warrants the girls were referred to as "jade cocoons" and the boys as "little hands."

Wang Hung-hsü also reported the following conversation that occurred when the imperial entourage reached Hu-ch'iu in 1707. Fan P'u told his relative Ch'eng: "There is a senior Chinese official who says that I am no good, and that I didn't go to pay reverence to the imperial entourage." Ch'eng asked, "Was it a eunuch who told you about this?" Fan P'u: "It was not a eunuch. It was the person who stands number one before the Emperor who told me." So I asked Wang, "Who is this number-one man?" Wang, in turn, asked Ch'eng whether the number-one man was a guards-officer-of-the-presence, or someone at an even higher level. But Ch'eng was too frightened to name names. I was sure at least that the leak did not come from my guards officer Mau, even though I did not yet know who the number-one man was.

In checking on crimes I have this rule: never to pardon without reflection, but also never to believe lightly what others say to me or make their words the grounds for unreasonably scorning or disgracing someone. But I heard more and more news of my son's reckless, violent, and insulting behavior, until finally on October 11, 1708, I told my guards officers Uši and Cangšeo, and the eunuch Ts'un Chu, to transmit an edict to all my entourage: "Anything you hear or see must be truthfully reported to me. If you fail to mention things, and we get to the stage of people being killed, will you still be able to keep it concealed and not report it? Concealing and not reporting will be considered a crime committed by you. And if Uši, Cangšeo, or Ts'un Chu—those three—conceal one word of this my edict, or don't deliver it clearly so that all understand it, then let them be executed."

Six days later I made Yin-jeng, Second Son and Heir-Apparent, kneel before the entourage outside my traveling palace, and had this edict read out:

"I have held the glorious inheritance of Emperors Ch'ing T'ai-tsu, T'ai-tsung, and Shih-tsu for forty-eight years, with care and with attention, compassionate to my officials and nourishing my people, seeking only tranquillity for the country.

"Now I see that Yin-jeng rejects the virtues of his ancestors, and disobeys my own orders. He is dissolute, tyrannical, brutal, debauched—it's hard to even speak about it. I've tolerated him for twenty years, but he's grown even worse, scorning and tyrannizing all at court—the princes, nobles, greater and lesser officials—and monopolizing power. He has assembled his clique. He spies on my person. He checks up on every single one of my routine actions. The country only has one ruler—how is it that Yin-jeng recklessly attacks princes and officials, brutally beats them? Prince Nersu, Beile Haišan, Duke Puci have all been beaten by him. From topmost officials to common soldiers, few have not suffered from him. I knew all about his behavior, but I didn't say a word about it to any of the officials since, if any of them talked about his conduct, he would hate them for it and have them beaten."

Having made up my mind, I had Yin-jeng dismissed from

his position as Heir-Apparent and ordered the six sons of Song-gotu executed. To the senior Manchu officials I gave as clear an explanation for my anger as I could write: "Over the years I have read the histories, and have always been very careful not to let women from outside wander in and out of the palace. Nor have I let pretty young boys wait upon me. I keep my body pure, and don't have any flaws. Guwamboo and Uši are here and have attended to my person since childhood; they know about every detail of my conduct. Now that the Heir-Apparent's conduct has come to this, I cannot overcome my anger and sorrow."

Yet, as I had Uši tell the guards officers and troops, I would kill no more people; they were not to be frightened, I would listen to no more accusations, I would pardon the rest of them; perhaps I had not made myself clear, being so angry and upset and grieved. And I began to wonder why Yin-jeng had behaved as he had, when he had been taught so well, raised so carefully. What of his other habits: sleeping by day, eating at midnight, drinking tens of cups of wine without ever getting drunk, eating seven or eight bowls of rice without being full? He saw spirits, was restless, constantly changed his residence; on rainy nights, in thunderstorms, he was so scared he didn't know where to turn. In ceremonies to the gods he was so frightened he couldn't perform the proper rituals. His actions were erratic, his words all awry. It was almost as if he were directed in some way by demons. I recalled that he used often to visit his women in the Chieh-fang Palace—which was a dark, shady, dirty place. Many who lived there grew ill and died. The bad emanations could have produced some evil spirit that entered Yin-jeng on one of his visits there. If he had been rendered mad that would explain his conduct, and even such odd facts as his inability to win the affection of his own favored retainers.

And then on November 26 I got the news, from my Third Son Yin-chih, that Yin-jeng had indeed been bewitched. Yin-chih had a Mongol groom, Bahan Gorong, who had been skilled in medicine since childhood and also knew the art of laying curses on people. Yin-t'i, the Eldest Son, learning of this, had summoned Bahan Gorong and two other lamas to use their arts to cast spells on Yin-jeng. I sent guards officers to search Yin-t'i's palace, and they found the magical objects buried there. The objects were designed to conjure up nightmare demons, and I heard from Yin-jeng's keepers that, on the 28th, when the objects were dug up, Yin-jeng had a sudden epileptic seizure, took on a strange appearance, and almost killed himself. His eunuchs had to hold him down, encircling him, until after a while he came to, frightened and bewildered. And my dead grandmother came to me in a dream, her face deeply sorrowful, and sat in silence some distance from me, not like her usual self at all.

I had read about demonic possession, but always said that it was not something one could completely believe in. Now I began to realize that by these means people's minds can indeed be changed. I had believed completely that Yin-jeng had committed all the evil acts he was accused of. Now I wondered.

After all, there were other sons. Yin-t'i, the Eldest, who had had the spells cast, I arrested—he had been as violent as Yin-jeng, and was cruel and stupid. He had tortured Yin-jeng's craftsmen and some of them had committed suicide. Obviously he should never be my successor, even if he had personally been loyal to me, and protected me. He had even dared to suggest that Yin-jeng was so unpopular that I could have him killed without any blame attaching to me, and I could then name Yin-ssu, my Eighth Son, as Heir-Apparent. For had not Chang Ming-te, the seer who could read the future in men's faces, said that Yin-ssu "must come to greatness"?

Acting on this information, I appointed investigators to check the physiognomist Chang; they reported that he had been recommended to Prince Bumba by his chamberlain Alu, and that Bumba in turn recommended him to Yin-t'i. In interrogation Chang testified: "I spoke wildly, saying that the Heir-Apparent was cruel, and that if we met I would kill him. And I made up a story about having sixteen men of unusual skills, and that two of them should be summoned to see the Prince. And I egged on the Prince to listen to me, planning to get lots of money. Then Duke Puci recommended me to Yin-ssu, and I read his face for him, saying: 'Lively and alert, kind and sincere, happiness and long life stretch before you. Truly it is a face of Greatness.'" The investigators recommended that Chang be beheaded, but I said: "Chang Ming-te's criminal behavior was so monstrous he should be put to the lingering death. When the sentence is carried out let all those who were implicated with him in the case be present, so that they can watch."

Yin-ssu I arrested; and I nearly killed my Ninth Son and Fourteenth Son when they tried to defend him further, though finally I pardoned them, as I did the others. There were too many people implicated: Yin-ssu's wet-nurse's husband's uncle had schemed with Sunu, who in turn sought vengeance for his grandfather, executed by my great-grandfather T'ai-tsu long ago. And Yin-ssu's wife was Prince Yolo's granddaughter, while Yolo's consort was Songgotu's younger sister, and their offspring as "uncles" showed no respect for Yin-ssu's wife. I could do nothing but urge them to obedience once again: "All of you my sons know that I am your ruler and father; no matter what I may order you to do, you should do it obediently. That is the first step to behaving properly as my subjects and my sons. If you don't remember this, then later, when I am dead, you can lay my body out in the Ch'ien-ch'ing Palace, strap on your armor, and fight it out."

By mid-December officials were beginning to memorialize for the restoration of Yin-jeng, but I warned them that just because I was talking with Yin-jeng again, that did not mean I had forgiven him. The question was still open: "Those of you who want the deposed Heir-Apparent restored must not be joyful; those who don't want the deposed Heir-Apparent restored must not grieve." So I called a great meeting of all senior officials at the Ch'ang-ch'un Garden on December 25, and ordered my Mongol son-in-law, Prince Bandi, to lead the discussions. My Eldest Son Yin-t'i, I said, had acted so badly that he could not be considered; "but apart from him, discuss whom you would like from among all the other sons, and I will follow your advice." The discussions went on all day, though most officials were too scared to speak out, save for a small group who recommended Yin-ssu. This group consisted of Mingju's son K'uei-hsü, Ebilun's son Alingga, and T'ung Kuo-k'ang's son Olondai, joined by Wang Hung-hsü. I rejected this recommendation, saying: "The establishment of an heir-apparent is of crucial importance, and you must use all your skills in discussing it. My Eighth Son has had no experience, and has just been found guilty. Moreover, his mother's family is a very lowly one. Think again."

The arguments and discussions dragged on, as the eunuchs Liang Chiu-kung and Li Yü moved back and forth with messages between my chambers and the meeting hall. But finally I saw that many officials were still intimidated, and that the matter was too important to be left to oral transmissions by two eunuchs—even trusted ones such as these. So I arranged for the officials to meet with me face to face, and also for each one to write his own decision on a piece of paper, which he would give me to look at. But as it had grown dark, I sent the officials home to think about the problem overnight, charging them to return at dawn the following day.

The next day I told them of my dreams concerning Yin-jeng, and my realization that demonic possession was possible. "Are you all agreed now?" "Yes, we are all agreed." "Since you are all agreed, you can all see this edict that I have written out with my own brush in vermilion: 'When I seized Yin-jeng I had made no plans involving others; because it was the correct thing, it had to be done, so I seized him and had him locked up. The whole country thought my action was correct. As I now consider the whole business, I'm not clear in my own mind; checking each item through in detail, there are some things that fit perfectly and others that seem to have no form at all. Moreover, the mental illness that affected him seems to have grown better. Not only did all the officials grieve, I also grieved. Now that he is getting better, it's good fortune for me and for my officials. I let people look after him, but kept passing on my instructions that he not be taken far away from me. I am not now in any hurry to re-establish Yin-jeng as Heir-Apparent, but just want all of you officials to know what my thoughts are. There will be absolutely no vengeance from Yin-jeng, that I can guarantee.'"

On December 28 I shelved Bandi's recommendation that Yin-jeng be restored. On January 8 I restored Yin-ssu to his princedom. Then, on March 2, I summoned all the chamberlains of the Imperial Bodyguard, the Grand Secretaries, and the Board presidents, determined to find out who was behind the Yin-ssu clique. Again the discussions went on all day—and would all night too, I said, until we got to the root of it—until at last Chang Yü-shu said Maci had told him that "the majority favor Yin-ssu." Maci angrily corrected this; his exact words, he said, had been "It is not yet decided. I hear that in the group there are some who favor the Eighth Son." And he shook his sleeves in contempt and left my presence. So I ordered Prince Cuntai to investigate Maci, and they found that he deserved death for his conduct, together with his brothers, that their relatives should be dismissed and their families banished to Heilungchiang. But I spared Maci, and ordered him to be put under house arrest and guarded by Yin-ssu. Bandi and the others again requested the restoration of Yin-jeng, and this time I agreed. For I had been weak and ill, and Yin-jeng had tended me lovingly; all the demonic influences to which he had been subjected by the curses had passed away. I had trusted in Heaven and in my ancestors and they, mindful of my years of toil, had helped me in my weakness. In the middle of March I went journeying, by land and by boat, with Yin-jeng, and my Fourth, Seventh, Eighth, Thirteenth, Fourteenth, Fifteenth, and Sixteenth Sons. Five inches of snow fell, promising good fortune to the country. And in April, with Unda and Li Kuang-ti presiding, we restored Yin-jeng to his former position of Heir-Apparent.

Then in December 1711 it all started again, in winter, in the Ch'ang-ch'ün Garden. I said: "There are great officials forming factions around the Heir-Apparent. You are all people I selected for senior office, and have been favored for fifty years. What is the meaning of this cleaving to the Heir-Apparent? I think Ošan knows about this matter."

General Ošan: "I have been nourished and chosen by the Emperor. If I knew of this, how would I dare conceal it?"

Board of War president Gengge: "Truly I know nothing about it. Had I known, I would have reported it."

Board of Punishments president Ch'i-shih-wu: "I never go anywhere. I really know nothing about this."

I said: "I've known of this for a long time. As my inquiries did not bring out the full truth I sent this message to General Dutu: 'Someone has confessed and given evidence about your clique. Report all the facts to me. If you don't, you and your family will be killed.' So Dutu wrote it all out in a memorial." And I took out General Dutu's palace memorial and showed it to them.

Then I had the bondservant superviser Chang Po-liang led out, and told him to look over the lieutenant-generals; and, calling forward General Uli, I asked Chang Po-liang: "Are you sure this is the man?" "Yes, I am sure." And I said, "Suman has gone on a journey, but why hasn't General Yangdai come?" Someone answered, "He didn't come because he's sick." I asked Chang Po-liang, "Was Yangdai one of them?" And Chang said, "There was one old general."

So I turned to General Yatu and asked, "Did you know what Ošan was up to or not?" "I have often heard Ošan publicly say that he's grateful for the Emperor's favors and seeks to serve him. I know nothing about this secret business." "Yatu, are you one of them?" "No."

I said to General Ošan and the rest: "I am not getting complete testimony. How could I want to harm those who are not involved? You have been saying that I am old, and you have formed cliques, acting recklessly without fear. But now you are in my presence, what trouble can you cause? How can you let your faces look up at the light of day? Among my officials there are many who have not joined your cliques. Seeing them, are you not ashamed?"

Uli said: "You have favored me with lieutenant-general's rank, and I am a member of the Imperial Clan; how could I have agreed to take part in such a business? My house is near Ošan's, and certainly I have been there for drinking parties. But I am not guilty of forming a clique with him."

Ch'i-shih-wu said: "By nature I am unable to get people to like me, and I have no friends. I have been under the Emperor's scrutiny for a long time. I don't know why Dutu should hate me enough to implicate me. I know nothing about this whole business. Ošan invited me to dinner once, and I invited him once; if we formed any clique, then certainly we should be executed."

"You said you never went anywhere. Why are you now bringing up these invitations to dinners?"

"Ošan's mother is from the Tunggiya clan, and calls me uncle; that's why there were these dinner invitations."

To this I responded: "You, Ch'i-shih-wu, are an absolutely worthless person, below the dogs and swine. What profit can men derive from joining cliques with such trash? Gengge was a household slave of Songgotu; he groveled before Songgotu in Ula, and offered up the ritual utensils. In the Songgotu case he should have been executed, but I gave him a special pardon, and he repays my favor by plotting in cliques. All your conduct must spring from Gengge."

Gengge prostrated himself and protested: "I have received great favors from the Emperor. If I am guilty of this, let me be put to the lingering death."

I answered: "Songgotu's clique has not been all cut off; you want to be Songgotu's avengers. Your fathers and grandfathers were all slaves in Songgotu's household—everyone in the Plain Yellow Banner knows all about this case. And this Ošan once claimed to be a member of the Gorolo clan, hoping to be enrolled in one of the Imperial Banners. I did not permit this and he's had a grudge against me ever since. And he had no thoughts for my favors, but rebelliously forms a clique, a complete ingrate." I ordered that Ošan, Gengge, Ch'i-shih-wu, and Uli be arrested and tried. Ch'i-shih-wu and Ošan were proved to be involved with Tohoci, commandant of the Peking troops; their plots and corruption were widespread. For people who "never went anywhere" the evidence showed that they did a lot, and asked a great many people to drink with them. When it was proved also that they had stolen large sums of money, I ordered them executed.

Throughout these hearings, Yin-jeng's name remained omnipresent. I told the Imperial Clan: "All these cases are because of Yin-jeng. What Yin-jeng has been doing is known to everyone in the country, great or small. If only he was filial at heart and benevolent in actions, then the whole country would know he was my son, and would not be alienated." Instead, he surrounded himself with venal toadies. By the winter of 1712 his madness was back and I could bear no more; he spied on people in the privies, he spat and swore at his retinue and his consorts and showed no remorse, and once again I canceled his titles and had him put under guard.

Each person has sons he loves deeply, and sons he does not love deeply. For many years I bore my suffering silently; it was hard and only I could have done it, while Yin-jeng's foodstuffs and clothes and display doubled mine. Those he wanted me to censure I censured, those he wanted me to punish I punished, those he wanted me to exile I exiled. Only those he wanted me to kill did I not kill. As I yielded, he remained unchanging in evil; my heart was ash, hope gone. The officials feared, saying, "One out of the two sides means death," thinking if they chose the wrong one to be loyal to, the other would kill them. Yin-jeng's consorts' hearts grew cold, and I was sure that not one would weep if he were dismissed. His guards officers sweated in their yellow jackets, overworked, unsmiling. Daily I sent ten of my own guards officers to keep an eye on him, but it was as if to Yin-jeng they had no eyes, and he continued to let every kind of person pass through his gate. As my face grew thin and sickly everyone kept quiet, no officials spoke out to comfort me. I said: "Now that I have come to my final decision, there's no use now to send in words of comfort. The first time I dismissed him I was truly enraged and sorrowful, but this time I think nothing of it, I carry it through chatting and smiling." I told the Court that I had killed only a few people on the first occasion, and I would kill only one or two on the second. Let the rest stop their worrying and cleave in loyalty to me—then there would be a time of Great Peace. As for those in the future who chose to memorialize, requesting Yin-jeng's restoration on the grounds that he had again changed his ways and now followed goodness—they would be executed. Yin-t'i, the Eldest Son, was still in confinement. And in 1714, for ceaseless arrogance and plotting, for talking of my death and boasting of his backers, for offering me a present of dying falcons, I once again imprisoned Yin-ssu, the Eighth Son.

I used to say to my sons: Seek joyfulness when you can,

for seeking joy leads to an auspicious atmosphere. After meals we would talk about pleasant things and set our eyes on rare antiques, so we digested easily and our bodies flourished.

I used to say to them: Judge your man by looking carefully into his eyes; the eyes will show if there is any evil lurking there; the pupils should be clear, not blurred with worry or uncertainty. Don't look around while sitting or look back while walking; we Manchus have never tolerated that.

I told them how many ways there are of finding the principles of morality: through reading, through lectures, through reflection, through experience. I said: Let true reverence be in you always. This reverence means love and attention even to the smallest things. When there is nothing of importance to do, hold yourself firm with this reverence. When problems arise use reverence in handling them. Be as attentive in the end as at the beginning, take the long view. If this becomes a habit you will be at peace, for with this reverence in your heart the true heart will be profoundly lodged in the center, just as the master of his own home is able to keep all his family affairs in order.

I told them to be careful with their subordinates, for such men learn subtly to match their masters' inclinations and to tempt them with their own desires, for they seek nothing but their own profit. Yet at the same time, masters should try to be neither too harsh nor too lenient with servants; they should punish them if they need it, and not just nurse their anger, for that will frighten the servants and be of no value. That is the principle of using people. Remember it.

Despite my warnings, officials continued to bring up the matter of the succession. In 1713, Chao Shen-ch'iao memorialized that a new heir-apparent should be named, and I had his memorial returned. In 1717, Wang Shan and a group of censors memorialized also on the same topic, and I told them that their action was improper. Then the ignorant young Hanlin scholar,

Chu T'ien-pao, requested the restoration of Yin-jeng himself, saying Yin-jeng had become benevolent and filial, ever more sagelike and worthy; that I was to blame because I would not meet him face to face; that the tragedy of his case could be compared with that of Han Wu-ti's heir-apparent, who was driven to suicide; and that General Fiyanggu sought to destroy him. I found that Chu T'ien-pao had been encouraged in his treason by his own father, and that both had been connected with others in a clique. Once more I outlined, for their benefit, Yin-jeng's proven faults, and I added the new ones we had discovered—that he had written letters in invisible ink to certain senior Manchu nobles, to see if he might be made a military commander; that he had falsely claimed that I had been praising him; that he had used his wife's doctor to smuggle out his letters for him; that he had sworn at the tutor Hsü Yüan-meng; that he had reviled his uncles and cousins; and that he had turned his back on me when in my presence. So there was no doubt that he must still be kept locked up. As for the Chus, father and son, their guilt could not be forgiven. At first I ordered that Chu T'ien-pao be beheaded and his father be put to the lingering death afterward. Then I relented, and merely made the father watch while the son was publicly beheaded.

I used to say to my sons: "When spring arrives the times are in tune, the flowers spread out their best brocade, and the birds call their countless lovely songs. This should be even more true for men in this world: enjoying tranquillity, resting at home, and content in their work, they should naturally speak fine words and do good deeds, and so have no need for shame in this life."

I used to say to them: "In spring and summer the little ones should play outside in the garden. There's no need to stop them."

VI   *Valedictory*

On December 23, 1717, the Emperor went to the Eastern Chamber of the Ch'ien-ch'ing Palace and ordered all his sons, the Manchu and Chinese Grand Secretaries and subchancellors, the officials of the nine chief ministries, the chief supervisors of imperial instruction, the censors and intendants, to assemble there.

The following edict was issued:

When I was young, Heaven gave me great strength, and I didn't know what sickness was. This spring I started to get serious attacks of dizziness and grew increasingly emaciated. Then I went hunting in the autumn beyond the borders, and the fine climate of the Mongolian regions made my spirits stronger day by day, and my face filled out again. Although I was riding and shooting every day, I didn't feel fatigued. After I returned to Peking the Empress Dowager fell ill, and I was dejected in mind; the dizziness grew almost incessant. Since there are some things that I have wanted to say to you on a normal day, I have specially summoned you today to hear my edict, face to face with me.

The rulers of the past all took reverence for Heaven's laws and reverence for their ancestors as the fundamental way in ruling the country. To be sincere in reverence for Heaven and ancestors entails the following: Be kind to men from afar and keep the able ones near, nourish the people, think of the profit of all as being the real profit and the mind of the whole country as being the real mind, be considerate to officials and act as a father to the people, protect the state before danger comes and govern well before there is any disturbance, be always diligent and always careful, and maintain the balance between leniency and strictness, between principle and expediency, so that long-range plans can be made for the country. That's all there is to it.

No dynasty in history has been as just as ours in gaining the right to rule. The Emperors T'ai-tsu and T'ai-tsung initially had no intention of taking over the country; and when T'ai-tsung's armies were near Peking and his ministers advised him to take it, he replied: "The Ming have not been on good terms with our people, and it would be very easy to conquer them now. But I am aware of what an unbearable act it is to overthrow the ruler of China." Later the roving bandit Li Tzu-ch'eng stormed the city of Peking, the Ming Emperor Ch'ung-chen hanged himself, and the officials and people all came out to welcome us. Then we exterminated the violent bandits and inherited the empire. In olden times, it was Hsiang Yü who raised an army and defeated the Ch'in, yet the country then passed to the Han, even though initially Emperor Han Kao-tsu was only a local constable on the Ssu River. At the end of the Yüan, it was Ch'en Yu-liang and others who rebelled, yet the country then passed to the Ming, even though initially Emperor Ming T'ai-tsu was only a monk in the Huang-chüeh Temple. The forebears of our dynasty were men who obeyed Heaven and lived in harmony with other men; and the empire was pacified. From this we can tell that all the rebellious officials and bandits are finally pushed aside by truly legitimate rulers.

I am now close to seventy, and have been over fifty years on the throne—this is all due to the quiet protection of Heaven and earth and the ancestral spirits; it was not my meager virtue that did it. Since I began reading in my childhood, I have managed to get a rough understanding of the constant historical principles. Every emperor and ruler has been subject to the Mandate of Heaven. Those fated to enjoy old age cannot prevent themselves from enjoying that old age; those fated to enjoy a time of Great Peace cannot prevent themselves from enjoying that Great Peace.

Over 4,350 years have passed from the first year of the Yellow Emperor to the present, and over 300 emperors are listed as having reigned, though the data from the Three Dynasties—that is, for the period before the Ch'in burning of the books—are not wholly credible. In the 1,960 years from the first year of Ch'in Shih-huang to the present, there have been 211 people who have been named emperor and have taken era names. What man am I, that among all those who have reigned long since the Ch'in and Han Dynasties, it should be I who have reigned the longest?

Among the Ancients, only those who were not boastful and knew not to go too far could attain a good end. Since the Three Dynasties, those who ruled long did not leave a good name to posterity, while those who did not live long did not know the world's griefs. I am already old, and have reigned long, and I cannot foretell what posterity will think of me. Besides which, because of what is going on now, I cannot hold back my tears of bitterness; and so I have prepared these notes to make my own record, for I still fear that the country may not know the depth of my sorrow.

Many emperors and rulers in the past made a taboo of the subject of death, and as we look at their valedictory decrees we find that they are not at all written in imperial tones, and do not record what the emperor really wanted to say. It was always when the emperors were weak and dying that they found some scholar-official to write out something as he chose.

With me it is different. I am letting you know what my sincerest feelings are in advance.

When I had been twenty years on the throne I didn't dare conjecture that I might reign thirty. After thirty years I didn't dare conjecture that I might reign forty. Now I have reigned fifty-seven years. The "Great Plan" section of the *Book of History* says of the five joys:

The first is long life;
The second is riches;
The third is soundness of body and serenity of mind;
The fourth is the love of virtue;
The fifth is an end crowning the life.

The "end crowning the life" is placed last because it is so hard to attain. I am now approaching seventy, and my sons, grandsons, and great-grandsons number over one hundred and fifty. The country is more or less at peace and the world is at peace. Even if we haven't improved all manners and customs, and made all the people prosperous and contented, yet I have worked with unceasing diligence and intense watchfulness, never resting, never idle. So for decades I have exhausted all my strength, day after day. How can all this just be summed up in a two-word phrase like "hard work"?

Those among the rulers of earlier dynasties who did not live long have all been judged in the Histories as having caused this themselves through their own wild excesses, by overaddiction to drink and sex. Such remarks are just the sneers of pedants who have to find some blemishes in even the purest and most perfect of rulers. I exonerate these earlier rulers, because the affairs of the country are so troublesome that one can't help getting exhausted. Chu-ko Liang said: "I shall bow down in service and wear myself out until death comes," but among all the officials only Chu-ko Liang acted in this way. Whereas the emperor's responsibilities are terribly heavy, there is no way he can evade them. How can this be compared with being an official? If an official wants to serve, then he serves; if he wants to stop, then he stops. When he grows old he resigns and

returns home, to look after his sons and play with his grandsons; he still has the chance to relax and enjoy himself. Whereas
the ruler in all his hard-working life finds no place to rest. Thus,
though the Emperor Shun said, "Through non-action one governs," he died in Ts'ang-wu [while on a tour of inspection]; and
after four years on the throne Emperor Yü had blistered hands
and feet and found death in K'uai-ch'i. To work as hard at government as these men, to travel on inspection, to have never a
leisure moment—how can this be called the valuing of "non-
action" or tranquilly looking after oneself? In the *I Ching*
hexagram "Retreat" not one of the six lines deals with a ruler's
concerns—from this we can see that there is no place for rulers
to rest, and no resting place to which they can retreat. "Bowing
down in service and wearing oneself out" indeed applies to
this situation.

All the Ancients used to say that the emperor should concern himself with general principles, but need not deal with
the smaller details. I find that I cannot agree with this. Careless handling of one item might bring harm to the whole world,
a moment's carelessness damage all future generations. Failure
to attend to details will end up endangering your greater virtues. So I always attend carefully to the details. For example:
if I neglect a couple of matters today and leave them unsettled,
there will be a couple more matters for tomorrow. And if tomorrow I again don't want to be bothered, that will pile up even
more obstructions for the future. The emperor's work is of
great importance, and there should not be delays, so I attend
to all matters, whether they are great or small. Even if it is just
one character wrong in a memorial, I always correct it before
forwarding it. Not to neglect anything, that is my nature. For
over fifty years I have usually prepared in advance for things—
and the world's millions all honor my virtuous intentions.
How can one still hold to "there being no need to deal with the
smaller details"?

I was strong from my childhood onward, with fine muscles;

I could bend a bow with a pull of 15 *li*, and fire a fifty-two-inch arrow. I was good at using troops and confronting the enemy, but I have never recklessly killed a single person. In pacifying the Three Feudatories and clearing out the northern deserts, I made all the plans myself. Unless it was for military matters or famine relief, I didn't take funds from the Board of Revenue treasury, and spent nothing recklessly, for the reason that this was the people's wealth. On my inspection tours, I didn't set out colored embroideries, and the expenses at each place were only 10,000 or 20,000 taels. In comparison, the annual expense on the river conservancy system is over 3,000,000 —so the cost was not even one per cent of that.

When I studied as a child, I already knew that one should be careful with drink and sex, and guard against mean people. So I grew old without illness. But after my serious illness in the forty-seventh year of my reign, my spirits had been too much wounded, and gradually I failed to regain my former state. Moreover, every day there was my work, all requiring decisions; frequently I felt that my vitality was slipping away and my internal energy diminishing. I fear that in the future if some accident happened to me I would not be able to say a word, and so my real feelings would not be disclosed. Wouldn't that be regretful? Therefore I am using this occasion when I feel clear-headed and lively to complete my life by telling you all that can be revealed, item by item. Isn't that wonderful?

All men who live must die. As Chu Hsi said, "The principle of the cyclical cosmic forces is like dawn and night." And Confucius said, "Live contentedly and await Heaven's will." These sayings express the great Way of the Sages, so why should we be afraid? I have been seriously ill recently: my mind was blurred and my body exhausted. As I moved around, if no one held me up by the arms it was hard for me to walk. In the past I fixed my mind on my responsibilities to the country; to work "until death comes" was my goal. Now that I am ill I am querulous and forgetful, and terrified of muddling right with wrong, and leaving my work in chaos. I exhaust my mind for the country's sake, and fragment my spirits for the world. When your wits aren't guarding your body, your heart has no nourishment, your eyes can't tell far from near nor ears distinguish true from false, and you eat little and have a lot to do—how can you last long? Moreover, since the country has long been at peace and people have grown lazy, joy goes and sorrows mount, "peace" departs and "stagnation" comes. When the head is crammed with trifles, the limbs are indolent—until everything is in ruins and you inevitably bring down at random and together calamities from Heaven and destruction for men. Even if you want to do something, your vitality is insufficient, and by then it's too late to admit your mistakes. No more can you be roused up, and moaning in your bed you'll die with eyes open—won't you feel anguish just before you die?

Emperor Wu-ti of the Liang was a martial dynastic founder, but when he reached old age he was forced by Hou-ching into the tragedy at T'ai-ch'eng. Emperor Wen-ti of the Sui also was a founding emperor, but he could not anticipate the evil ways of his son Yang-ti and was finally unable to die in peace. There are other examples, like killing oneself by taking cinnabar, or being poisoned and eating the cakes, or the case of Sung T'ai-tsu, when people saw the candlelight from afar. There are records of all kinds of suspicious cases—are these not tracks of the past that we can see? All these happened because [the emperors] didn't understand in time. And all brought harm to country and people. Han Kao-tsu told Empress Lü about the mandate; T'ang T'ai-tsung decided on the heir-apparent with Chang-sun Wu-chi. When I read such things I feel deeply ashamed. Perhaps there are mean persons who hope to use the confusion, and will act on their own authority to alter the succession, pushing someone forward in expectation of future rewards. As long as I still have one breath left, how could I tolerate that sort of thing?

My birth was nothing miraculous—nor did anything extraordinary happen when I grew up. I came to the throne at eight, fifty-seven years ago. I've never let people talk on about supernatural influences of the kind that have been recorded in the Histories: lucky stars, auspicious clouds, unicorns and phoenixes, *chih* grass and such like blessings, or burning pearls and jade in the front of the palace, or heavenly books sent down to manifest Heaven's will. Those are all empty words, and I don't presume so far. I just go on each day in an ordinary way, and concentrate on ruling properly.

Now, officials have memorialized, requesting that I set up an heir-apparent to share duties with me—that's because they feared my life might end abruptly. Death and life are ordinary phenomena—I've never avoided talking about them. It's just that all the power of the country has to be united in one person. For the last ten years, I've been writing out (and keeping sealed) what I intend to do and what my feelings are, though I haven't finished yet. Appointing the heir-apparent is a great matter; how could I neglect it? The throne of this country is of the utmost importance. If I were to relieve myself of this burden and relax in comfort, disentangling my mind from every problem, then I could certainly expect to live longer. You officials have all received great mercies from me—how can I attain the day when I will have no more burdens?

My energies have shrunk, I have to force myself to endure, and if everything finally goes awry, won't the hard work of the last fifty-seven years indeed be wasted? It is my intense sincerity that leads me to say this. Whenever I read an old official's memorial requesting retirement, I can't stop the tears from flowing. You all have a time for retiring, but where can I find rest? But if I could have a few weeks to restore myself and a chance to conclude my life with a natural death, then my happiness would be indescribable. There is time ahead of me; maybe I will live as long as Sung Kao-tsung. We cannot tell.

Not until I was fifty-seven did I begin to have a few white

hairs in my beard, and I was offered some lotion to make it black again. But I laughed and refused, saying: "How many white-haired emperors have there been in the past? If my hair and whiskers whiten, won't that be a splendid tale for later generations?" Not one man is now left from those who worked with me in my early years. Those who came later to their new appointments are harmonious and respectful with their colleagues, they are just and law-abiding, and their white heads fill the Court. This has been the case for a long time, and for this I am grateful.

I have enjoyed the veneration of my country and the riches of the world; there is no object I do not have, nothing I have not experienced. But now that I have reached old age I cannot rest easy for a moment. Therefore, I regard the whole country as a worn-out sandal, and all riches as mud and sand. If I can die without there being an outbreak of trouble, my desires will be fulfilled. I wish all of you officials to remember that I have been the peace-bearing Son of Heaven for over fifty years, and that what I have said to you over and over again is really sincere. Then that will complete the fitting end to my life.

I've been preparing this edict for ten years. If a "valedictory edict" is issued, let it contain nothing but these same words.

I've revealed my entrails and shown my guts, there's nothing left within me to reveal.

I will say no more.

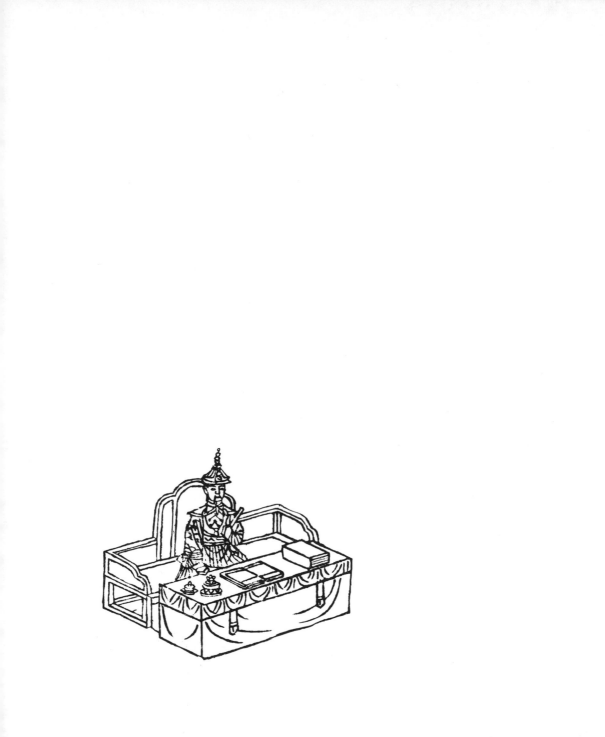

Seventeen Letters

to Ku Wen-hsing, Chief Eunuch, Spring 1697

The following sequence of seventeen letters was written by K'ang-hsi in 1697 to one of his most trusted eunuchs. The letters are here translated in full because they show the Emperor's informal style and the way he bunched his ideas, and are thus a valuable addition to the rest of the book, which is mainly a montage from fragments. Sealed up in a box within the Imperial Palace, the letters were discovered by scholars after the 1911 revolution and were subsequently transcribed and published. Probably no such sequence of letters has survived from any other emperor in China's history.

Second Month, Eighth Day

On the 7th we passed the fork in the road at Pa-ta-ling and camped. On the 8th we camped at Huai-lai hsien. The weather is completely different from that in Peking; I really feel the cold. Some time ago the silk store had two fur coats, one wolf and one desert fox, though they had not been faced. Have these two coats finished, using Yü satin for the sleeves and Ling-ning silk for the bodies; when they are done, send them along with one of the batches of memorials. They musn't be made too tight. Because the lot you sent along with the memorials last time were too tight, they were really uncomfortable. You must be careful.

When I left, the consort Te-fei was slightly ill. Is she quite better now? I hope that the princes who had the measles are all better—and of course that the palaces are now all clear and auspicious.

The camels and horses on this trip are sleek and lovable, and walk well. Ever since leaving the city I've kept on getting the most excellent news. I am in fine health.

Second Month, Twenty-Second Day

During this last thirty-day period since I left the City, I've passed through San-yün. To the south I've seen as far as Wei-chou, Ying-chou, Yen-men, and Ning-wu. To the north I've seen as far as P'ien-kuan and Sha-hu-k'ou. I've camped in Huai-jen, Ma-i, and Shou-chou. I have looked at the topography. This is an area of ancient battlefields, now at peace, with carefree people. All, from the white-haired oldest to the youngest being carried, bow down to the ground before my horse, no differently from those on my Southern Tours. The people are sincere in spirit and customs. Because last year's harvest was excellent, there's plenty of grain and fodder.

I'm happy in mind, well in body. It's a little warmer than it was in Ta-t'ung. Part of the river is unfrozen, part still frozen. All the retinue are well. Pass this news on to those in the palace.

Second Month, Twenty-Eighth Day

Since sending off my last letter to you, we've been through the area of Ta-shui-k'ou, north of the Ning-wu Pass. We've also passed K'o-lan-chou and Ho-ch'ü, and arrived at San-ch'a-p'u. On the 26th we reached Li-chia-kou. There was no water there, but the local officials at I-ching were ready with three hundred large jars of water. I was moving along the road, when I saw people coming from Li-chia-kou talking excitedly. They said that three days ago the dry river which runs from K'o-lan-chou, and is called the Hsiao-tsun River, had a flash flood which came to within seven miles of Li-chia-kou to the south. The local officials feared that mud would cover the imperial road, so they held it back with a dike. Other people were saying that the three prongs of this dry river today had water that would reach down to Han-chia-lou, and the local people were blocking that up as well.

I truly didn't believe this, and when I got there went to

take a look. It was true. Then I had the dike opened, and by early evening the river water had reached the imperial camp at Li-chia-kou with a depth of two feet. So the three hundred jars were never used.

The 27th we journeyed to Nien-wu village, through 56 *li* of high mountains and peaks linked without a break. I have never been through such unpleasant mountains. Had not the local people heard that I was coming and competed to clear the way, we'd never have been able to get through. The previous day there had been a snowfall; the wind piled it up, drift on drift, along the edges of the road so that the road itself was perfectly all right for those pushing carts. One *li* before the camp there was also a little stream of clear water with a lovely taste. Everyone among the retinue's officials and troops saw for themselves what happened on these two days, and I said: "This is no more than chance; there is nothing so unusual about it."

On the 28th we reached Pao-te-chou, on the bank of the Yellow River. I took a little boat and went fishing; the river was full of *shih-hua* fish—they taste fresh and delicious, one can't describe it in words. There's every kind of food here, but the white noodles are best of all. These are all little details; I don't write about them for outside transmittal, but just let you people in the palace know them.

Third Month, Fourth Day

Since crossing the river we've passed through Fu-ku-hsien and Shen-mu-hsien and other places and are now near Yü-lin. The characteristics of these Shensi mountains and rivers make for quite different kinds of scenery—there are fine places and there are unpleasant places. The good aspects are that the customs are pure and honest, the people's hearts are like those of the men of old, the water and soil are good, there are no strange diseases, there's plenty of food, in the mountains pine trees and cedars grow—they are beautiful when seen from a distance.

What I call "unpleasant" places are those that have the [Great] Wall forts on the crests of the hills, while all the villages themselves are in the sides of the broken cliffs—people make caves and live in them. The peaks are not really peaks, the roads are not really roads, it's ridiculous.

To the south I've traveled through Chihli, Shantung, Chiangnan, and Chekiang, as far as Shao-hsing, a distance of 4,000 *li*; to the north I've been over 2,000 *li* to the Kerulen River; in the east I've reached Ula in Kwantung, over 2,000 *li*. Now I have passed through Shansi and Shensi on a western trip of over 2,000 *li*. Rivers, lakes, mountains, deserts, and the Gobi— all deserted—I've been through them all. None of them has the scenery or the prosperous people of the South.

On the 4th we stopped at Shen-mu-hsien, and in the late afternoon some of Galdan's brigands were brought to our camp, and all the Manchus and Chinese, civilian or military, of whatever rank, were excited and pleased. So you can see the truth of the saying that "Everyone has the right to execute treasonous officials and brigands"; how can it just be accidental?

Though I am a traveler in the distant mountain passes, I am determined to wipe out the brigands, concentrating on gaining my goal. Moreover, it's the beginning of the late spring and the ice is not yet melted—the Ch'ing-ming festival is near, but the wind is still cold. I don't know if it's been like this in Peking this year or not.

I'm in very good health, there's ample food and drink on the route, the white noodles are outstanding. Is everyone well in the palace? The Galdan business should be over fairly soon, it's just that I can't give a definite date.

When I was in Shen-mu I got a couple of local delicacies and sent them to the [consorts in the] Yen-hsi and I-k'un Palaces, so they can take a look and smile. Please also offer up a box of the Shen-mu white noodles in greeting.

Third Month, Fifth Day

When I get to Ninghsia I'm going to wait for people to come from Galdan before I decide on the use of troops. The camels and horses are sleek; if we have to go somewhere we can move immediately. The Ninghsia area is fine, and everything is very cheap. There are no flowering plants, though.

Both the seal and the box of the last lot of documents you sent me had been opened. So I'm sealing this up on the outside. When you next send some reports, seal them up in the same way.

Third Month, Seventh Day

Among the local produce that the Moslems of Hami sent to me along with the [captured] Galdan bandits, only the sun-dried muskmelon had a really beautiful taste. I'm sending off some to you, but as I'm afraid you won't know what to do with it, I'll specifically write it out for you:

> After you have washed it clean in either cold or hot water, steep it in hot water (but only for a short time), and then eat it either cold or hot. It tastes fresh and the juice is like the honeyed juice of a dried peach. Where there are holes, fill them up with little grapes.

Tell the consorts about this. This is a trifling matter, but my heart is truly far away with you—don't laugh at me for this.

Also Third Month, Seventh Day

When I passed through the Ordos area, a great many Mongol princes' consorts came to greet me. Get one floss silk dress and one cotton dress from each of the consorts and concubines, and send them along with the next batch of documents to me.

My female attendant Hsü and the two other females don't have enough underwear, jackets, middle-length garments, silk shirts, silk middle-length garments, and satin socks to be worn with boots. Tell the consorts in the Yen-hsi Palace to decide on the amount, and send them along to me with the documents when they're finished.

Third Month, Twenty-Eighth Day

Since the last batch of reports were sent, I've been out hunting with the Green Standard troops of the Third Border division. There were an incredible number of hares and birds. On the 22nd, at Hsing-wu camp, the hunting circle was quite filled with hares; I shot 311 of them. On the 23rd, at Ch'ing-shui fort, there were as many hares again but I couldn't shoot them all, and stopped after a hundred or so.

On the 24th we camped at Kuang-ch'eng on the banks of the Yellow River. The 25th we crossed and camped on the other bank. On the 26th we reached Ninghsia. Though the scenery here is not up to that in the South, it's like heaven to earth in comparison with what I've just traveled through. Everything we need is here and food prices are cheap. From the western Ho-lan Mountains to the Yellow River on the east, all the cities are surrounded with paddy fields. Of the nine border divisions fixed by the Ancients I have now visited seven; and, of those I've seen, only Ninghsia bears talking about. I've obtained various local products here in Ninghsia. Offer them to the Empress Dowager. Give the other things to the consorts and concubines, and distribute them according to the list.

I reached Ninghsia on the 26th, and on the 27th sent off P'an Liang-tung with presents of local products. All those that have names on, distribute accordingly. Those without names will be explained orally to you by P'an Liang-tung.

Intercalary Third Month, Fifteenth Day

I've been in Ninghsia nineteen days. [Today] I'm going to Pai-t'a, on the bend of the Yellow River—it's 400 *li* from Ninghsia, and is the home of Ha-lun, the Tu-leng duke. Once I get to Pai-t'a I'll assess the situation and make my plans. From now on I'm gradually getting nearer to Peking.

Intercalary Third Month, Eighteenth Day
Although the purpose of this expedition was to finish off Galdan, I also wanted to deal with the Ölöds beyond the western border. There are many different groups of them and we must curb them if we are to have a lasting peace. At the time of leaving Peking I didn't make a clear statement about this, but since I left I have sent men to every area, announcing my intentions. Besides those I've announced at intervals as having come over to us, the entire tribe of Ölöds who live in or around Hsihai have now declared their allegiance, and have already started the journey to come to me. I raise my hands to my forehead, I am so very pleased.

To be virtuous and so be granted the protection of heaven and earth, and without one man being killed to have tens of thousands come over—truly that exceeded my expectations. Everyone in camp who heard about it congratulated each other and thought it a great joy. Because I'm sending a report on this, I write to you also.

Intercalary Third Month, Twenty-Third Day
When I was in Ninghsia I grew very tired and depressed, but since going through the pass I've been feeling invigorated. The water and soil are good, I've left behind the scenes of Shansi and Shensi, with their yellow sands and frightening cliffs, and that really makes me happy. We've been moving downstream recently and had many chances to ride in the boats. There are few fish in the Yellow River, but on the banks, among the willows, tall grass, and reeds, there are wild pigs, horses, deer, and other things.

Intercalary Third Month, Twenty-Sixth Day

The cucumbers that you just sent me are excellent—you must send some along in future every time there is a delivery of memorials. Also some white radish and eggplant.

I've already reached Pai-t'a and have specially sent Liu Hou-erh to take my greetings to the Empress Dowager; there is no other job for him to do. This man is peculiar and his gall is great. How can he be my personal attendant? He's really loathsome. Don't have him sent back here. Lock him up in the Ching-shih-fang, keep him there and don't let him go home.

Fourth Month, First Day

On the 1st I personally reviewed the cavalry. Within the next few days we'll settle the matter of the grain transport, and then choose a day to start back. I'll probably be in Peking around the summer solstice. You shouldn't let many people know about this, just the consorts and concubines.

Fourth Month, Third (?) Day

I'm on the edge of the Yellow River; day by day with the Mongols from all the various tribes I play around and laugh. I'm in excellent spirits. I've been on lots of journeys, but never have I been so happy and satisfied. Tell those close to me so that they don't worry. If I take the Chang-chia-k'ou route, it is 900 *li* to Peking; if I follow the Sha River via Ta-t'ung, it is 1,200 *li*.

I've sent people to Ninghsia for food and noodles. The noodles are even better than those for imperial use in the capital. Grapes are very good. We're near the frontier, so have everything. The only sad thing is that the weather is not cold so the river is not frozen, and it's hard to move along. You people at home were afraid I wouldn't like the cold. That's a real joke.

The second-day report said that 50 *li* upstream at Hsi-erh-ha there are two bridges of ice, over one *li* in length. But there's no other ice either up- or downstream. I have sent someone to check. If it is true, that will be a very strange thing.

Fourth Month, Seventh Day

Everything is finished here, and we'll be returning partly on the land route, partly by water, and should reach Peking around the summer solstice.

Fourth Month, Seventeenth Day

Previously I wrote the sentence "Determined to wipe out the brigands, concentrating on gaining my goal."

Now Galdan is dead, and his followers have come back to our allegiance. My great task is done. In two years I made three journeys, across deserts combed by wind and bathed with rain, eating every other day, in the barren and uninhabited deserts—one could have called it a hardship but I never called it that; people all shun such things but I didn't shun them. The constant journeying and hardship has led to this great achievement. I would never have said such a thing had it not been for Galdan.

Now heaven, earth, and ancestors have protected me and brought me this achievement. As for my own life, one can say it is happy. One can say it's fulfilled. One can say I've got what I wanted.

In a few days, in the palace, I'll tell you all about it myself. It's hard to tell it with brush and ink—these are just the main points.

Fourth Month, Twenty-Ninth Day

On the 29th I passed Sha-hu-k'ou; we'll travel outside the border to Chang-chia-k'ou and so to Peking, arriving probably about the fifth month, fifteenth day. Previously I said we'd arrive at the summer solstice, but I was delayed by stormy waves on the Yellow River. Here beyond the border it's crisp, not very hot; in the mornings some people even had to wear sleeveless leather jerkins. The water and grass along the route are quite different from those on the western frontier.

I am healthy. All the retinue are well. One can say, "My mind is expanded and my body at ease," and we're coming home.

The "Final" Valedictory Edict

K'ang-hsi died on the thirteenth day of the eleventh month of the sixty-first year of his reign: December 20, 1722. At the time of his death, the following edict was issued to the people as being the Emperor's "final" valedictory edict.

The rulers of the past all took reverence for Heaven's laws and reverence for their ancestors as the fundamental way in ruling the country. To be sincere in reverence for Heaven and ancestors entails the following: Be kind to men from afar and keep the able ones near, nourish the people, think of the profit of all as being the real profit and the mind of the whole country as being the real mind, protect the state before danger comes and govern well before there is any disturbance, be always diligent and always careful. So might you be able to make long-range plans for the country.

I am now close to seventy, and have been sixty-one years on the throne—this is all due to the quiet protection of Heaven and earth and the ancestral spirits; it was not my meager virtue that did it.

*We find from the Histories that** over 4,350 years have passed

*Passages added by the framers of the "final" edict are indicated here by italics.

from the first year of the Yellow Emperor to the present, and three hundred and one emperors are listed as having reigned. *Very few emperors have ruled as long as I have.* When I had been twenty years on the throne I didn't dare conjecture that I might reign thirty. After thirty years I didn't dare conjecture that I might reign forty. Now I have reigned sixty-one years. The "Great Plan" section of the *Book of History* says of the five joys:

> The first is long life;
> The second is riches;
> The third is soundness of body and serenity of mind;
> The fourth is the love of virtue;
> The fifth is an end crowning the life.

The "end crowning the life" is placed last because it is so hard to attain. I am now approaching seventy, *and have the world as my possession,* and my sons, grandsons, and great-grandsons number over one hundred and fifty. The country is at peace and happy. *You can say that my good fortune has been extensive. Even if I should suddenly die my mind would be truly content. I have thought that ever since I came to the throne, even though I would not dare myself to say that we have* improved all manners and customs, and made all the people prosperous and contented; *I tried to emulate the wise rulers of the Three Dynasties, and desired to bring lasting peace to the whole earth, and make all men happy in their work.* I have worked with unceasing diligence and intense watchfulness, never resting, never idle. So for decades I have exhausted all my strength, day after day. How can all this just be summed up in a two-word phrase like "hard work"?

Those among the rulers of earlier dynasties who did not live long have all been discussed in the Histories as having caused this by drink and sex. Such remarks are just the sneers of pedants who have to find some blemishes in even the purest and most perfect of rulers. I *now* exonerate these earlier rulers, *saying that* because the affairs of the country are so troublesome one can't help getting exhausted. Chu-ko Liang said, "I shall bow down in service and wear myself out until death comes," and only Chu-ko Liang acted in this way. Whereas the emperor's responsibilities are terribly heavy, there is no way he can evade them. How can this be compared with being an official? If an official wants to serve, then he serves; if he wants to stop, then he stops. When he grows old he resigns and returns home, to look after his sons and play with his grandsons; he still has the chance to relax and enjoy himself. Whereas the ruler in all his hard-working life finds no place to rest. Thus, though the Emperor Shun said, "Through non-action one governs," he died in Ts'ang-wu; and after four years on the throne Emperor Yü had blistered hands and feet and found death in K'uai-ch'i. To work as hard at government as these men, to travel on inspection, to have never a leisure moment—how can this be called the valuing of "non-action" or tranquilly looking after oneself? In the *I Ching* hexagram "Retreat" not one of the six lines deals with a ruler's concerns—from this we can see that there is no place for rulers to rest, and no resting place to which they can retreat. "Bowing down in service and wearing oneself out" indeed applies to this situation.

No dynasty in history has been as just as ours in gaining the right to rule. The Emperors T'ai-tsu and T'ai-tsung initially had no intention of taking over the country; and when T'ai-tsung's armies were near Peking and his ministers advised him to take it, he replied: "The Ming have not been on good terms with our people, and it would be very easy to conquer them now. But I am aware of what an unbearable act it is to overthrow the ruler of China." Later the roving bandit Li Tzu-ch'eng stormed the city of Peking, the Emperor Ch'ung-chen hanged himself, and the officials and people all came out to welcome us. Then we exterminated the violent bandits and inherited the empire. *We made a study of the Rituals, and buried Ch'ung-chen in accordance with them.*

Initially, Emperor Han Kao-tsu was only a local constable on the Ssu River, and Ming T'ai-tsu was only a monk in the Huang-chüeh Temple. It was Hsiang Yü who raised an army and defeated the Ch'in, yet the country passed to the Han. At the end of the Yüan, it was Ch'en Yu-liang and others who rebelled, yet the country then passed to the Ming. The forebears of our dynasty were men who obeyed Heaven and lived in harmony with other men; and the empire was pacified. From this we can tell that all the rebellious officials and bandits are finally pushed aside by truly legitimate rulers. Every emperor and ruler has been subject to the Mandate of Heaven. Those fated to enjoy old age cannot prevent themselves from enjoying that old age; those fated to enjoy a time of Great Peace cannot prevent themselves from enjoying that Great Peace. Since I began reading in my childhood, I have managed to get a rough understanding of the constant historical principles. Also, during the years of my strength, I could bend a bow with a pull of 15 *li*, and fire a fifty-two-inch arrow. I was good at using troops and confronting the enemy, but I have never recklessly killed a single person. In pacifying the Three Feudatories and clearing out the northern deserts, I made all the plans myself. Unless it was for military matters or famine relief, I didn't take funds from the Board of Revenue treasury, and spent nothing recklessly, for the reason that this was the people's wealth. On my inspection tours, I didn't set out colored embroideries, and the expenses at each place were only 10,000 or 20,000 taels. In comparison, the annual expense on the river conservancy system is over 3,000,000—so the cost was not even one per cent of that.

Emperor Wu-ti of the Liang was a martial dynastic founder, but when he reached old age he was forced by Hou-ching into the tragedy at T'ai-ch'eng. Emperor Wen-ti of the Sui also was a founding emperor, but he could not anticipate the evil ways of his son Yang-ti and was finally unable to die in peace.

All these events happened because [the emperors] didn't understand in time.

I have over one hundred sons and grandsons. *There is nobody among the princes, ministers, officials, soldiers, and people—nor among the Mongols—who does not feel affection for me in my old age. Now, although I am dying of old age, I am content. The descendants of Emperor T'ai-tsu's son Prince Li [Daisan] and of the other glorious princes are all living at peace. My Fourth Son Yin-chen—Prince Yung—has a noble character and profoundly resembles me; it is definite that he has the ability to inherit the empire. Let him succeed me to the throne and become emperor. Obedient to the rituals, don the mourning clothes for twenty-seven days, then doff them. Announce this to the people, make it known to all.*

> A comparison of this "final" edict with the draft valedictory, translated in full as Part VI of this volume, shows that the document is, in fact, a scissors-and-paste reordering of ten blocks of sentences from the draft edict, with the addition of a lengthy and optimistic concluding passage. The result is bland and generally warm-hearted, dignified in a stereotyped way, but totally misleading as to K'ang-hsi's actual state of mind. Among the passages of the draft valedictory edict that were omitted from the "final" edict were these words of K'ang-hsi's:

". . . I am already old, and have reigned long, and I cannot foretell what posterity will think of me. Besides which, because of what is going on now, I cannot hold back my tears of bitterness; and so I have prepared these notes to make my own record, for I still fear that the country may not know the depth of my sorrow.

"Many emperors and rulers in the past made a taboo of the subject of death, and as we look at their valedictory decrees we find that they are not at all written in imperial tones, and do not record what the emperor really wanted to say. It was always when the emperors were weak and dying that they found some scholar-official to write out something as he chose."

The other major passages omitted from the final valedictory are the following:

K'ang-hsi's opening remarks on his dizziness and depression.

K'ang-hsi's statement that the records for the period of the Three Dynasties and before were not accurate, because the Ch'in had burned so many texts; accordingly, "totally credible" history only begins with the Ch'in Dynasty, and K'ang-hsi had ruled the longest of any man from that period.

K'ang-hsi's insistence that a good emperor must concern himself with the details of administration, and not be content only to deal with general principles.

The lengthy passage in which K'ang-hsi reflects on his various illnesses, his lack of efficiency caused by declining mental and physical powers, and the significance of death.

The long list of examples of treachery or stupidity that can be found in traditional Chinese history, related to the succession question.

The forthright statement of disbelief in omens and miraculous events as these have been customarily related to the emperor's person and actions in dynastic histories.

The blunter passages on the difficulty that emperors have in relaxing, and the impossibility of their finding repose by retirement, as officials can (though some calmer passages on this theme were included).

And, finally, the concluding section on his white

hairs, his disillusionment, and his anguished plea that these his final words be respected and preserved.

From this list of omissions we can see how anxious the drafters of this "final" valedictory edict (we don't know if they were court officials, K'ang-hsi's son Yung-cheng, Manchu advisers, or confidential secretaries) were to preserve the dignity of the imperial image. K'ang-hsi had originally presented himself as a man in pain and a man with doubts; he had also expressed skepticism about the value and honesty of the way (he guessed) he himself would be enshrined in the historical tradition. The "final" valedictory edict shows how right K'ang-hsi was to be skeptical—he emerges only as a shadow, his platitudes enshrined and his forcefulness and anger and honesty and pain all—alike—removed.

It is a pleasure for the historian, after two hundred and fifty years, to relegate the "final" edict to an appendix, and to let K'ang-hsi's original draft speak for itself.

Abbreviations Used in the Notes

*(For full data on the following references,
see the alphabetical listings in the Bibliography.)*

BH   Brunnert and Hagelstrom, *Present Day Political Order of China,* transliterations and translations of offices in the Ch'ing Dynasty bureaucracy.

ECCP   *Eminent Chinese of the Ch'ing Period,* a two-volume biographical dictionary.

KHTYC   *K'ang-hsi Ti yü-chih wen-chi,* the literary works of the K'ang-hsi emperor—containing edicts, essays, and poems.

KKWH   *Ku-kung wen-hsien,* quarterly periodical of the Palace Museum (Taipei), of which the first nine volumes contain photo-reproductions of K'ang-hsi's vermilion endorsements to the palace memorials.

SL   *(Ta-Ch'ing Sheng-tsu Jen Huang-ti) Shih-lu,* the *Veritable Records* of the K'ang-hsi reign, a daily chronological account of the official business of the Chinese Empire.

THKY   *T'ing-hsün ko-yen,* conversations, observations, and aphorisms of K'ang-hsi.

YC   *(Ch'ing Sheng-tsu) Yü-chih,* letters, notes, and fragments in K'ang-hsi's own hand.

Notes

(Notes are keyed to the text by page and line numbers. For example, 16/34—17/7 indicates page 16, line 34, through page 17, line 7.)

NOTES TO "K'ANG-HSI'S REIGN"

xi   **K'ang-hsi**   There have been no lengthy biographical studies of K'ang-hsi in Chinese, and only three in Western languages: Joachim Bouvet's flattering portrait, which appeared in French in 1699, based on a combination of firsthand experience and hearsay; Eloise Hibbert's breezy presentation of 1940, drawn mainly from Jesuit sources; and Lawrence D. Kessler's unpublished Ph.D. dissertation of 1969, which draws on a wide range of Chinese sources but is limited to the years of K'ang-hsi's youth, entitled "The Apprenticeship of the K'ang-hsi Emperor, 1661–1684."

In Japan, four biographies of K'ang-hsi have been published in the twentieth century: Nishimoto Hakusen's *Koki Taitei* (K'ang-hsi the Great) in 1925; Nagoya Yoshiro's *Taitei Koki* (The Great K'ang-hsi) in 1938; Tagawa Daikichiro's *Seiso Koki tei* (Sheng-tsu, the K'ang-hsi Emperor) in 1944; and, most recently, Mano Senryu's 1967 study *Koki Tei* (Emperor K'ang-hsi). In 1941 Gotō Sueō also published a complete Japanese translation of Bouvet's 1699 portrait. All these authors saw K'ang-hsi as a wise and strong ruler, who happily combined martial skills with a knowledge of science and the Confucian virtues, and several of them thought K'ang-hsi (as a conquering Manchu ruler) could act as an exemplar for the Japanese in China in the twentieth century: thus Nishimoto reprinted his book in 1941 with the observation that this study of an alien ruler would serve as a good model for the Japanese, while Nagoya subtitled his book "The Principles for Governing China" and noted in his conclusion that it could be "a point of reference" for the Japanese involved with China. Tagawa was also interested in the early strength of the Jesuits in China, as well as K'ang-hsi's views on progress and technology; Mano concentrated more on comparing K'ang-hsi (favorably) with Louis XIV, and with emphasizing his humanity—by 1967 Japanese scholars studying the K'ang-hsi reign were no longer so tightly linked to considerations of *Realpolitik*.

With the exception of Lawrence Kessler's study, however, the above works are not fully tied into original Chinese sources and, besides that, rely rather heavily on the Jesuit image first developed by Bouvet. Accordingly, though there is naturally overlap at times, I have not constantly referred across to items that also occur in these varied biographies, but have concentrated on citing those original Chinese sources that I feel to be definitely reliable.

Two recent Chinese articles are also worthy of mention. Liu Ta-nien's *"Lun K'ang-hsi"* appeared in China in 1961 with this full and informative English "translation" of the title: "Emperor K'ang-hsi, the Great Feudal Ruler Who United China and Defended Her Against European Penetration." Here we see the emergence of what may become a dominant theme in later writings— K'ang-hsi as the shrewd anti-imperialist. Liu also has an extremely illuminating comparison of K'ang-hsi and Peter the Great, based on a consideration of the freedom of operation permitted to them by the economic realities of their respective societies. Some of Liu's arguments were criticized by Yüan Liang-i in his 1962 essay *"Lun K'ang-hsi ti li-shih ti-wei"* (A Discussion of K'ang-hsi's Position in History). Yüan agreed that K'ang-hsi was a great historical figure, but felt that Liu had over-emphasized the military power of the West in the seventeenth century, had oversimplified the economic realities of the time—particularly the different types of dominant landlords—and had underplayed Manchu–Han racial tensions.

The best brief, scholarly introduction to K'ang-hsi's reign remains that by Fang Chao-ying in *Eminent Chinese of the Ch'ing Period*, pp. 327–31.

xiii/24–32 **Letter to Ku Wen-hsing** Cf. Appendix A, p. 160, below.

xxii/4 **Yourcenar** Marguerite Yourcenar, *Mémoires d'Hadrien* (Paris: Plon, 1953); Eng. transl. *Memoirs of Hadrian* (New York: Farrar, Straus and Young, 1954).

xxiv/32–4 **Quotation** *SL*, 3684 (276/16).

xxv/31–3 **Quotation** *"Une heure n'est pas qu'une heure, c'est un vase rempli de parfums, de sons, de projets et de climats. Ce que nous appelons la réalité est un certain rapport entre ces sensations et ces souvenirs qui nous entourent simultanément"* (Marcel Proust, *A la Recherche du temps perdu*, XV: *Le Temps retrouvé* [Paris: Gallimard, 1949 edn.], p. 35).

Notes to Part i, "In Motion"

5 **Poem** *KHTYC*, p. 1308.

7/1–15 **Gardens** Kao Shih-ch'i, *P'eng-shan mi-chi*, p. 1.

7/16—8/4 **Plants** *THKY*, pp. 59b–60; *SL*, 2093 (155/5b), and *YC*, p. 13; Kao Shih-ch'i, *P'eng-shan mi-chi*, p. 1.

8/4–5 **Ginseng** *SL*, 2093 (155/6b).

8/5–8 **Ilha muke** *YC*, p. 17. *Ilha muke* is literally "river flower," following Norman, *Manchu Dictionary*, pp. 291 and 211.

8/8 **Wild barley** *YC*, p. 17b. Norman, *Manchu Dictionary*, p. 68, *cing k'o muji.*

8/10–22 **Hunting parks** Bell, *Journey*, pp. 164–71. *KHTYC*, vol. II, ch. 33, pp. 11–16; Carroll Malone, *Peking Summer Palaces*, pp. 21–4. (References to falconry are rare, but cf. General Lan Li's gift of six in *Sheng-tsu wu-hsing Chiang-nan*, p. 4; the reference to special "falcon and hound guards officers" in *SL*, 3628 (272/11); and

Gerbillon's letter in du Halde, *General History,* IV, 309, 310, 317, and especially 319, where Gerbillon mentions K'ang-hsi as having 25 to 30 falcons, each in the care of one officer. For earlier periods, cf. Schafer, "Falconry in T'ang Times." For Buglio's book on European falconry, written at K'ang-hsi's request, cf. Dehergne, *"Fauconnerie, plaisir du roi."*)

8/23–5 **Air and soil** Cf. the Valedictory Edict, pp. 141–51, and Verbiest letter in d'Orléans, *Conquerors,* p. 107.

8/26 **Quotation** A phrase of Pereira's that K'ang-hsi particularly liked: Pereira letter in d'Orléans, *Conquerors,* p. 144.

8/26–34 **Weather** *YC,* p. 4, where K'ang-hsi talks of feeling *"ch'ing-hsien"* rather than *"wei-ch'ü"*; and K'ang-hsi's letters in *YC,* pp. 1b and 8b.

9/1–7 **Fruit and nuts** D'Orléans, *Conquerors,* pp. 105, 135, 142; Gerbillon letter in du Halde, *General History,* IV, 327; "ulana" in Norman, *Manchu Dictionary,* p. 416, is *prunus humilis; YC,* three separate references on pp. 18 and 18b; *SL,* 1350 (101/20).

9/7–8 **Tea** D'Orléans, *Conquerors,* p. 139.

9/9–13 **Fish** *SL,* 1350 (101/20); Kao Shih-ch'i, *Sung-t'ing hsing-chi,* p. 9b; du Halde, *General History,* IV, 358; *YC,* p. 18, K'ang-hsi sends 50 fish preserved in fat or brine to the Empress Dowager, and 150 to his consorts and concubines.

9/13–16 **Venison** Kao Shih-ch'i, *Sung-t'ing hsing-chi,* p. 15b; du Halde, *General History,* IV, 360, 362, 365; d'Orléans, *Conquerors,* p. 141.

9/17 **Bear's paw** Kao Shih-ch'i, *Hu-ts'ung tung-hsün jih-lu,* p. 8b.

9/19–28 **Animals killed** *SL,* 3797 (285/9b–10).

9/29–32 **Quotation** *SL,* 3298 (247/12b).

9/32—10/2 **Stags** Du Halde, *General History,* IV, 321–2 and 369–70.

10/3 **Arrows** Ibid., p. 359.

10/4–12 **Other hunts** Kao Shih-ch'i, *Hu-ts'ung hsi-hsün jih-lu,* pp. 3–4; d'Orléans, *Conquerors,* pp. 112, 139–40, 146; du Halde, *General History,* IV, 379.

10/13–19 **Tigers** Kao Shih-ch'i, *Hu-ts'ung hsi-hsün jih-lu,* p. 3; *SL,* 1430 (107/9b) and 2550 (190/8).

10/20–1 **Leopard and bear** *SL,* 2550 (190/8b) and 2553 (190/14).

10/21–5 **Sheep** *SL,* 2757 (205/13). The source adds that the arrow also broke a lahari *(ilex latifolia)* tree, which seems to be making a good story too good.

10/25–8 **Crossbow** *THKY,* p. 90.

10/28—11/6 **Gunpowder** *THKY,* p. 50; d'Orléans, *Conquerors,* pp. 123–4; *SL,* 3558 (267/16b).

11/7–8 **Over rocks** Kao Shih-ch'i, *Hu-ts'ung hsi-hsün jih-lu,* pp. 3–4.

11/9–17 **Na Hari** *SL,* 1832–3 (136/11b, 12b, 13); Norman, *Manchu Dictionary, na* and *hari, ha* and *hada.* For the area of these hunts, cf. *Ch'ing-tai i-t'ung ti-t'u,* p. 104, column "East, one."

11/18–24 **Dangerous hunts** *THKY,* pp. 97 and 49b–50.

11/24–8 **Dogs** Kao Shih-ch'i, *Hu-ts'ung tung-hsün jih-lu,* p. 5.

11/29–31 **Accidents** Du Halde, *General History,* IV, 365 and 369.

11/32–4 **Wang** *Wang Chih nien-p'u,* p. 36.

12/1 **Verbiest** *Flettinger MS.,* fol. 2319v.

12/2 **Mucengge** Chang Ying, *Nan-hsün,* p. 17.

12/3–5 **Borden** *SL,* 2873 (213/29b).

12/6–9 **Boys riding** *THKY,* pp. 106b–107.

12/10–21 **Prayers** De Harlez, *Religion nationale,* pp. 141–3.

12/22–33 **Riders** *THKY,* pp. 106b–107.

12/34—13/3 **Discipline** *SL,* 1436 (108/8).

13/3–9 **Periodicity** *THKY,* p. 71b.

13/10–22 **Maneuvers** *SL,* 1437 (108/10); Kao Shih-ch'i, *Hu-ts'ung tung-hsün jih-lu,* p. 5; Bell, *Journey,* p. 169; *SL,* 2511 (186/17); du Halde, *General History,* IV, 320, and d'Orléans, *Conquerors,* p. 137.

13/23–8 **Northern areas** *SL,* 2470 (183/23) and 3035 (227/9b).

13/28–34 **Supplies** *SL,* 2470 (183/24).

14/1–7 **Sekse** *SL,* 2307–8 (171/26b–27); *Ch'ing-shih,* p. 2578

14/7–16 **Water types** *YC,* p. 7; *SL,* 2306 (171/23b).

14/17–25 **Bad water** *THKY,* pp. 28b and 35; *YC,* p. 20; *SL,* 2688 (200/11b); cholera is *huo-luan.*

14/26—15/7 **Base camps** *THKY,* pp. 20b–21; *YC,* pp. 9 and 13b.

15/8–23 **Rain** The *Records of Sunshine and Rain* are the *Ch'ing-yü lu; YC,* pp. 14b–15.

15/24–7 **Lengths** *SL,* 2093 (155/6b).

15/28—16/1   **Observations**   *SL,* 3558 (267/16), for flags; 2076 (154/4), for gnomon; d'Orléans, *Conquerors,* p. 116, for charts.

16/2–5   **Constellations**   *SL,* 1882 (139/31b–32); Ts'an and Tsui are both in the constellation Orion.

16/6–10   **Geography**   *SL,* 3559 (267/17).

16/11–19   **Refreshments**   *SL,* 2345 (174/2), for troops; 2309 (171/29b), for carters; 2470 (183/24), for vendors.

16/20–2   **Merchants**   *Sheng-tsu ch'in-cheng shuo-mo jih-lu,* p. 6b.

16/22–5   **Rewards**   *SL,* 2340 (173/32); *Sheng-tsu ch'in-cheng shuo-mo jih-lu,* p. 3.

16/25–33   **Horses**   *SL,* 2309 (171/29), an edict just on this topic; *THKY,* pp. 21 and 33b–34b; *YC,* p. 4b.

16/34—17/7   **Behavior**   *Sheng-tsu hsi-hsün jih-lu,* p. 25b; *SL,* 2280–1 (169/20b–21) and 2346 (174/3).

17/8–20   **K'ang-hsi on march**   *THKY,* pp. 33b–34; *SL,* 2308 (171/28); Kao Shih-ch'i, *Hu-ts'ung tung-hsün jih-lu,* p. 3b; *Sheng-tsu ch'in-cheng shuo-mo jih-lu,* p. 4.

17/20–4   **Quotation**   *SL,* 2911 (217/2).

17/24–8   **Common people**   *Sheng-tsu hsi-hsün jih-lu,* p. 9b; Kao Shih-ch'i, *Hu-ts'ung hsi-hsün jih-lu,* p. 1.

17/29—18/1   **Veterans**   *THKY,* p. 104; *Sheng-tsu ch'in-cheng shuo-mo jih-lu,* p. 6; *SL,* 2879 (214/10).

18/2–6   **Archery**   *Sheng-tsu hsi-hsün jih-lu,* pp. 11 and 20.

18/7–11   **Fuel**   *SL,* 1544 (115/24).

18/11–16   **Drill**   *SL,* 2041 (151/14b) and 2167 (160/25b), for heavy-pull (*keng*) bows; 2114 (156/19b), for fowling pieces; 1570 (117/16), for ambidexterity.

18/17–19   **Exams**   *SL,* 2702 (201/20). On this occasion, in 1700, K'ang-hsi said the candidates were the best he had seen in "any of the twelve or thirteen examinations" he had attended.

18/20–1   **Marching**   *THKY,* pp. 34b–35.

18/21–2   **Smallpox**   *THKY,* p. 25. The phrase for inoculation is *chung tou;* cf. Wong and Wu, *History of Chinese Medicine,* section on "variolation."

18/22–4   **Swimming**   *THKY,* pp. 28b–29.

18/25–31   **Frontiers**   *YC,* pp. 4b, 6, 8b—all letters to Ku Wen-hsing written on the 1696 Galdan campaign; *SL,* 1911–12 (141/22b–23).

18/31—19/13 **Logistics** *SL*, 2264 (168/15); 2266 (168/20); 2274 (169/8).

19/14—20/6 **Route orders** *SL*, 2280–2 (169/20–4), in sequence sections 2–6; 6; 7 and 8; 14; 13; 17.

20/7–18 **Galdan debates** *SL*, 2315 (172/5b) (Ahmad, *Sino-Tibetan Relations in the Seventeenth Century*, indicates many translated Tibetan sources relevant to this campaign), and the debates spread over *SL*, 2319–22 (172/13–19).

20/19–26 **Galdan's character** *SL*, 1119 (83/18b); 2295 (171/2b); 2313 (172/2); 2321 (172/18b).

20/26–34 **Tracking Galdan** *SL*, 2320 (172/16); 2325–33 (173/1, 10b, 12, 13b, 17, 18).

21/1–10 **Quotation** *SL*, 2334 (173/19b).

21/11–14 **Jao Modo** *SL*, 2337–8 (173/26–7).

21/14–19 **Dalai Lama** Outline of story, *SL*, 2361–5 (175/5–14); possible explanations for K'ang-hsi's confusion over the fifth Dalai Lama's death are discussed by Ahmad, *Sino-Tibetan Relations*, pp. 44–53. The Dalai Lama had been dead fifteen years.

21/20–2 **Second campaign** *Sheng-tsu ch'in-cheng shou-mo jih-lu*, pp. 8b–11. This source supplements *SL*, and the Chinese and Tibetan documents translated in Ahmad, *Sino-Tibetan Relations*, pp. 310–23.

21/23–32 **Third campaign** *SL*, 2415–16 (180/6b–7).

21/32—22/6 **General Wang** *SL*, 2433 (181/13).

22/7–14 **Military Classics** *SL*, 3249 (243/17–18). The term K'ang-hsi used for *Seven Military Classics* was *Wu-ching ch'i-shu*.

22/14–31 **Galdan's death** Cf. K'ang-hsi letters to Ku Wen-hsing, below, and rescripts to Ts'ao Yin in *KKWH*, 2/1/129. Also *SL*, 2462 (183/7); *ECCP*, pp. 267–8; *YC*, pp. 6b–7.

22/32—23/12 **Bear** Du Halde, *General History*, IV, 365–7, description by Gerbillon.

NOTES TO PART II, "RULING"

27 **Poem** *KHTYC*, p. 2477.

29/1–6 **Giving life** *SL*, 3165 (236/14). *Sheng-tsu Jen Huang-ti ch'i-chü chu*, p. 422.

29/6–16 **Punishment** *I Ching* (Wilhelm), pp. 217 and 676; *SL*, 1487 (112/1).

29/17—30/9 **Hu** *SL*, 1966 (146/3–4). Full title, *BH*, no. 933. Other members of the family were also executed by strangling. For a parallel case of local gentry terrorizing their neighborhood, cf. *Wen-hsien ts'ung-pien*, pp. 113–29.

30/9–15 **Yambu** *SL*, 2740 (204/3b). Cf. *SL*, 1639 (122/13), for another warning execution.

30/16–26 **Disobedience** *SL*, 755–6 (55/26b–27), for Malangga; 783 (57/26), for two officers; 2496 (185/15), for Sekse.

30/27—31/14 **Treason** Staunton, *Penal Code*, pp. 269–70, for lingering death. On Chu Yung-tso, cf. *SL*, 3167 (236/17) (also Spence, *Ts'ao Yin*, pp. 234–6, on I-nien); Chu San T'ai-tzu is in *SL*, 3145 (235/9) (case starts *SL*, 3103 [232/10b]; for detailed reports on the case, cf. "*Chu San T'ai-tzu an*"); *SL*, 3116 (233/8), for Chu as a rallying point. Ilaguksan background, *SL*, 2273 (169/6b). The hunt for Ilaguksan, *SL*, 2468 (183/19b–20) and 2479–80 (184/6b–8). Execution in *SL*, 2500 (185/23). *SL*, 2541 (189/14b), for Galdan. *SL*, 1336 (100/11b), for Wu's corpse. *SL*, 1336–7 (100/11b–14), for Keng and other rebels.

31/15–19 **Urgency** Mingju urges immediate execution, *SL*, 1336 (100/12b); for Heir-Apparent case, cf. Part V, "Sons," below.

31/20–5 **Mercy** *THKY*, pp. 38b and 80b–81. Cf. *SL*, 3365–6 (272/6b–7), for example of a fat eunuch arriving with an imperial reprieve just after the criminal has been executed.

31/26–34 **Reprisals** *SL*, 622 (45/4), for gates closed; *SL*, 625 (49/9) and 627 (45/13b–14), on Yang; *SL*, 668 (48/23b), on bandits.

32/1–18 **Edict** *SL*, 692 (50/16). (Though when General Laita took along women—on his own initiative—K'ang-hsi regarded it as insignificant; *Pa-ch'i t'ung-chih*, ch. 152, pp. 28b–29.)

32/19–23 **Barge pullers** *SL*, 1388 (104/15).

32/24—33/4 **Review procedures** *THKY*, p. 38b; *SL*, 2767–8 (206/14b–16); *Li Kuang-ti nien-p'u*, ch. 2, p. 56. An eye-witness account of this whole procedure is in Han T'an, *Yu-huai-t'ang wen-kao*, ch. 8, pp. 14–17b.

33/5–8 **Categories** *SL*, 2700 (201/16). Sun, *Ch'ing Administrative Terms*, no. 1718.

33/9–20 **Murder weapons** *SL,* 3371–2 (252/18b–19).

33/20–2 **Reprieves** *SL,* 2768 (206/16); 2927 (218/6b); 2621 (195/18b).

33/23–31 **Wife-killers** Han T'an, *Yu-huai-t'ang wen-kao,* ch. 8, p. 16b.

33/31—34/9 **Other murders** Han T'an, *Yu-huai-t'ang wen-kao,* ch. 8, p. 14b. Other examples are in Wu, "Emperors at Work," p. 218.

34/9–14 **Fan Sung** *SL,* 2700 (201/15b–16).

34/15–22 **Good points** *THKY,* p. 109. The example of Dantsila is in *THKY,* pp. 79b–80, and *ECCP,* p. 268.

34/23–30 **Russians** Fu Lo-shu, *Documentary Chronicle,* I, 76, 91, 121. For her translations of documents covering the whole run of these Russian campaigns and the Nerchinsk negotiations, cf. ibid., pp. 56–103. A comprehensive survey of this period, with detailed references to Russian and Chinese sources, is Mancall, *Russia and China: Their Diplomatic Relations to 1728.* Cf. also the useful Fletcher article "Aleksandrov on Russo-Ch'ing Relations."

34/30—35/9 **Miao** *THKY,* p. 39b; *SL,* 1415 (106/18).

35/10–14 **Disarm** *SL,* 3018–19 (225/16b–17).

35/15–27 **Shih Lang** *SL,* 1550 (116/8); *THKY,* p. 80; *ECCP,* p. 653; *Li Kuang-ti nien-p'u,* ch. 1, p. 39, lists arguments for letting the Dutch run the island. Cf. *ECCP,* pp. 653–4, for biographies of Shih Shih-lun and Shih Shih-p'iao.

35/28—36/10 **"San-fan War"** *SL,* 1047–8 (76/6–8), 1054 (78/19), 1084 (80/27b), 1140 (85/12).

36/11–33 **Giyešu** *SL,* 1171 (88/2b) and 1172 (88/3). *SL,* 1185–6 (89/2b–3), on Icangga.

36/33—37/9 **Rebel deaths** *SL,* 1312–13 (98/16–17).

37/9–11 **Other executions** *SL,* 1336–7 (100/11b–13), 1356 (102/4), 1357 (102/5).

37/12–20 **Amnesties** *SL,* 1311 (98/13), 1367 (102/25), 1378 (103/20b).

37/21—38/9 **Edict on war** *SL,* 1320 (99/8), and *KHTYC,* pp. 211–13 (12/6b–9).

38/10–17 **Commissioners** *SL,* 599 (43/5); those sent to Keng and Shang were Chinese.

38/17–29 **Preparations** *SL,* 599 (43/6), on appointees; 600 (43/9), on Manchurian estimates; 612–13 (44/8–9), on standardization. Contingency plans are discussed in *SL,* 617 (44/17b). Details of these preparations are not traceable, but it is interesting that K'ang-hsi spent a good deal of time with Mishan, Molo, and Mingju at the Nan-yüan (*SL,* 572 [41/3b]) and just at this time made the trusted Wang Hsi the Chinese Board of War president (*SL,* 588 [42/11b]). Part of the diaries for this period are preserved in *Sheng-tsu Jen Huang-ti ch'i-chü chu. SL,* 602 (43/11b), for Manchu watchmen.

38/30 **Samha and Dangguri** They were two of the four Manchus mentioned above; *SL,* 614 (44/12).

38/31–3 **Šodai** *Pa-ch'i t'ung-chih,* ch. 155, pp. 25–27b; *SL,* 614 (44/12b).

38/34—39/5 **Optimism** *SL,* 663 (48/13), chooses princes; 616–17 (44/16b–17), gives presents; 623 (45/5), prays.

39/5–7 **Blunders** Some graphic K'ang-hsi comments on this may be found in *SL,* 820 (60/3b–4), 1085 (80/29), and 1223 (91/25b–26).

39/7–9 **Chinese generals** Contrast *SL,* 751 (55/18b), anger at Manchus, with *SL,* 752 (55/20b), warm praise for Chinese generals. For a survey of the entire war, drawn from Chinese sources, cf. Tsao, *The Rebellion of the Three Feudatories.* Also cf. the various cross-references in the *ECCP* biographies of Wu San-kuei, Shang Chih-hsin, and Keng Ching-chung. A detailed study of the organizational background of the three feudatories is given by Kanda Nobuō in *"Heiseiō Go Sankei no Kenkyū."*

39/10–20 **Criticisms** *THKY,* pp. 17–19.

39/21 **Lasari** Loving edict for Lasari in *SL,* 1152 (86/7b). Biography in *Pa-ch'i t'ung-chih,* ch. 236, p. 20. Also praised in *Hui-tien shih-li,* p. 17,586 (1052/2b).

39/21–4 **Troubles** *SL,* 1160 (87/3), burning of T'ai-ho Palace; 1107 (82/18), earthquakes; 1160–1 (87/4b–5), falls sick.

39/25–34 **Songgotu and Wei** *THKY,* pp. 8b–9, and *ECCP,* pp. 663–6, for Songgotu; *SL,* 2203 (163/17), and *ECCP,* pp. 848–9, for Wei Hsiang-shu. Also *SL,* 1435 (108/6), for Songgotu's wealth; and *SL,* 2203 (163/17), for Wei's hatred of Songgotu.

40/1–26 **Moralists** *SL,* 2203 (163/17) and 1610 (120/15), K'ang-hsi's general comments; 1499 (112/2b) and 2146 (159/3b), need for less talk; 2763 (206/5b) and 2900 (216/3), on Li Kuang-ti (biography,

ECCP, pp. 473–5); 3246–7 (243/12b–13), on P'eng P'eng (biography, *ECCP,* pp. 613–14); 2770–1 (206/20–1), on P'eng's anger; 2763 (206/5b) and 2836 (211/16), on Chao Shen-ch'iao (biography, *ECCP,* p. 80); 2764 (206/8), on Shih Shih-lun (*ECCP,* pp. 653–4, includes K'ang-hsi comments); 2882 (214/16b), on Yang Ming-shih.

40/27—41/1 **Chang P'eng-ko** Lists of best officials in *SL,* 2703 (201/21) and 2734 (203/19b); and discussion in Wu, *Communication and Control,* p. 24. The spirit of the waters (*ho-po*) is discussed in Werner, *Chinese Mythology,* p. 159; and the hierarchy of river gods, in ibid., pp. 433–6. *SL,* 2752 (205/3b), on drop in river level; 2944 (219/19b), on Bannermen.

41/2–11 **Cliques** *SL,* 2409 (179/9) and 2210 (164/3b–4). K'ang-hsi's views on earlier high-level Manchu cliques are in *SL,* 3133 (234/13).

41/11–15 **Fire** *SL,* 1528 (114/24). For K'ang-hsi's personal supervision of extinguishing a fire at Prince Giyešu's palace, cf. *SL,* 1728 (128/23b).

41/16–25 **Impeachments** *SL,* 2734 (203/19), on Bannermen; Manchus in the examination case of 1711–12 are discussed in Spence, *Ts'ao Yin,* pp. 240–54, and in Wu, *Communication and Control,* pp. 142–8; *SL,* 2732–3 (203/16b–17b), on good soldier; 2236 (166/7), on favorites.

41/26–32 **Hated officers** *SL,* 2409 (179/9). K'ang-hsi made the interesting observation to Wei Hsiang-shu that people had often tended to overrate memorials by past officials if the memorialist died for his views, even though the memorial, in and of itself, was no better than other memorials written by the same man; *Wei Hsiang-shu nien-p'u,* p. 52.

41/32—42/4 **Wen-pao** *SL,* 2468–9 (183/20b–21) and 2472 (183/28b).

42/4–11 **Information** *SL,* 2472 (183/28). Also cf. the succinct discussions in Wu, *Communication and Control,* chs. 3, 5, 6, and his amplifications of certain points in "A Note on the Proper Use of Documents," and Spence, *Ts'ao Yin,* passim. A statement on confidentiality, dated 8/8/2, is one of the earliest K'ang-hsi edicts through which his voice clearly appears. *KHTYC,* pp. 57–8, and *SL,* 439 (31/1b).

42/11–16 **Memorials** *SL,* 3533 (265/14b). The most important technical analysis of this memorial system is Wu, "The Memorial Systems of the Ch'ing Dynasty." An early example (1689) of such a check over an open memorial is in *Lu Lung-chi nien-p'u,* p. 25b. Liu Yin-shu is discussed in *KKWH,* 3/1/116–17. For another example of a senior official losing his sight, cf. *Nien Keng-yao che,* p. 3.

42/17–23 **In Manchu** Wu, *Communication and Control,* p. 43, and *KKWH,* 1/2/213 and 217.

42/24–9 **Secrecy** *SL,* 3019 (225/17).

42/30—43/14 **Audiences** *SL,* 1445 (109/2), on military men. General discussion in *Communication and Control,* p. 22. *T'ien Wen nien-p'u,* p. 26, officials sit; Wu, "Emperors at Work," p. 224, *n.* 22, on deaf official. Direct questions are in *Kuo Hsiu nien-p'u,* p. 32. For a gentler example of probing family questions, cf. *Wei Hsiang-shu nien-p'u,* p. 50b. *SL,* 2566 (191/16b), on note taking.

43/15–18 **Tours in North** Gerbillon letters in du Halde, IV, 348–9 and 378.

43/18–25 **Tours in South** *Sheng-tsu wu-hsing Chiang-nan,* pp. 13b, 25b, 32b, 36b, 39b.

43/25–7 **Anonymous** *SL,* 540 (38/24).

43/27–32 **Exaggerated** Gerbillon letter in du Halde, IV, 352–3.

43/33–4 **Impartiality** *SL,* 3165 (236/13) and 3356 (251/16b). Spence, *Ts'ao Yin,* pp. 253–4.

44/1 **Puppets** *SL,* 2002 (149/19).

44/2–3 **Honorifics** *SL,* 2745 (204/14b).

44/4–22 **Manchus and Chinese** *SL,* 3409–10 (255/18b–19), on general traits; *SL,* 2479 (184/5), Manchus are tough. Manchu scholars are discussed in *SL,* 2570–1 (191/24b–25). Also K'ang-hsi's praise for Lasari, modified praise for K'u-le-na and Ko-ssu-t'ai, in *SL,* 1681 (125/21b). *SL,* 1446 (109/4b), ride horses into yamen; *KKWH,* 1/3/177, disrupt courts. *SL,* 1573 (117/22), on Shao-kan; 1769 (131/21), on dice; 2847 (212/9–10), on army gambling; 2527 (188/6), on nobility; 2883 (214/17b) and 3008 (224/27), on Han T'an's drinking; 1706 (127/11b), on chess. *THKY,* pp. 27–8, 92b–93b, for drink as a curse.

44/22–6 **Yang and Yin** *SL,* 3409 (255/18b).

44/27–31 **Praise** *SL,* 3409 (255/18b) and 3782–3 (284/4b–5).

44/32—45/14 **Hexagram Ch'ien** For a detailed example of K'ang-hsi reading the *Book of Changes,* cf. study of hexagram no. 16, *Yü,* as described by the lecturer-diarists in *Sheng-tsu Jen Huang-ti ch'i-chü chu,* pp. 485, 488, 491. The commentary on *Ch'ien* is in *I Ching* (Wilhelm), pp. 9 and 383; K'ang-hsi discusses it in *SL,* 1533 (115/2).

45/15–22 **Hexagram Feng** *SL,* 1483 (111/30b), and *I Ching* (Wilhelm), p. 670, hexagram no. 55, Commentary. For third line, cf. *I Ching* (Wilhelm), p. 215.

45/22–6 **Status** *THKY,* pp. 23b and 33.

45/28—46/8 **Eunuchs** *SL,* 2206 (163/24b), on Ch'ien case; *THKY,* p. 33b, for chats; *SL,* 3211 (240/10), on numbers; 2079 (154/9), on poverty; 1530 (114/28), on memorials.

46/9–20 **Work loads** *Sheng-tsu hsi-hsün jih-lu,* p. 5, for Ch'in example; *THKY,* p. 38, has four-hundred-per-day figure.

46/20–34 **Fulata** *SL,* 760 (56/3).

47/1–11 **River works** *THKY,* p. 74, general principles; *THKY,* pp. 91b–92, on prices; *THKY,* pp. 72–73b, on promotions. Rivers were inspected on the Southern Tours, Spence, *Ts'ao Yin,* ch. 4. Maps were made by guards officer Mau, *SL,* 1816 (135/7b).

47/12–20 **Chang** *KKWH,* 1/4/180.

47/20—48/13 **Pirates** *SL,* 2863 (213/9), on "bird boats"; 3385–6 (254/2–3b), on supplies; 3652–3 (274/8–9), map bases; *KKWH,* 1/1/68, forced ashore; 1/3/151, Shih's special forces; 1/4/94–5, firearms; *SL,* 3386 (254/3b), as advisers; 2896 (215/20), as messengers; traced by agents in 2863 (213/9); lured by decoys in 3166 (236/15).

48/14–21 **Vessels** *SL,* 3385–6 (254/2b–3).

48/21–3 **Western** *SL,* 3379 (253/10b). Transl. Fu Lo-shu, *Documentary Chronicle,* I, 118.

48/24–31 **Types** *SL,* 2866 (213/15) and 3067 (229/13b), for ex-merchants; *KKWH,* 1/3/145, on local no-goods. K'ang-hsi's rescript in *KKWH,* 1/3/151, deals with need for checking.

48/32—49/5 **Salt** *KKWH,* 1/4/93, with K'ang-hsi's interlinear comment "Good," and 1/4/101.

49/5–18 **Miners** *KKWH,* 1/3/147. Cf. also Sun, "Mining Labor in the Ch'ing Period," pp. 50–5. The buying of information, *kou-hsien*, is discussed in *KKWH*, 1/3/150. *Li Kuang-ti nien-p'u*, ch. 2, p. 59, deals with closure of mines.

49/19—50/3 **Provincials** *SL*, 3246 (243/12b), Fukien; 2700 (201/16), Shensi; 2741 (204/6), and *Sheng-tsu wu-hsing Chiang-nan*, p. 48, on Shantung; *SL*, 2735 (203/22), Khalkas; *Sheng-tsu hsi-hsün jih-lu*, p. 6, Shansi; *SL*, 2003 (148/21b) and 1878 (139/23b–24), on Kiangsu.

50/4–11 **Worthless** *SL*, 2229 (165/22), for examples; 2055 (152/17b–18), on where born.

50/12–23 **Military** *SL*, 2222 (165/7b) and 2818 (210/8).

50/24–31 **Examiners** Tso Pi-fan, in Spence, *Ts'ao Yin*, pp. 241–9, for corruption; *SL*, 1605 (120/6), can't understand; 1765–6 (131/14b–15), know nothing; 2882 (214–16b), insist on memorization; 3009 (224/30), back own locals. Makers of false claims are in *SL*, 2662 (198/23b–24). On the examination systems in general, cf. Shang Yen-liu, *Ch'ing-tai k'o-chü*. On the candidates' preparation and life-styles, cf. Chang Chung-li, *The Chinese Gentry*, and Ho Ping-ti, *The Ladder of Success*.

50/31—51/11 **Candidates** *SL*, 3425 (256/22), on styles; 2662 (198/24), on wealth; 3859 (290/30b), in Hanlin; 1706 (127/11), can't punctuate; 1682 (125/23), on Bannermen; 3330 (249/19), for accents.

51/12–26 **Examining** *Ku Ssu-li nien-p'u*, p. 9b, has details on re-examining *chü-jen*; it is also mentioned in *SL*, 2642 (197/8). For K'ang-hsi's attention to a *chü-jen* candidate caught with a cross-registration problem, cf. *Sheng-tsu wu-hsing Chiang-nan*, p. 31. For a different example, cf. *Ch'ien Ch'en-ch'ün nien-p'u*, p. 19b: K'ang-hsi gives Ch'ien a present of an ornamental purse since his mother's illness had prevented him attending a special examination. *Mao Ch'i-ling nien-p'u*, p. 20, describes the *po-hsüeh*. Ti I, *Ch'ang-ch'un yüan yü-shih kung-chi*, describes taking a Manchu exam.

51/27–31 **Truly good** Mei Ku-ch'eng, *KKWH*, 1/4/78–9 (and for K'ang-hsi's knowledge of Ku-ch'eng's grandfather Mei Wen-ting, cf. *Li Kuang-ti nien-p'u*, ch. 1, pp. 50b–51, and ch. 2, pp. 17, 18b, 25b). Minggantu, *Ch'ing-shih lieh-chuan*, ch. 71, p. 52b. Wang Lan-sheng, *SL*, 3804 (286/3b). Kao Shih-ch'i, *P'eng-shan mi-chi*, p. 3. Li Tu-no, *ECCP*, p. 491. For others in this general category of special favor, cf. the supplement to Fang Chao-ying, *Chin-shih t'i-ming*, p. 245.

51/32—52/2 **Scholarly governors** Fang Chao-ying, *Chin-shih t'i-ming*, pp. 40−1, for the class of 1685.

52/3−21 **Ch'en** *Ch'ing-shih lieh-chuan*, ch. 14, p. 13, for Ch'en; his memorials are in *KKWH*, 2/1/105−15. K'ang-hsi comments "*Chu-t'i*"—"You should use an open memorial for this"—on one early memorial; and criticizes him in *KKWH*, 2/1/111; the later memorials in 2/1/115−28 are all factual, with little comment by K'ang-hsi. (Ch'en was later made president of the Board of Works.)

52/22−34 **Wang** *KKWH*, 1/1/60−6. Biographical details are in *Kuo-ch'ao ch'i-hsien lei-cheng*, pp. 3567−8 (60/42−3).

53/1−3 **Transfers** *SL*, 1455 (109/21), transferred to *Fu-tu-t'ung*, *BH*, no. 720.

53/3−20 **Chang** *Kuo-ch'ao ch'i-hsien lei-cheng*, p. 3580 (61/7), transferred to *ts'ang-ch'ang shih-lang*, *BH*, no. 564. *Chang Po-hsing nien-p'u*, ch. 1, pp. 27b−28, has K'ang-hsi's 1707 speech. *SL*, 3531 (265/9), condemned to death; and pardoned in 3544 (266/11b). Contrast with much more favorable version of Chang's retirement in *Chang Po-hsing nien-p'u*, ch. 2, p. 15.

53/21—54/11 **Ting** *SL*, 3328 (249/15), on first assessments. Wang's 1711 discussion is in *KKWH*, 1/1/63−4. On the *ting* system, cf. Ho Ping-ti, *Studies on the Population of China*, pp. 24−35. From Ho's analysis we can see that K'ang-hsi must have been thinking about the North China adult-male-population *ting* rather than a broader-based unit of land. An extremely clear survey of the Ch'ing tax structure is given by Wang Yeh-chien, "The Fiscal Importance of the Land Tax During the Ch'ing Period."

54/12−34 **Ting status** Whole paragraph from *SL*, 3328 (249/15−16b), on rebates. On taxes, cf. also *SL*, 3305 (248/5−6) and 3355 (251/13−14). The phrase for untaxed population increase was "*yung-pu-chia-fu tzu-sheng jen-ting*." *SL*, 3438 (257/19), gives an annual population increase of 60,455 to a base of 23,587,224. Then for some years it was steady around the 24,000,000 mark. Cf. *SL*, passim, end of twelfth month of each year.

55/2−16 **Hu** *KKWH*, 1/3/179.

55/16−25 **K'ang-hsi's decision** *SL*, 3355 (251/13−14b).

55/26−33 **Winter of 1672** *SL*, 568 (40/20b). K'ang-hsi's phrase was *"yü-ch'i to-i-shih, pu-ju sheng-i-shih."*

55/34—56/8 **Ts'ao** *KKWH*, 2/1/136 (slightly changing translation in Spence, *Ts'ao Yin*, p. 186). *KKWH*, 1/4/94, comment to Shih I-te; 1/4/217, to Chang Ku-chen.

56/9−25 **Marsai** *SL*, 1635 (122/5b−6).

56/26—57/2 **Lang** *KKWH*, 1/4/66−7.

56/35—57/11 **The Mean** Legge, *The Chinese Classics*, I, 395−6, *Doctrine of the Mean*, XIV, 1, 3, 4. Paragraph 4 is quoted by K'ang-hsi in *SL*, 3667 (275/10b), and the passage is praised by him in *YC*, p. 21.

57/12−15 **Apply ourselves** *THKY*, p. 116.

57/15−18 **Droughts** *THKY*, p. 83.

57/18−35 **Hexagram Kuai** *Li Kuang-ti nien-p'u*, ch. 1, p. 45, describes drawing the hexagram, *I Ching* (Wilhelm), pp. 168−9. Mingju's dismissal is in *Ch'ing-shih*, p. 2569; the tables show the dramatic turnover in the second month. Impeachments are given in *SL*, 1795−6 (133/17−20b).

58/1−19 **Auguries** *SL*, 3230 (242/4b), not shunned; 2077 (154/6), to be simply stated; 2413 (170/1b) and 2504 (186/4b), on eclipses; 2196 (163/4b) and 2062 (153/8), on locusts.

58/19—59/12 **Fate** *THKY*, pp. 69b−70, on shaping forces; *THKY*, pp. 76b−77, on minds and forecasts; *SL*, 1342 (101/4) and 1346 (101/11), for soothsayer Chu. K'ang-hsi sent Nien Keng-yao to blindman Lo in 1721. Cf. *Nien Keng-yao che*, p. 47.

59/13−18 **As a youth** "Foreknowledge"—*yü-chih*. *SL*, 3638 (273/3b−4); presumably this inspired the brief comment in *THKY*, p. 19: "In heavy rains and thunderstorms never stand under large trees."

59/18−22 **Book of Changes** *SL*, 1572 (117/19b), on *Book of Changes;* 1483 (111/29b), on its complexity.

59/22−5 **Human voice** *SL*, 3225 (241/13b). "Primal sound" is *yüan-yin*.

59/26−31 **Calligraphy** *THKY*, pp. 3 and 100. Kao Shih-ch'i, *P'eng-shan mi-chi*, pp. 1 and 3. *SL*, 2908 (216/19), on Manchu calligraphy.

59/31−4 **Invocation** *SL*, 1589−90 (119/2b−3).

63 **Poem** *KHTYC*, p. 2428.

65/1–11 **Ask questions** *THKY*, pp. 9b–10.

65/12—66/5 **Artisans** *THKY*, pp. 48b–49. *YC*, p. 18b, for old Chou; *YC*, p. 19b, for Chu.

66/6–15 **Lu deer** *YC*, p. 17b, and *THKY*, p. 47.

66/15–32 **Instruments** Following Legge, *The Chinese Classics*, IV, 346. *THKY*, pp. 46b–47, K'ang-hsi discusses the stanza. He has a lengthy discussion of harmonies in *THKY*, pp. 86b–88b.

66/33—67/11 **Tides** *YC*, p. 16b.

67/12–31 **"Principle" of Things** *THKY*, p. 41b, on awareness; *THKY*, p. 61, on antiques; *THKY*, p. 68b, for Antoine Thomas (cf. Pfister, *Jesuits*, no. 163); *THKY*, pp. 88b–89, and Fu Lo-shu, *Documentary Chronicle*, I, 52, on lions; Verbiest letter in d'Orléans, *Conquerors*, p. 111, on sea-lions.

67/32—68/10 **Western skills** *THKY*, pp. 64b–65, clocks; Kao Shih-ch'i, *P'eng-shan mi-chi*, p. 2 (part transl. in Fu Lo-shu, *Documentary Chronicle*, I, 113), glassware; *THKY*, p. 63, lacquer.

68/11–19 **Ask questions** *THKY*, pp. 1b–3.

68/19—69/6 **Strange things** Pereira letter in d'Orléans, *Conquerors*, pp. 142–3 (for Thomas Pereira, cf. Pfister, *Jesuits*, no. 142); Fu Lo-shu, *Documentary Chronicle*, I, 133, for fireflies and mammoths; *SL*, 2699 (201/13), on grains of blood.

69/7–20 **Shrines** Chang Ying, *Nan-hsün hu-ts'ung chi-lüeh*, p. 18; Spence, *Ts'ao Yin*, ch. 4, for Southern Tours; *SL*, 1530 (114/27b), on Wu-t'ai-shan; 1564 (117/3b), on Mount T'ai and suicides.

69/20–5 **Confucius' home** Visit summarized in *SL*, 1575–8 (117/25–31); it is described in detail by K'ung Shang-jen, *Ch'u-shan i-shu chi*.

69/26—71/5 **At the home** K'ung Shang-jen, *Ch'u-shan i-shu chi*, pp. 10–15. Quotations slightly abbreviated. The passage on K'ung's age is in ibid., p. 20b. For another example of K'ang-hsi's interest in a famous old tree, cf. Chang Ying, *Nan-hsün*, pp. 6b–7.

71/6–30 **At the tomb** K'ung Shang-jen, *Ch'u-shan i-shu chi*, pp. 17b–21.

71/31–3 **Presents** K'ung Shang-jen, *Ch'u-shan i-shu chi*, pp. 22 and 24b. *SL*, 1578 (117/31).

71/34—72/8 **Boats** "Junk" here is *sha-ch'uan; SL,* 1567 (117/10). *SL,* 3598 (270/15), does not date this visit to Soochow, but it seems probable that this was when K'ang-hsi investigated boat building as well. *THKY,* pp. 71b–72, for the "yellow boat," *huang-ch'uan.*

72/9–24 **Western astronomy** *THKY,* p. 86. Edicts transl. in Fu Lo-shu, *Documentary Chronicle,* I, 35–8, 44–6, 58, 93. Verbiest letter in d'Orléans, *Conquerors,* pp. 96 and 129.

72/25—73/2 **Western calculations** *Lettres édifiantes,* VII, pp. 186–9, on Euclid and long hours; *YC,* p. 16b, on cannon; *Flettinger MS.,* fol. 2322, on organ and fountain; windmill in *Flettinger MS.,* fol. 2321. Summary of Verbiest's mechanical work in Spence, *To Change China,* pp. 26–8. Details in Bosmans, *Verbiest. THKY,* p. 57b, for Yin-t'i. *Lettres édifiantes,* VIII, p. 88.

73/2–5 **Music and painting** Kao Shih-ch'i, *P'eng-shan mi-chi,* p. 3b, and Pfister, *Jesuits,* p. 382, for Pereira and music. For Pedrini, cf. Pfister, *Jesuits,* p. 384, *n.* 1, stating he became "court musician" in 1711. Rosso, *Apostolic Legations,* p. 300 (and *K'ang-hsi yü Lo-ma shih-chieh,* no. 6), shows Pedrini teaching the Third, Fifteenth, and Sixteenth sons of K'ang-hsi. There is an imperial discussion of the eight-note scale and matters of harmony in *SL,* 2076 (154/3b). For Yin-chih (K'ang-hsi's Third Son) and music, cf. *Fang Pao nien-p'u,* p. 11b, and for K'ang-hsi's belief in Yin-chen (later the Yung-cheng emperor) as skilled in musical matters, cf. *YC,* p. 19b. For Gherardini's work at court, cf. *Gherardini MS.;* K'ang-hsi had Westerners paint portraits of some of his concubines, and he showed them to Kao Shih-ch'i (*P'eng-shan mi-chi,* p. 4); also transl. Fu Lo-shu, *Documentary Chronicle,* I, 113.

73/5–19 **More calculations** *Lettres édifiantes,* VII, 190–1, on volumes and spheres; *SL,* 3271 (245/9–11), on river works and circumferences; 2076 (154/4), on lock gates.

73/20—73/33 **Horizons and eclipses** *THKY,* p. 8, admits mistakes; *YC,* p. 16b, on Pierre Jartoux (Pfister, *Jesuits,* no. 260); *SL,* 3224 (241/11b–12), on earth's curvature; 2925 (218/1b), on solar eclipse; 3467–8 (260/10b–11), latitudes.

73/33—74/10 **Maps** *THKY,* pp. 68b–69b. Pfister, *Jesuits,* no. 236, for Jean-Baptiste Régis, and no. 171, for Joachim Bouvet. For concluding edict, cf. *SL,* 3773–4 (283/10b–12b). The maps are analyzed and reproduced in Fuchs, *Jesuiten-Atlas.* Governor Liu's remarks are in *KKWH*, 3/1/126–7. Xavier-Ehrenbert Fridelli in Pfister, *Jesuits*, no. 274.

74/10–12 **Little new** Hashimoto Keizo, "*Mei Wen-ting*," p. 497; *ECCP*, pp. 570–1; and *Li Kuang-ti nien-p'u*, ch. 2, p. 17 (K'ang-hsi receives Mei's work in 1703), and ch. 2, p. 25b (K'ang-hsi discusses the book in 1705 with Mei, and praises him). The work in question was Mei's *Li-hsüeh i-wen*; ch. 46, pp. 1 and 2, records discussions with K'ang-hsi, and p. 3 has a concise passage on the similarities and differences between Chinese and Western methods of calculation.

74/13–30 **Origins** *SL*, 3271 (245/10b), for algebra; *YC*, p. 17, for polar angles; magic squares in *YC*, p. 11b. Needham, *Science and Civilization*, III, 57. For K'ang-hsi cautions about *Ho-t'u lo-shu*, cf. *THKY*, p. 76.

74/31—75/4 **Errors** *SL*, 2925 (218/1b–2), basic; 3307 (248/10b), small.

75/5–11 **Know a fraction** Rosso, *Apostolic Legations*, pp. 305 and 268, on Bouvet, and p. 376, for smiling. *K'ang-hsi yü Lo-ma shih-chieh*, no. 14.

75/12–17 **Misled** Rosso, *Apostolic Legations*, pp. 285 and 287; *K'ang-hsi yü Lo-ma shih-chieh*, no. 5. Also *YC*, p. 16.

75/18–28 **de Tournon** Rouleau, "de Tournon" (an erudite and fascinating essay, based on the transcripts from Stumpf's diary, amplified by Candela's diary), pp. 285, 313, and pp. 316–17, *ns.* 12 and 14.

75/29—76/21 **Biased** Rosso, *Apostolic Legations*, p. 329; *YC*, 15b–16; Rouleau, "de Tournon," pp. 288–9, 292–5, 302, and pp. 309–10, *n.* 78.

76/22—77/17 **Audience starts** Rouleau, "de Tournon," pp. 313–16.

77/18—78/16 **Audience continues** Rouleau, "de Tournon," pp. 315–16, 318, and p. 318, *n.* 18.

78/17—79/15 **Audience ends** Rouleau, "de Tournon," pp. 319–21.

79/16–30 **Rites** Rosso, *Apostolic Legations*, pp. 138–45.

79/31—80/9 **Maigrot** Rosso, *Apostolic Legations*, pp. 339–40 (*K'ang-hsi yü Lo-ma shih-chieh*, no. 11) and 358 (*K'ang-hsi yü Lo-ma*, no. 13).

80/9–23 **Animals and angels** Rosso, *Apostolic Legations*, pp. 340, 353 (*K'ang-hsi yü Lo-ma*, nos. 11 and 13), and 366, Maigrot leaves.

80/24–9 **Yin-jeng** *Lettres édifiantes*, IX, 398.

80/30–3 **Spirits and fears** *THKY*, pp. 61b–62.

80/33–4 **Pronunciations** *THKY*, p. 55; theme of sounds developed, *SL*, 3225 (241/13) and 3804 (286/3).

81/1 **Society of Peter** Rosso, *Apostolic Legations*, p. 348 (*K'ang-hsi yü Lo-ma*, no. 13), for Peter (*po-to-lo hui*) and Jesuits (*yeh-su-hui*).

81/2–8 **Quarrels** Rosso, *Apostolic Legations*, p. 237 (*K'ang-hsi yü Lo-ma*, no. 1), Bouvet and Mariani; ibid., pp. 234–5, on Portuguese and French, and p. 311 (*K'ang-hsi yü Lo-ma*, no. 7), on the devil.

81/9–26 **K'ang-hsi's threats** Rosso, *Apostolic Legations*, pp. 244 (*K'ang-hsi yü Lo-ma*, no. 4) and 368 (*K'ang-hsi yü Lo-ma*, no. 13).

81/27—82/9 **Missionary residence** Rouleau, "de Tournon," p. 296, *n.* 60; Rosso, *Apostolic Legations*, p. 239 (*K'ang-hsi yü Lo-ma*, no. 2). K'ang-hsi uses the literal phrase *pai-jen* for "white men." For difficulties in leaving China, cf. remarks in *Gherardini MS.*, letter no. 6, November 1701, to his brother.

82/9–14 **Certificates** Rouleau, "de Tournon," p. 268, *n.* 7, and p. 287, *n.* 47. Rosso, *Apostolic Legations*, pp. 171–8, and p. 171, *n.* 59, for Ripa's description of the *p'iao* certificate.

82/15–26 **Anxiety about West** *SL*, 3598 (270/11b); Fu Lo-shu, *Documentary Chronicle*, I, 106 and 122–3.

82/26–31 **Ch'en Mao** Fu Lo-shu, *Documentary Chronicle*, I, 123–6; de Mailla's letter to de Colonia, *Lettres édifiantes*, XIV, 86; and remarks on the Ch'en Mao text in Rosso, *Apostolic Legations*, p. 315.

82/32—84/6 **Three Jesuits** *Lettres édifiantes*, XIV, 129–33. An abbreviated Chinese version is translated in Rosso, *Apostolic Legations*, p. 321.

84/7–9 **Drops in the ocean** Rouleau, "de Tournon," p. 315, *n.* 8, and p. 320.

84/10–24 **Wild teachings** Rosso, *Apostolic Legations*, p. 376 (*K'ang-hsi yü Lo-ma*, no. 14). A similar bunching of Christians, Buddhists, and Taoists is in Fu Lo-shu, *Documentary Chronicle*, I, 105. *Lettres édifiantes*, XIII, 381–4, for censor on Virgin Mary; *Flettinger MS.*, fol. 2323v, on Verbiest discussion; Bell, *A Journey from St. Petersburg to Pekin*, p. 154, on Noah; *Lettres édifiantes*, VII, 140–1, request for miracles.

84/25-32 **Buddhist regulations** *Hui-tien shih-li,* pp. 11,735-6 (501/1-4) and 11,737 (501/5).

84/33-4 **Christians** *Flettinger MS.,* fol. 2320v. Yang Kuang-hsien gave the enormous estimate of one million Chinese Christians in 1660 (Fu Lo-shu, *Documentary Chronicle,* I, 36). Between 1694 and 1703 Jesuits guessed that six hundred adults a year were being converted in Peking (*Lettres édifiantes,* VI, 79).

85/1-10 **Sects banned** *THKY,* pp. 40 and 43; De Groot, *Religious Persecution,* pp. 153-4; *Hui-tien shih-li,* p. 6838 (132/4). *SL,* 3188 (238/7b), and general ban of erotic works in 1737 (129/14b).

85/11-14 **Books banned** Wang Hsiao-ch'uan, *Yüan Ming Ch'ing . . . shih-liao,* p. 22; *Hui-tien shih-li,* p. 14,867 (767/3). *SL,* 3307 (248/9). *ECCP,* p. 701, for view that K'ang-hsi erroneously connected Tai with the wrong Fang family. Also Goodrich, *The Literary Inquisition of Ch'ien-lung,* pp. 77-8.

85/15—86/8 **Tai case** Tai Ming-shih, *Nan-shan chi,* pp. 419-20. The first part is translated in Lucien Mao, "Tai Ming-shih," pp. 383-4. "Clear wind" is *ch'ing-feng* and could be a pun for "Ch'ing Dynasty Wind." *SL,* 3322 (249/3) and 3381 (253/13).

86/9-31 **History writing** *SL,* 2078 (154/7), emperor's responsibility; 2930 (218/11b-12), Sung and Yüan; 2409 (179/10), do not ridicule; 3211-12 (240/10b-11), Ch'ung-chen absurdities; 3366 (252/7), questions Yüan; 3397 (254/26b), questions Chang P'eng-ko; 3398 (254/27), checks on Chang Hsien-chung's sons.

86/32—87/17 **Credibility** *SL,* 3645 (273/18), on Hsiang Yü, and 2078-9 (154/8-9), on Ming factions.

87/17—88/2 **Eunuch interviews** *SL,* 2846 (212/7), 3211 (240/9) (*lao-pan* for "old comrade"), 3397 (254/26b), 3454 (259/7b). Wang's suicide is in *SL,* 2846 (212/7b).

88/3-14 **Sources on Ming** *SL,* 1484 (111/32) ("gazette" is *ti-pao*); 3645 (273/18), on private histories; 1505 (113/6) and 1484 (111/32b), too much material; 1948 (144/15), on distortions.

88/15-20 **K'ang-hsi checks** *SL,* 1484 (111/32b), on bias; 2077-8 (154/6b-7), on checking through; also 1530 (114/28).

88/20-9 **Accept criticism** *SL,* 1505 (113/6b), proud Hanlin scholars; 1625 (121/18), 1957 (145/9), and 2029 (150/17b-18), on K'ang-hsi's readings; 995 (73/21b), T'ang T'ai-tsung.

88/29—89/1 **Keep original drafts** *SL*, 1746 (130/4).

89/1–11 **Evaluations** *SL*, 2409 (179/10), on Hung-wu; 2077 (154/6b), on Hsüan-te; Ch'ung-chen exonerated in 3944 (297/8). ("Emperor who destroyed his country" is *wang-kuo chih-chün*.)

89/12–20 **The facts** *SL*, 1718 (128/3b) and 1746 (130/4). "Shared opinion" is *kung-lun*.

89/21–32 **Ch'i and Ch'ü** *SL*, 2865 (213/13).

NOTES TO PART IV, "GROWING OLD"

93 **Poem** *KHTYC*, p. 2468.

95/1–5 **Kao's medicine** Kao Shih-ch'i, *Sai-pei hsiao-ch'ao*, p. 1, for *i-yüan-san*, and pp. 4b, 6, and 9, for other symptoms. Chang Lu, *I-t'ung*, ch. 16, p. 96b, on *i-yüan* formula. These, and the following drug and plant identifications, are taken from Bretschneider, *Botanicon Sinicum*, from Wallnöfer, *Chinese Folk Medicine*, and from *Chung-kuo i-hsüeh ta-tzu-tien*.

95/5—96/4 **Wang's medicine** The incident is in *Wang Chih nien-p'u*, pp. 40b–41. For the formula, cf. Niu Hsiu, *Ku-shen hsü-pien*, p. 6437. According to this source, Wang Chih also claimed that *ts'ui-hsien* pills had given him the energy to enjoy sixty-eight lovers of both sexes in the previous forty years. Chang Lu, *I-t'ung*, ch. 14, p. 113.

96/5–9 **Wei's medicine** *Wei Hsiang-shu nien-p'u*, p. 63. *Liu chün-tzu t'ang* is analyzed in *Chung-kuo i-hsüeh ta-tzu-tien*, p. 433, and in Chang Lu, *I-t'ung*, ch. 16, p. 53b.

96/9–13 **Dr. Li** *KKWH*, 1/4/192–5. The details here are rich enough to constitute a valuable source for medical study.

96/14–17 **Old folk** *YC*, pp. 20b–21.

96/18–33 **Drugs** *THKY*, pp. 56 and 98–9. *SL*, 586 (42/8) and 3281 (246/2b). "Restoratives" are *tzu-pu*.

96/33—97/6 **Regimens** *SL*, 3076 (230/7); *KKWH*, 1/2/195, instructions to Sung Lao; *THKY*, pp. 3b and 56b–57. "Massages" are *t'ui-mo*.

97/6–28 **Diets** *YC*, p. 22, goose and fish; Bell, *Journey*, p. 136, described this not roasting as a general rule at court; *Ch'a Shen-hsing* *nien-p'u*, pp. 14b−15; Yang's case is in Hsü Ping-i, *Kung-yin ta-chia chi*, p. 2, and Tung Wen-chi, *En-tz'u yü-shu chi*, p. 1b. "Strengthening prescriptions" are *yang-sheng shu*. *THKY*, pp. 14b−15, on Lao-tzu; *THKY*, p. 48, for what suits you.

97/28—98/2 **Plain peasant food** *THKY*, pp. 35b and 37b.

98/3−6 **North and South** *THKY*, pp. 62b−63.

98/6−11 **Wang** *Wang Chih nien-p'u*, p. 28.

98/12−16 **Frankness** *THKY*, pp. 97b−98.

98/16−28 **Specialists** *Hui-tien shih-li*, p. 18,117−18 (1005/3b−6), for Court. Dr. Min, *KKWH*, 1/4/118. On special drugs to cure the King of Korea's eye problems, cf. *SL*, 3651 (274/5); *SL*, 576 (41/12), on drugs for officials.

98/29−31 **Precautions** *Hui-tien shih-li*, pp. 18,119−20 (1105/7b−8).

98/32−4 **Quinine** Spence, *Ts'ao Yin*, p. 260.

99/1−5 **Doctors** For these Chinese Court doctors, cf. Kao Shih-ch'i, *Sai-pei hsiao-ch'ao*, pp. 1, 6b, 9; for the Western doctors and pharmacists and for Brother Frapperie, who served from 1700 to 1703, cf. letters in PRO, SP9/239 (reference as under *Gherardini MS.*), nos. 12 and 13. Also Pfister, *Jesuits*, pp. 555−7 (Rhodes), 476 (Baudino), 622 (Viera), 563 (Frapperie).

99/6−11 **Lan Li** Ch'en K'ang-ch'i, *Lang-ch'ien chi-wen san-pi*, ch. 4, pp. 13b−14b. Another example of K'ang-hsi's curiosity over wounds is given by Kao Shih-ch'i, *Sung-t'ing hsing-chi*, p. 28b, where they examine a Mongol veteran with twenty-four battle scars on his body.

99/12−32 **Harmony of treatment** *THKY*, p. 56, for *jorhai*, equivalent to the Western *sonchus asper*; Wang Hao, *Sui-luan chi-en*, p. 288 (p. 3), on Ch'a-sheng; *YC*, p. 11, for stopping bleeding; *SL*, 2825 (210/21b), prevent colds; *YC*, p. 17b, for *yengge*; *YC*, p. 20b, for *t'ung-kuan* and *chiu-ho*.

99/33—100/5 **Prescriptions** *THKY*, pp. 98b−99, and *SL*, 3076 (230/7).

100/6−8 **Not intelligent** *SL*, 1613−14 (120/22b−23). Large sections of this medical text have been translated—Veith, *Huang-ti nei-ching*.

100/8−19 **Shallow teaching** *THKY*, p. 98, seek money; *YC*, p. 20b, wild questions; *SL*, 3341 (250/18b), just stay alive.

100/20—101/4 **Eunuch Ku** This whole paragraph from *YC*, pp. 19b–20. The "five viscera" are heart, lungs, liver, kidneys, and stomach.

101/5—102/25 **Taoists** *THKY*, pp. 85–6, general remarks. Detailed passage on Hsieh and Wang in *YC*, pp. 21–2. *SL*, 1881 (139/30), book thrown back.

102/26–32 **Shamans** De Harlez, *Religion Nationale*, pp. 116–17.

102/33—103/6 **Teeth** *THKY*, pp. 44 and 84b–85.

103/7–30 **Daily care** *THKY*, p. 3b, body and mind; *THKY*, p. 68, warm clothes; *THKY*, pp. 74b–75, don't bank stoves; *THKY*, p. 75, hat flaps; *THKY*, pp. 3b–4, bear the heat; *THKY*, p. 4, coolness in self; *THKY*, p. 70, observe taboos; *YC*, p. 14b, vile smells; *THKY*, p. 9, avoid filth; *THKY*, p. 70b, not over-clean.

103/31–4 **Defects** *THKY*, p. 65b–66.

104/1–15 **Holding up** *THKY*, p. 89b, on taboo; *THKY*, p. 67, on the pain. *SL*, 3667 (275/10b), for help; 3679 (276/5), for foot bound and padded chair. *SL*, 3313 (248/22b), held at rituals; *THKY*, p. 90, on today's youth; *THKY*, pp. 67b–68, bear pain calmly.

104/16—105/12 **Grandmother** *SL*, 1775 (132/1b), prayed for; K'ang-hsi reconnoiters Wu-t'ai-shan in *SL*, 1430 (107/19); describes scenery in a letter, *YC*, p. 1; *THKY*, p. 49b, no head for heights; her final remarks in *SL*, 1494 (112/15–16), dated 22/9/23–4 (eunuch Chao Shou-pao in *KHTYC*, p. 260). In a rare error *Hui-tien shih-li*, p. 9261 (311/16b), says it was the Empress Dowager Hsiao-hui, not K'ang-hsi's grandmother, who accompanied K'ang-hsi. But *SL*, 1491 (112/10b), and other texts are quite clear it was the grandmother. Cf. also *THKY*, pp. 13–14.

105/13–21 **Her death** *SL*, 1776 (132/4), and *THKY*, pp. 83b–84b.

105/22–33 **Care for old** *YC*, p. 10b. Charles Dolzé in PRO, SP9/239 (full reference under *Gherardini MS.*), no. 13, from Gerbillon to Le Gobien, Peking, 8 October 1701. K'ang-hsi ordered Dolzé attended by Gherardini and two Chinese "officers" and other attendants. He also ordered Bouvet and Belleville to come from Peking to keep Dolzé company. (This source is a valuable addition to Pfister, *Jesuits*, no. 230, biography of Dolzé; it also adds to Pfister, no. 237, on Brother Charles de Belleville.) *SL*, 2640 (197/4b), for Princess Shu-hui.

105/34—106/18 **Presents** *KHTYC*, p. 135, for Shu-hui; *THKY*, p.

100b, for pleasure; Spence, *Ts'ao Yin*, p. 147, for Empress Dowager; *KHTYC*, p. 264, and *SL*, 2701 (201/18b), for grandmother; *Flettinger MS.*, fol. 2319v, for Yin-jeng; Gerbillon letter in du Halde, *General History*, IV, 224, for Songgotu, though in this case K'ang-hsi said that he wanted it back later on! *Chang Po-hsing nien-p'u*, ch. 1, p. 29; Kao Shih-ch'i, *P'eng-shan mi-chi*, p. 4b; *YC*, p. 12b, for Li Kuang-ti. The principles of spontaneity are repeated by K'ang-hsi in *THKY*, pp. 35b, 36b, 37, 45.

106/19-29 **Quiet sitting** *P'eng Ting-ch'iu nien-p'u*, p. 18; *THKY*, p. 20b; *YC*, p. 14b. "True quietness" is *chen-ching*.

106/30—107/32 **Adept Wang** *KKWH*, 1/3/180, includes K'ang-hsi's rescripts. "Entering the darkness" is *miao-min*. The stages of Confucius are discussed in *THKY*, pp. 11b-12b, and the Yellow Emperor's in Veith, *Huang-ti nei-ching*, pp. 99-100. For K'ang-hsi's thorough reading of this work, cf. *SL*. 1613-14 (120/22b-23).

107/33—108/8 **Family deaths** *SL*, 3858-9 (290/12b-13) (where K'ang-hsi says he was sent to live outside the Forbidden City with his wet nurses, because he had not had smallpox, and so had no chance to have even "one day's" company with his father or mother). Ceremonies at Shun-chih's death in *Hui-tien shih-li*, pp. 11,103-4 (456/12-14). Manchu practices are in de Harlez, *Religion nationale*, p. 48. *Ch'ing Huang-shih ssu-p'u*, p. 48, on mother. Family's burial rites in *Hui-tien shih-li*, 11,111-13 (456/27b-32); summary in *SL*, 159 (9/14b); cremations in *ECCP*, pp. 302 and 258.

108/8-19 **Mausolea** *SL*, 155 (9/5) and 158 (9/14b), not allowed visit; tomb areas in De Groot, *The Religious System of China*, III (Book 1), 1290; other concubines' tombs in *Hui-tien shih-li*, p. 10,806 (432/16b); the geomancers are named in *SL*, 230 (14/28). This memorial, in which their names appear, has been translated in Fu Lo-shu, *Documentary Chronicle*, I, 37-8. Vital pulses of the area in De Groot, *The Religious System of China*, III (Book 1), 1284-5. Tomb specifications and maintenance in *Hui-tien shih-li*, pp. 16,564-9 (943/2-12) and 16,585 (945/6).

108/20-2 **Age itself** *Feng P'u nien-p'u*, p. 17b; *SL*, 3225 (241/13b) and 3287 (246/14b).

108/23—109/2 **Old advisers** *SL*, 2173-4 (161/10b-11), for Grand

Secretaries; *Huang Tsung-hsi nien-p'u,* ch. 2, p. 12 (Huang, a well-known scholar, refused to serve the Ch'ing out of loyalty to the fallen Ming; his biography is in *ECCP,* pp. 351–4); *SL,* 1832 (136/11b), on Shih Lang; *Feng P'u nien-p'u,* pp. 15b–16, 19, 20b.

109/3–22 **Old and ill** *SL,* 1832 (136/11b–12), make concessions; 1653 (123/14), when able to walk; 2169 (161/1b), rice gruel; 2927 (218/5), not impeached; distinguishing offices in 2737 (203/26b) (though in *SL,* 2732 (203/16), K'ang-hsi had praised Chang P'eng-ko for his vigorous inspection tours while holding senior office as Director of River Conservancy); *KKWH,* 1/4/97, for different climates.

109/23–34 **Incompetence** *SL,* 1707 (127/14), 1769 (131/22b), 1843 (137/6b); 2121 (157/13), for Chin Fu; 2671 (199/5), for Li Ping; 3031 (227/2), really lazy; 2992 (223/15) and 2671 (199/6), remove some.

110/1–22 **Hexagrams** *SL,* 3618–19 (271/24b–25), anticipating the language of the Valedictory Edict as translated in Part VI. *I Ching* (Wilhelm), pp. 49 and 447. Both hexagrams are named in the Valedictory Edict, *SL,* 3667 (275/10b).

110/23–30 **River crossings** *SL,* 3032 (227/3b–4), is an example of less vivid language being used than in the earlier text, here *KHTYC,* p. 1516.

110/31—111/19 **Tolerances** *THKY,* p. 43b, on heat; *SL,* 1896 (140/23b), poor eyes; *THKY,* p. 99b, and *SL,* 2278 (169/15), moxa treatment; *SL,* 3099 (232/2), on "dizziness" (*t'ou-hsüan*); 3166 (236/16) and 3175 (237/5), thin and weak; 3639 (273/5b), on Tsewang Araptan; 3663 (275/1b–2), voice hoarse.

111/20—112/7 **Memory** *SL,* 2563 (191/10b), Alantai and Icangga; 3087 (231/6b), secretaries less good; *Sheng-tsu hsi-hsün jih-lu,* p. 23b, applied memory; *SL,* 3644 (273/15), E-tu-le-hu; 3661 (274/25b), "dizziness"; 3340 (250/16b), forgets books; 2911 (217/1b–2), part of contents; 3644 (273/15), tells Maci.

112/8–17 **Study young** *THKY,* pp. 113b–114.

117 **Poem** *KHTYC*, pp. 546–7. Prince Yin-jeng was now ten.

119–122 **Genealogy** All births, ages, and titles are taken from the comprehensive imperial genealogy *Ch'ing Huang-shih ssu-p'u*, ed. by T'ang Pang-chih. For brevity I have used the following translations: *huang-hou*, empress; *kuei-fei*, imperial consort; *fei*, consort; *pin* and *kuei-jen*, concubine; *kung-jen*, palace attendant. Additional information on the family background of many of the consorts is in *Ch'ing lieh-ch'ao hou-fei chuan-kao*. Jung-fei lived on until 1727. Fourth Son Yin-chen became the Emperor Yung-cheng, and his mother was then named empress retroactively. Consort Tunnggiya was named empress in 1689, when she was fatally ill; cf. *SL*, 1908 (141/16b). The last birth is given in *SL*, 3697 (277/17b), without the concubine's name.

123/1–18 **Used to say** *THKY*, p. 59, little ones; *THKY*, p. 29, swearing; *THKY*, p. 29b, anger; *THKY*, p. 22, desires; *THKY*, p. 96, quoting Confucius, on sex and fighting; *THKY*, p. 89b, on palace women; *THKY*, p. 65, old rugs; *THKY*, p. 14b, fur rugs; *THKY*, p. 48, Keng's coat; *THKY*, p. 1, birthdays.

124/1–4 **One old teacher** *THKY*, p. 9b, presumably referring to guards officer A-shu-mo-erh-ken (cf. Part I, "In Motion"). The passage also echoes the *Doctrine of the Mean*, XIV, 5 (Legge, *Chinese Classics*, I, 396).

124/5–10 **Stay Manchu** *THKY*, pp. 104–5, though in 1683 K'ang-hsi did decree that thereafter the menu for New Year's feasts should be Chinese, not Manchu: *SL*, 1513 (113/21b). *THKY*, p. 57, for wide spaces.

124/11–18 **Students** *THKY*, pp. 114 and 101b, quoting *Doctrine of the Mean*.

124/19–24 **Training** *THKY*, pp. 109b and 113. The passage echoes *Doctrine of the Mean*, XX, 9 (Legge, *Chinese Classics*, I, 407).

124/25–8 **Spoiling** *THKY*, pp. 23 and 71.

124/29–33 **Entrusted sons** *SL*, 3152–3 (235/24b–25) and 3345 (250/26b).

124/34—125/12 **Raising Yin-jeng** *SL*, 796 (58/19b), raised myself; *KHTYC*, I, 150, smallpox; *SL*, 3133 (234/13), emperor as nurse;

teachers in, 3132 (234/11); *ECCP,* p. 710, also discusses his tutor, T'ang Pin; *Weng Shu-yüan nien-p'u,* pp. 33b–34; Han T'an, *Yu-huai t'ang wen kao,* ch. 22, p. 23, on painting; *SL,* 3130 (234/8b), studies government; *ECCP,* p. 924, acts as regent.

125/13–25 **Perversity** *SL,* 2493 (185/9), Yin-jeng's cooks; 2613 (195/2b), Third Son; 1995–6 (148/6b–7), Eldest Son; 3152–3 (235/24b–25), Fourth Son.

125/25–34 **Excesses** *SL,* 3128 (234/3). For the Heir-Apparent struggles, cf. Wu, *Communication and Imperial Control,* passim and especially pp. 52–65. Professor Wu is currently completing a full-length study of the succession problem.

126/1–15 **Songgotu** *SL,* 2816 (210/3), 2849 (212/13b–14), 2850–1 (212/16–17). The exact date Songgotu was killed is not known, but in *SL,* 3136 (234/19b), K'ang-hsi says he "put him to death" (*chih yü ssu*).

126/15–21 **Suspicion** *SL,* 3127–8 (234/2–4); K'ang-hsi is referring to the fact that Yin-jeng's mother died in childbirth.

126/22—127/30 **Wang's investigation** K'ang-hsi's edict is printed in facsimile in *KKWH,* 1/1/78, Wang's reports in 1/1/96–100. Also for 1707 entourage in *KKWH,* 46/4/18–19, and *SL,* 3066 (229/12). The sons on this tour were Yin-jeng, and the First, Thirteenth, Fifteenth, and Sixteenth (*SL,* 3048 [2284b]).

127/31–4 **Checking crimes** *SL,* 3125 (233/26b).

128/1–11 **Edict in 1708** *SL,* 3126 (233/27). The role of guards officers in the Ch'ing is a major unstudied subject, with the exception of Saeki Tomi's recent article *"Shindai no jiei ni tsuite."*

128/12—129/1 **Edict of dismissal** *SL,* 3127–8 (234/2–3). The six sons of Songgotu are listed in *SL,* 3129 (234/5), and were dead by the next day (234/6).

129/1–11 **Bodily purity** *SL,* 3130 (234/7).

129/12–16 **Pardons** *SL,* 3129 (234/6b).

129/16–32 **Demonic possession** K'ang-hsi discussed these symptoms in two edicts, *SL,* 3131 (234/9b–10) and 3132 (234/11b). "Demons" are *kuei-wu;* "evil spirits," *hsieh-mei;* "mad," *k'uang-chi.*

129/33—130/15 **Evidence** *SL,* 3146 (235/12), on "magical objects" (*chen-ya-wu*); 3149 (235/17), on "nightmare demons" (*yen-mei*); 3151 (235/21b), dream of grandmother.

130/16–20 **Doubts** *SL*, 3149 (235/17) and 3151 (235/22).

130/21–31 **Yin-t'i** *SL*, 3128–9 (234/4b–5), 3136 (234/20b), 3137 (234/22b).

130/32—131/14 **Physiognomist** *SL*, 3138 (234/24b) and 3143 (235/5b).

131/15–17 **Nearly killed** *SL*, 3138 (234/24). This, as K'ang-hsi seizes a dagger and runs at his sons, being held back by Fifth Son Yin-ch'i, is perhaps the most vividly presented episode in *SL*.

131/18–30 **Others implicated** *SL*, 3144 (235/8b) and 3145 (235/9). K'ang-hsi uses almost the same language when attacking Yin-ssu in 1714, *SL*, 3479 (261/9b).

131/31—133/15 **Restoration debates** *SL*, 3149–52 (235/17–23). Yin-ssu's mother was from a bondservant (*pao-i*) family. Evidence of K'ang-hsi's trust for Liang is in *YC*, p. 21; for Li Yü, in *KKWH*, 1/1/96, and Rosso, *Apostolic Legations*, p. 235.

133/16–18 **Bandi and Yin-ssu** *SL*, 3154 (235/27–28b).

133/18—134/10 **March 1709 debates** *SL*, 3160–2 (236/4b–7), for the prolonged and heated debate; 3163 (236/9b), on Maci's anger; 3163 (236/10b), Cuntai's investigation; 3164 (236/11), Maci spared; 3165 (236/13), Yin-jeng restored; 3168 (236/19b and 20b), auspicious journey; 3174 (237/4), formal restoration.

134/11—136/25 **December 1711 debates** Following dialogue all from *SL*, 3310–11 (248/15–18b). Arrests and punishments of the clique in *SL*, 3311 (248/18b), 3323 (249/5b), 3335 (250/5b), and 3337 (250/10b).

136/24–34 **Yin-jeng dismissed** *SL*, 3335 (250/6b) and 3352–3 (251/7b and 9b). For four discussions by K'ang-hsi of Yin-jeng's behavior, cf. *YC*, p. 10.

137/1 **Loved sons** *SL*, 3311 (248/18).

137/2–29 **Dismissal explained** *SL*, 3353–4 (251/10b–12), and formal edict to the country on Yin-jeng's dismissal, *SL*, 3369 (252/14).

137/30–3 **Yin-ssu** *SL*, 3478–9 (261/8b–9b). A curious episode is described in *SL*, 3586–7 (269/20–1): Yin-ssu was seriously ill in his gardens near the Ch'ang-ch'ün Palace road, and it was possible that he might die there. K'ang-hsi ordered the other sons to debate whether or not Yin-ssu should be moved, to avoid any adverse influences on K'ang-hsi as he traveled past; they decided (with only Yin-t'ang, Eighth Son, angrily dissenting) that Yin-ssu must be moved. Other K'ang-hsi comments on Yin-ssu are in *SL*, 3586 (269/20), 3592 (270/3), and 3610 (271/8b).

137/34—138/20 **I used to say** *THKY*, pp. 21b–22, seek joyfulness; *THKY*, p. 75b, after meals; *THKY*, pp. 40b–41 (quoting Mencius), look in eyes; *THKY*, p. 41, don't look around; *THKY*, p. 115, find morality; *THKY*, p. 2, on "reverence" (*ching*).

138/21–8 **Subordinates** *THKY*, pp. 2b, 23b–24, 32b.

138/29—139/6 **Restoration memorials** *SL*, 3378 (253/8), Chao Shen-ch'iao; *Wen-hsien ts'ung-pien*, pp. 106–7, *SL*, 3672 (275/20), *ECCP*, p. 830, for Wang Shan; scholar Chu T'ien-pao's memorial can be partly reconstructed by the sentences quoted by K'ang-hsi in *SL*, 3691 and 3693 (277/6, 6b, 10, 10b).

139/7–9 **Clique charged** *SL*, 3541 (266/5).

139/10–18 **New faults** *SL*, 3691 (277/6b) and 3693 (277/10).

139/18–22 **Chus punished** *SL*, 3694 (277/11) and 3703 (277/30b). For punishments of the rest of the clique, cf. 3692–3704 (277/8–31).

139/23–31 **Spring arrives** *THKY*, p. 115b.

139/30–2 **Little ones** *THKY*, p. 59.

NOTES TO PART VI, "VALEDICTORY"

143—151 This whole edict is printed in *SL*, 3665–9 (275/5–13).

144/10 T'ai-tsu and T'ai-tsung were K'ang-hsi's Manchu ancestors Nurhaci and Abahai.

146/6–10 **The five joys** Following the translation in Legge, *Chinese Classics*, p. 343.

147/11 **Hexagram "Retreat"** This is *Tun*, the thirty-third hexagram.

149/7–8 **Peace and stagnation** The eleventh and twelfth hexagrams, *T'ai* and *P'i*.

149/16–29 **Emperors** In each of these examples, the emperors died in mysterious or tragic circumstances. The episodes are all discussed in the traditional dynastic histories.

Note to Appendix A, "Seventeen Letters to Ku Wen-hsing . . ."

157—166 These letters were printed in *YC*, pp. 35–9 (or pp. 2–9 in the original pagination). The editors of *Chang-ku ts'ung-pien* were confused over the dating of *two* series of letters, and thinking that they related to *one* Northern Tour, printed them all in one long jumbled sequence. If we allot serial numbers to these *YC* letters, we find that the correct sequence for the "Seventeen Letters to Ku Wen-hsing, Chief Eunuch, Spring 1697," is the following: 4, 5, 6, 7, 8, 9, 10, 14, 15, 16, 17, 18, 19, 33, 20, 23, 26. The other letters refer to the campaign of 1696.

Note to Appendix B, "The 'Final' Valedictory Edict"

169—173 This edict is printed in *SL*, 3980–2 (300/7–11).

Bibliography

AHMAD, ZAHIRUDDIN. *Sino-Tibetan Relations in the Seventeenth Century.* Rome: Istituto Italiano per il Medio ed Estremo Oriente, 1970. (Also Index volume, comp. by Christiane Pedersen [Rome: I.I.M.E.O., 1971].)

BELL, JOHN. *A Journey from St. Petersburg to Pekin, 1719–1722,* ed. J. L. Stevenson. Edinburgh University Press, 1965.

BRUNNERT, H. S., and V. V. HAGELSTROM. *Present Day Political Organization of China,* Eng. transl. by A. Beltchenko and E. E. Moran. Shanghai, 1912.

BOSMANS, H. *"Ferdinand Verbiest, directeur de l'observatoire de Peking (1623–1688)." Revue des Questions Scientifiques,* LXXI (1912), 195–273 and 375–464.

BOUVET, JOACHIM. *Histoire de l'empereur de la Chine.* The Hague, 1699; reprinted Tientsin, 1940.

BRETSCHNEIDER, EMILII VASIL'EVICH. *Botanicon Sinicum: Notes on*

Chinese Botany from Native and Western Sources. 3 vols., *Journal of the North China Branch of the Royal Asiatic Society,* new ser., XVI, XXV, XXIX.

CH'A SHEN-HSING 查慎行 (compiler Ch'en Ching-chang 陳敬璋). *Ch'a T'a-shan nien-p'u* 查他山年譜 (Chronological Biography of Ch'a Shen-hsing), in *Chia-yeh t'ang ts'ung-shu* 嘉業堂叢書, 1918.

CHANG CHUNG-LI. *The Chinese Gentry: Studies on Their Role in Nineteenth-Century China.* Seattle: University of Washington Press, 1955.

CHANG LU 張璐. *I-t'ung* 醫通, 16 *chuan.* Completed before 1705, printed in *Chang Shih i-shu* 張氏醫書 (The Medical Works of Chang Lu), n.p., n.d. Preface by Chu I-tsun, dated 1709.

CHANG PO-HSING 張伯行. *Chang Ch'ing-k'o kung nien-p'u* 張清恪公年譜 (Chronological Biography of Chang Po-hsing), in *Cheng-i-t'ang chi* 正誼堂集, 1739.

CHANG YING 張英. *Nan-hsün hu-ts'ung chi-lüeh* 南巡扈從紀略 (Records from the Retinue on a Southern Tour), in *Chao-tai ts'ung-shu* 昭代叢書, 5th ser., *chuan* 7.

CH'EN K'ANG-CH'I 陳康祺. *Lang-ch'ien chi-wen, san pi* 郎潛紀聞三筆 (Collected Essays). 1883 edn.

CH'IEN CH'EN-CH'ÜN 錢陳羣. *Ch'ien Wen-tuan kung nien-p'u* 錢文端公年譜 (Chronological Biography of Ch'ien Ch'en-ch'ün), in *Hsiang-shu-chai ch'üan-chi* 香樹齋全集, 1894 edn.

The Chinese Classics, transl. by James Legge. 5 vols. Taipei: Wen-hsing shu-tien reprint, n.d.

Ch'ing Administrative Terms: A Translation of the Terminology of the Six Boards with Explanatory Notes, transl. and ed. by Sun E-tu Zen. Cambridge: Harvard University Press, 1961.

Ch'ing Huang-shih ssu-p'u 清皇室四譜 (The Ch'ing Imperial Family: Emperors, Consorts, Princes, Princesses), ed. by T'ang Pang-chih 唐邦治. Taiwan: Wen-hai Ch'u-pan-she, Chin-tai Chung-kuo shih-liao ts'ung-k'an, no. 71 (1966).

Ch'ing lieh-ch'ao hou-fei chuan kao 清列朝后妃傳稿 (Draft Biographies of Ch'ing Dynasty Empresses and Consorts), comp. by Chang Ts'ai-t'ien 張采田. 2 *chuan.* 1929.

Ch'ing-shih 清史 (History of the Ch'ing Dynasty). 8 vols. Taipei: Kuo-fang yen-chiu yüan, 1961.

Ch'ing-shih lieh-chuan 清史列傳 (Ch'ing Dynasty Biographies). 10 vols. Taipei: Chung-hua shu-chü reprint, 1962.

Ch'ing-tai i-t'ung ti-t'u 清代一統地圖 (China's National Atlas of the Ch'ing Dynasty; 1st edn., 1760). Taipei: Kuo-fang yen-chiu yüan reprint, 1966.

Chung-kuo i-hsüeh ta-tzu-tien 中國醫學大辭典 (Dictionary of Chinese Medicine), ed. by Hsieh Kuan 謝觀. 4 vols. Shanghai: Shang-wu yin-shu-kuan, 1955.

Chu-san T'ai-tzu an 朱三太子案 (The Case of the Ming Prince Chu-san [in 1708]), in *Shih-liao hsün-k'an* 史料旬刊 (Collected Historical Documents), pp. 20–2. Taipei: Kuo-feng ch'u-pan-she, 1963.

DEHERGNE, J. *"Fauconnerie, plaisir du roi"* (transl. by Louis Buglio). *Bulletin de l'Université l'Aurore* (Shanghai), 3rd ser., vol. VII, no. 3 (1946), pp. 522–56.

A Documentary Chronicle of Sino-Western Relations (1644–1820), comp. and transl. by Fu Lo-shu. 2 vols. A.A.S. Monographs and Papers, no. 22. Tucson: University of Arizona Press, 1966.

DU HALDE, JEAN BAPTISTE. *The General History of China,* transl. by R. Brookes. 4 vols. London, 1741.

Eminent Chinese of the Ch'ing Period, ed. by Arthur W. Hummel. 2 vols. Washington, D.C.: U.S. Government Printing Office, 1943–44.

FANG CHAO-YING 房兆楹 and TU LIEN-CHE 杜聯喆. *Tseng-chiao Ch'ing-ch'ao chin-shih t'i-ming pei-lu* 增校清朝進士題名碑錄 (Listing, Supplement, and Index of Ch'ing Dynasty *chin-shih* Holders). Harvard-Yenching Institute Sinological Index ser., Supplement no. 19. Taipei: Ch'eng-wen reprint, 1966.

FANG PAO 方苞. *Wang-hsi hsien-sheng nien-p'u* 望溪先生年譜 (Chronological Biography of Fang Pao), in *Fang Wang-hsi ch'üan-chi* 方望溪全集, Ssu-pu ts'ung-k'an edn.

FENG P'U 馮溥. *I-chai Feng kung nien-p'u* 易齋馮公年譜 (Chronological Biography of Feng P'u), comp. by Mao Ch'i-ling 毛奇齡, in *Hsi-ho ho-chi* 西河合集, 1720 edn.

FLETCHER, JOSEPH. "V. A. Aleksandrov on Russo-Ch'ing Relations in the Seventeenth Century: Critique and Résumé." *Kritika,* VII (spring 1971), 138–70.

Flettinger MS. Notes written in Peking, 1688. Serial K.A. 1329, fols.

2319v–2324. The Hague: Dutch East India Company Archives.

FUCHS, WALTER. *Der Jesuiten-Atlas der Kanghsi-Zeit.* Peking: Fu-jen University, 1943.

Gherardini MS. Manuscript letters from G. Gherardini, dated Peking, November 1701, to his brother in Parma and friends in Paris and Nevers. London: PRO, catalogued under SP9/239.

GOODRICH, LUTHER CARRINGTON. *The Literary Inquisition of Ch'ien-lung.* New York: Paragon Book reprint, 1966.

GOTŌ SUEŌ 後藤末雄. *Koki-tei den* 康熙帝傳 (A Biography of the K'ang-hsi Emperor), transl. from Joachim Bouvet, *Portrait historique de l'empereur de la Chine,* 1697. Tokyo, 1941.

GROOT, J. J. M. DE. *The Religious System of China.* 6 vols. Taipei: Ch'eng-wen reprint, 1969.

GROOT, J. J. M. DE. *Sectarianism and Religious Persecution in China: A Page in the History of Religions.* 2 vols. in 1. Taipei: Literature House reprint, 1963.

HAN T'AN 韓菼. *Yu-huai-t'ang wen-kao* 有懷堂文稿 (Draft Collected Essays of Han T'an). N.p., 1703.

HARLEZ, CHARLES DE. "La Religion nationale des Tartares orientaux: Mandchous et Mongols, comparée à la religion des anciens chinois . . ." in *Mémoires Couronnés et Autres Mémoires,* XL (1887). Brussels: Royal Academy of Sciences, Letters and Fine Arts.

HASHIMOTO KEIZO 橋本敬造. "Baibuntei no rekisangaku—Koki nenkan no tenmon rekisangaku" 梅文鼎の曆算學–康熙年間の天文曆算學 (Mei Wen-ting, an Astronomer in the K'ang-hsi Period), in *Tōhō Gakuhō* 東方學報, XLI (March 1970), 491–518.

HIBBERT, ELOISE TALCOTT. *K'ang Hsi, Emperor of China.* London: Paul, Trench, Trubner & Co., 1940.

HO PING-TI. *The Ladder of Success in Imperial China: Aspects of Social Mobility, 1368–1911.* New York: Columbia University Press, 1962.

HO PING-TI. *Studies on the Population of China, 1368–1953.* Cambridge: Harvard University Press, 1959.

HSÜ PING-I 徐秉義. *Kung-yin ta-chia chi* 恭迎大駕紀 (Greeting the Emperor's Retinue), in *Chao-tai ts'ung-shu* 昭代叢書, 2nd ser., *chuan* 16.

HUANG TSUNG-HSI 黃宗羲. *Huang Li-chou hsien-sheng nien-p'u* 黃梨洲先生年譜 (Chronological Biography of Huang Tsung-hsi), in *Huang Li-chou i-shu* 黃梨洲遺書, 1873 edn.

(Ch'in-ting Ta-Ch'ing) Hui-tien shih-li (欽定大清) 會典事例 (Imperial Ch'ing Statutes and Precedents; 1899 edn.). 19 vols. Taipei: Ch'i-wen ch'u-pan-she reprint, 1963.

I Ching, or Book of Changes, Richard Wilhelm transl. rendered into English by Cary F. Baynes. Bollingen ser. XIX. Princeton University Press, 1967.

KANDA NOBUŌ 神田信夫. *"Heiseiō Go Sankei no kenkyū"* 平西王吳三桂の研究 (A Study on Wu San-kuei, P'ing Hsi Wang), in *Meiji Daigaku Bungakubu Kenkyu hokoku: Toyoshi* 明治大學文學部研究報告東洋史. Tokyo: Meiji University, 1952.

K'ang-hsi yü Lo-ma shih-chieh kuan-hsi wen-shu ying-yin pen 康熙與羅馬使節關係文書影印本 (Facsimile of the Documents Relating to K'ang-hsi and the Legates from Rome), ed. by Ch'en Yüan 陳垣. Peiping: Ku-kung po-wu yüan, 1932. (Transcriptions of these documents are also in *Wen-hsien ts'ung-pien* [Taipei: Kuo-feng ch'u-pan-she reprint, 1964], pp. 168–75.)

KAO SHIH-CH'I 高士奇. *Hu-ts'ung hsi-hsün jih-lu* 扈從東巡日錄 (Daily Record of Traveling in the Retinue on the Western Tour [of 1683]), in *Hsiao-fang-hu chai yü-ti ts'ung-ch'ao* 小方壺齋輿地叢鈔, 1st ser., *ts'e* 4, pp. 265–68.

KAO SHIH-CH'I 高士奇. *Hu-ts'ung tung-hsün jih-lu* 扈從西巡日錄 (Daily Record of Traveling in the Retinue on the Eastern Tour [of 1682]), in *Hsiao-fang-hu chai yü-ti ts'ung-ch'ao* 小方壺齋輿地叢鈔, 1st ser., *ts'e* 4, pp. 253–62 and supplement pp. 263–4.

KAO SHIH-CH'I 高士奇. *P'eng-shan mi-chi* 蓬山密記 (An Account of Meetings with K'ang-hsi in 1703), in *Ku-hsüeh hui-k'an* 古學彙刊, ed. by Teng Shih 鄧實. 1st ser., no. 12. Shanghai: Kuo-sui hsüeh-pao she, 1912.

KAO SHIH-CH'I 高士奇. *Sai-pei hsiao-ch'ao* 塞北小鈔 (Brief Record of the Northern Tour [of 1683]), in *Chao-tai ts'ung-shu* 昭代叢書, Tao-kuang edn., 3rd ser., *chuan* 12, pp. 1–19.

KAO SHIH-CH'I 高士奇. *Sung-t'ing hsing-chi* 松亭行紀 (A Record of the Tour [of 1681]), in *Chao-tai ts'ung shu* 昭代叢書, Tao-kuang edn., 3rd ser., *chuan* 10, pp. 1–33.

KESSLER, LAWRENCE D. "The Apprenticeship of the K'ang-hsi Emperor, 1661–1684." History Ph.D., University of Chicago, 1969. A part of this study appears in the same author's "Chinese Scholars and the Early Manchu State," *Harvard Journal of Asiatic Studies*, XXXI (1971), 179–200.

(KHTYC) K'ang-hsi ti yü-chih wen-chi 康熙帝御製文集 (The Literary Works of the K'ang-hsi Emperor). 4 vols., with continuous pagination. Taiwan: Hsüeh-sheng shu-chü reprint, 1966.

(KKWH) Ku-kung wen-hsien 故宮文獻 (Ch'ing Documents at the National Palace Museum). National Palace Museum, Taiwan; the sequence from vol. 1, no. 1, December 1969. Vol. 3, no. 1, December 1971, contains photo-offset reproductions of the palace memorials in the K'ang-hsi reign.

KU SSU-LI 顧嗣立. *Ku Lü-yu tzu-ting nien-p'u* 顧閭邱自訂年譜 (Chronological Biography of Ku Ssu-li), in *Ping-tzu ts'ung-pien* 丙子叢編, 1936 edn.

K'UNG SHANG-JEN 孔尚任. *Ch'u-shan i-shu chi* 出山異數記 (Memoir Concerning K'ang-hsi's 1684 Tour to Confucius' Former Home), in *Chao-tai ts'ung-shu* 昭代叢書, 2nd ser., *chuan* 18.

Kuo-ch'ao ch'i-hsien lei-cheng ch'u-pien 國朝耆獻類徵初編 (Biographies of Eminent Men in the Ch'ing Dynasty). 25 vols. Taipei: Wen-hai ch'u-pan she reprint, 1966.

KUO HSIU 郭琇. *Hua-yeh Kuo-kung nien-p'u* 華野郭公年譜 (Chronological Biography of Kuo Hsiu), in *Kuo Hua-yeh shu-kao* 郭華野疏稿, 1895 edn.

Lettres édifiantes et curieuses, écrites des missions étrangères. Nouvelle édition. Paris, 1781.

LI KUANG-TI 李光地. *Li Wen-chen kung nien-p'u* 李文貞公年譜 (Chronological Biography of Li Kuang-ti), in *Jung-ts'un ch'üan-shu* 榕村全書, 1829 edn.

LIU TA-NIEN 劉大年. *Lun K'ang-hsi* 論康熙 *Emperor K'ang-hsi, the Great Feudal Ruler Who United China and Defended Her Against European Penetration*, in *Li-shih yen-chiu* 歷史研究, III (1961), 5–21.

LU LUNG-CHI 陸隴其. *Lu Shih-yü nien-p'u* 陸侍御年譜 (Chronological Biography of Lu Lung-chi). Ch'ien-lung edn.

MALONE, CARROLL BROWN. *History of the Peking Summer Palaces*

Under the Ch'ing Dynasty. New York: Paragon Book reprint, 1966.

MANCALL, MARK. *Russian and China: Their Diplomatic Relations to 1728*. Cambridge: Harvard University Press, 1971.

MANO SENRYŪ 間野潛龍. *Koki-tei* 康熙帝 (Emperor K'ang-hsi). Tokyo, 1967.

MAO CH'I-LING 毛奇齡. *Mao Hsi-ho hsien-sheng chuan* 毛西河先生傳 (Chronological Biography of Mao Ch'i-ling), in *Hsi-ho ho-chi* 西河合集, 1720 edn.

MAO, LUCIEN. "Tai Ming-shih." *T'ien Hsia Monthly*, V, 382-99.

MEI WEN-TING 梅文鼎. *Li-hsüeh i-wen* 曆學疑問 (Problems in Astronomy), in *Mei-shih ts'ung-shu chi-yao* 梅氏叢書輯要. 8 vols. Taipei: I-wen yin-shu kuan reprint, 1971. *Chuan* 46-8.

NAGAYA YOSHIRŌ 長與善郎. *Taitei Koki* 大帝康熙 (K'ang-hsi the Great), in *Shina tōchi no yōdō* 支那統治の要道. Tokyo: Iwanami Shoten, 1938.

NEEDHAM, JOSEPH. *Science and Civilization in China*. Cambridge: Cambridge University Press, 1954-   .

Nien Keng-yao che 年羹堯摺 (The Palace Memorials of Nien Keng-yao), in *Chang-ku ts'ung-pien* 掌故叢編, pp. 186-225. Taipei: Kuo-feng ch'u-pan she reprint, 1964.

NISHIMOTO HAKUSEN 西本白川. *Koki taitei* 康熙大帝 (K'ang-hsi the Great). Tokyo: Daitō Shupansha, 1925.

NIU HSIU 鈕琇. *Ku-shen hsü-pien* 觚賸續編 (Collected Historical Materials), in *Pi-chi hsiao-shuo ta kuan hsü-pien* 筆記小說大觀續編. Taipei, 1962 reprint. Vol. 25, p. 6437.

NORMAN, JERRY. *A Manchu-English Dictionary*. Draft publication. Taipei, 1967.

ŌNO KATSUTOSHI 小野勝年. *Koki Roku Jun Banju Seiten ni tsuite* 康熙六旬萬壽盛典についこ (On the Imperial Collection on K'ang-hsi's Sixtieth Birthday), in *Tamura Hakushi Shōju Tōyō shi ronsō* 田村博士頌壽東洋史論叢 (Collected Essays on Asian History in Honor of Professor Tamura). Kyoto, 1968.

D'ORLÉANS, PIERRE JOSEPH. *History of the Two Tartar Conquerors of China*, transl. by the Earl of Ellesmere. Hakluyt Society, 1st ser. XVII (1854). New York: Burt Franklin reprint, n.d.

OXNAM, ROBERT B. "Policies and Institutions of the Oboi Regency, 1661–1669." *Journal of Asian Studies*, XXXII (1973), 265–86.

Pa-ch'i t'ung-chih (ch'u-chi) 八旗通志（初集）(The History of the Eight Banners; edn. of 1739). 40 vols. Taipei: Hsüeh-sheng shu-chü reprint, 1968.

P'ENG TING-CH'IU 彭定求. *Nan-yün lao-jen tzu-ting nien-p'u* 南畇老人自訂年譜 (Autobiography of P'eng Ting-ch'iu), in *Nan-yün wen-kao* 南畇文稿, 1880 edn.

PFISTER, LOUIS, S.J. *Notices biographiques et bibliographiques sur les Jésuites de l'ancienne mission de Chine*. 2 vols. Shanghai, 1932 and 1934, Variétés Sinologiques, nos. 59 and 60.

ROSSO, ANTONIO SISTO, O.F.M. *Apostolic Legations to China of the Eighteenth Century*. South Pasadena, Cal.: P.D. and Ione Perkins, 1948.

ROULEAU, FRANCIS A., S.J. "Maillard de Tournon, Papal Legate at the Court of Peking: The First Imperial Audience (31 December, 1705)." *Archivum Historicum Societatis Iesu*, LXII (1962), 264–323.

SAEKI TOMI 佐伯富. *Shindai no jiei ni tsuite: Kunshu dokusaiken kenkyu no ichi shaku* 清代の侍衞についこ：君主獨裁權研究の一齣 (On the Ch'ing Guards Officers: An Aspect of the Study of Despotic Power), in *Tōyōshi kenkyu* 東洋史研究, 27:2 (1968), 38–58.

SCHAFER, EDWARD H. "Falconry in T'ang Times." *T'oung Pao,* 2nd ser., XLVI (1959), 293–338.

SHANG YEN-LIU 商衍鎏. *Ch'ing-tai k'o-chü k'ao-shih shu-lu* 清代科舉考試述錄 (A Study of the Ch'ing Examination System). Peking, 1958.

Sheng-tsu ch'in-cheng shuo-mo jih-lu 聖祖親征朔漠日錄 (Daily Record of K'ang-hsi's Personal Campaign in the Northern Deserts), transcr. by Lo Chen-yü 羅振玉, in *Shih-liao ts'ung-pien* 史料叢編. Mukden, 1933.

Sheng-tsu hsi-hsün jih-lu 聖祖西巡日錄 (Daily Record of K'ang-hsi's Western Tour), transcr. by Lo Chen-yü 羅振玉, in *Shih-liao ts'ung-pien* 史料叢編. Mukden, 1933.

Sheng-tsu Jen Huang-ti Ch'i-chü chu 聖祖仁皇帝起居注 (The Official Diary of K'ang-hsi's Activities, 12th Year of His Reign, Months 1, 5–6, 10–12), in *Shih-liao ts'ung k'an* 史料叢刊, pp. 335–578. Taipei:

Wen-hai ch'u-pan-she reprint, with continuous pagination, 1964.

Sheng-tsu wu-hsing Chiang-nan ch'üan-lu 聖祖五幸江南全錄 (A Complete Record of K'ang-hsi's Fifth Southern Tour [in 1705]), Anon., in *Chen-ch'i t'ang ts'ung-shu* 振綺堂叢書, 1st ser.

(SL) Ta-Ch'ing Sheng-tsu Jen Huang-ti shih-lu 大清聖祖仁皇帝實錄 (The Veritable Records of the K'ang-hsi Reign). 6 vols. Taipei: Hua-wen shu-chü reprint, 1964.

SPENCE, JONATHAN. *To Change China: Western Advisers in China, 1620 to 1960.* Boston: Little, Brown, 1969.

SPENCE, JONATHAN. *Ts'ao Yin and the K'ang-hsi Emperor, Bondservant and Master.* New Haven and London: Yale University Press, 1966.

SUN E-TU ZEN. "Mining Labor in the Ch'ing Period." *Approaches to Modern Chinese History,* ed. by Albert Feuerwerker, Rhoads Murphey, and Mary Wright. Berkeley and Los Angeles: University of California Press, 1967. Pp. 45–67.

Ta Tsing Leu Lee; Being the Fundamental Laws, and a Selection from the Supplementary Statutes, of the Penal Code of China . . . , transl. by Sir George Thomas Staunton. Taipei: Ch'eng-wen reprint, 1966.

TAGAWA DAIKICHIRŌ 田川大吉郎. *Seiso Koki tei* 聖祖康熙帝 (Sheng-tsu, the K'ang-hsi Emperor). Tokyo: Kyobunkan, 1944.

TAI MING-SHIH 戴名世. *Nan-shan chi* 南山集 (Collection of Prose Writings). 2 vols. Taipei: Hua-wen shu-chü reprint, 1970.

(THKY) T'ing-hsün ko-yen 庭訓格言 (K'ang-hsi's Conversations with His Sons). N.d. Preface by Yung-cheng, 1730.

TI I 狄億. *Ch'ang-ch'un yüan yü-shih kung-chi* 暢春苑御試恭紀 (On Taking a Special Examination in the Ch'ang-ch'un Palace), in *Chao-tai ts'ung-shu* 昭代叢書, 2nd ser., *chuan* 17.

T'IEN WEN 田雯. *Meng-chai tzu-ting nien-p'u* 蒙齋自訂年譜 (Chronological Biography of T'ien Wen), in *Ku-huan-t'ang chi* 古歡堂集, n.d.

TSAO KAI-FU. "The Rebellion of the Three Feudatories Against the Manchu Throne in China, 1673–1681: Its Setting and Significance." History Ph.D., Columbia University, 1965.

Tung Wen-chi 董文驥. *En-tz'u yü-shu chi* 恩賜御書紀 (In Memory of the Emperor's Gift), in *Chao-tai ts'ung-shu* 昭代叢書, 2nd ser., *chuan* 15.

VEITH, ILZA. *Huang ti nei ching su wen (The Yellow Emperor's Classic of Internal Medicine).* Berkeley and Los Angeles: University of California Press, 1966.

WALLNÖFER, HEINRICH, and ANNA VON ROTTAUSCHER. *Chinese Folk Medicine,* transl. by Marion Palmedo. New York: Crown Publishers, 1965.

WANG CHIH 王隲. *Wang Ta-ssu-nung nien-p'u* 王大司農年譜 (Chronological Biography of Wang Chih), in *I-p'u chuan chia-chi* 義脯傳家集, K'ang-hsi edn.

WANG HAO 汪顥. *Sui-luan chi-en* 隨鑾紀恩 (Memoir on Favors Conferred in the Imperial Retinue), in *Hsiao-fang-hu chai yü-ti ts'ung-ch'ao* 小方壺齋輿地叢鈔, 1st ser., ts'e 4, pp. 286–99.

WANG HSIAO-CH'UAN王曉傳. *Yüan Ming Ch'ing san-tai chin-hui hsiao-shuo hsi-ch'ü shih-liao* 元明清三代禁燬小說戲曲史料 (Historical Materials on the Banning of Fiction and Drama During the Yüan, Ming, and Ch'ing Dynasties). Peking: Tso-chia ch'u-pan she, 1958.

WANG YEH-CHIEN. "The Fiscal Importance of the Land Tax During the Ch'ing Period." *Journal of Asian Studies,* IV (August 1971), 829–42.

WEI HSIANG-SHU 魏象樞. *Wei Min-kuo kung nien-p'u* 魏敏果公年譜 (Chronological Biography of Wei Hsiang-shu), in *Han-sung chi* 寒松集, 1810 edn.

WENG SHU-YÜAN 翁叔元. *Weng T'ieh-an tzu-ting nien-p'u* 翁鐵庵自訂年譜 (Chronological Biography of Weng Shu-yüan). K'ang-hsi edn.

Wen-hsien ts'ung-pien 文獻叢編 (Collected Historical Documents). 2 vols. Taipei: Kuo-feng ch'u-pan-she reprint, 1964.

WERNER, E. T. C. *A Dictionary of Chinese Mythology.* Shanghai, 1932; New York: The Julian Press reprint, 1961.

WILLS, JOHN E., JR. "Ch'ing Relations with the Dutch, 1662–1690." Ph.D., Harvard University, 1967.

WONG, K. CHIMIN, and WU LIEN-TEH. *History of Chinese Medicine.* Tientsin: The Tientsin Press, 1932.

WU, SILAS H. L. *Communication and Imperial Control in China: Evolution of the Palace Memorial System, 1693–1735.* Cambridge: Harvard University Press, 1970.

WU, SILAS H. L. "Emperors at Work: The Daily Schedules of the

K'ang-hsi and Yung-cheng Emperors, 1661–1735." *Tsing Hua Journal of Chinese Studies*, new ser., vol. VIII, nos. 1 and 2 (August 1970), pp. 210–27.

Wu, Silas H. L. "The Memorial Systems of the Ch'ing Dynasty (1644–1911)." *Harvard Journal of Asiatic Studies*, XXVII (1967), 7–75.

Wu, Silas H. L. "A Note on the Proper Use of Documents for Historical Studies: A Rejoinder." *Harvard Journal of Asiatic Studies*, XXXII (1972), 230–9.

(YC) *Ch'ing Sheng-tsu yü-chih* 清聖祖諭旨 (Edicts of K'ang-hsi), in *Chang-ku ts'ung-pien* 掌故叢編. Taipei: Kuo-feng ch'u-pan she reprint, 1964. Pp. 35–45. This reprint gives the original Chinese pagination of each document reproduced; to make it easier to find specific passages, I cite passages according to this original pagination.

Yüan Liang-i 袁良义. "*Lun K'ang-hsi ti li-shih ti-wei*" 論康熙的歷史地位 (A Discussion of K'ang-hsi's Position in History), in *Pei-ching-shih li-shih hsüeh-hui* 北京市歷史學會. Peking Historical Society, I and II (1961 and 1962), 232–57.

Index

Abahai, K'ang-hsi's grandfather, 105; *see also* T'ai-tsung, Ch'ing Emperor
acupuncture, 98
aged, the: care of, 104–6; in office, 108–9; respect for, xx
aging, 102–3, 107, 108–12, 148–51
agriculture, 57–8; farm acreage, xvi, 54
Albazin, siege and destruction of, xiv, 34
alchemy, external, 101–2
algebra, 74
ancestor worship, 79, 80, 143
appointments, favoritism in, 41, 50
archery, 10, 11, 12, 13, 18
astronomy, xviii, 15–16, 58, 73, 85
audiences, court, 42–3

Bandi, Prince, 132, 133
Banner system, xx–xxi; Chinese Bannermen, 41, 44, 51; Manchu Bannermen, 40, 41, 44
"bird boats," 47
Boards, Six, xv; *see also* Civil Office, Board of; Public Works, Board of; Punishment, Board of; Revenue, Board of; Rites, Board of; War, Board of
Book of Changes (I Ching), xviii, 11, 29, 44–5, 57, 59, 69, 74, 75, 147

Book of History, 87, 125, 146, 169, 170
Book of Poetry, 66
books: censorship, 85; Ch'in burning of, 71, 145, 174
Bouvet, Father Joachim, 72, 75, 80, 81
"Breakthrough," hexagram from *Book of Changes*, 57
Buddhists, 84
bureaucracy, xv–xvi

Calendrical Bureau, xviii
calendrical science, 74–5
calligraphy, 51, 59
Cangšeo, guards officer, 69, 128
Canton, 84
cartography, xviii, 73–4
catholicism, 81; *see also* Christians; missionaries
cauterization, 98, 111
Censorate, xv
censorship, 85; *see also* books
census reports, 54, 84
Ch'ang-ch'un Yüan Palace, xiv, 7, 8, 51, 73, 132, 134
Chang Hsien-chung, 86
Chang P'eng-ko, 40–1, 47, 86
Chang Po-hsing, 47, 51–2, 53, 106
Chang Ying, xxiv, 69, 125
Chang Yü-shu, 44, 96, 133
Chao Shen-ch'iao, 40, 138
Chekiang province, 42, 47, 50, 52, 53, 160

Ch'en Shang-i, 47, 48
Ch'en Yu-liang, 144, 172
Chiangnan, 42, 50, 109, 160
Ch'ien, hexagram from *Book of Changes*, 45
Ch'ien-ch'ing Palace, 66, 108, 142
chih fungus (or grass), 52, 71, 150
Chin Dynasty, 124
Ch'in Dynasty, 144, 172; book burning, 71, 145, 174
Chinese: Manchus compared to, 41, 43–4; Bannermen, 41, 44, 51
Ch'ing Dynasty, xiv, xxii, 128, 144; family tombs, 108; *Veritable Records* of, xxiii
Ching-ti, Han Emperor, 69, 71
chin-shih examinations, xvi, 50, 51, 52
Ch'i-shih-wu, 89, 134, 135–6
Christians, 79–81, 84; *see also* missionaries; Westerners in China
Ch'ü-fu, home of Confucius, 69–71
Chu Hsi, xviii, 67, 74, 148
chü-jen examinations, xvi, 50, 51
Chu-ko Liang, 146, 171
Ch'ung-chen, Ming Emperor, 86, 87, 88, 89, 144, 171
Chu San T'ai-tzu, Ming pretender, 30–1
Civil Office, Board of, xv, 38
Classic of Internal Medicine, 100
Classics: see Confucian *Classics*
cleanliness, 103
clocks, 68, 72
Confucian *Classics*, xii, xvi, xviii, 50, 71

Confucius, 69–71, 79, 80, 107, 148
Council of Princes and High Officials, xvii, 19, 38
counties (*hsien*), xvi, 109
Court Medical Department, 95, 98
Coxinga, 35

death penalty, xvii, 29–37, 85–6; lingering death, 30–1; review, 32–4
demonic possession, 129–30, 132, 134
descendants of K'ang-hsi, xx, 119–22, 173; factional feuding among sons, xx–xxi, xxv, 126, 128–39
de Tournon, Maillard, xviii, 75–9, 82, 84
diet, 97–8
discipline: in child raising, 124; military, 12, 13, 18, 19–20, 30
diseases, 14, 18, 95–6, 98
divination, 57–9, 71
Doctrine of the Mean, 56–7
drugs, 95–7, 99; Western, 97, 98–9
Dutu, General, 134, 135

eclipses, 58, 73
education, xvi, 112, 124–5; *see also* examination system; scholarship
emperor, office of, xii, 29, 143–51; Mandate of Heaven, 144–5, 172; responsibility, xvi–xvii, 146–7, 174; sources of information, 41–3, 47; succession to, 128–39, 149–50, 173, 174

Empress Dowager, xx, xxii, 39,
  96, 106, 124; illness and death
  of, 104–5, 143
"entering the darkness," Taoist
  concept, 107
*Eulogy for Governor-General Chao
  Hung-hsieh* (K'ang-hsi), 27
eunuchs, xv, 45–6
Europeans: *see* Westerners
examination system, xv, xvi,
  50–2
executions: *see* death penalty
"external alchemy," 101–2

farmland acreage, xvi, 54
favoritism: *see* appointments
Feng, hexagram from *Book of
  Changes,* 45
filial piety, xx, 69
"Fire on the Mountain," hexagram from *Book of Changes,* 29
fishing, 9
five joys, the, 146
Fiyanggu, General, 20, 21, 139
Fontaney, Jesuit, 72, 84
foods, 97–8
fortune-telling, 57–9
fu (prefectures), xvi
Fukien province, 47, 48, 49, 50,
  52, 85

Galdan, Zungar leader, xv, 30,
  31, 34, 125; campaigns against,
  13, 17, 18–22, 160, 161, 163, 165
Gengge, 134, 135–6
geomancy, 108
geography, xviii, 16, 73–4
Gerbillon, Jesuit, 72, 76, 77, 79
Gift for an Old Official (K'ang-
  hsi), 93
gift-giving, 105–6

glassware, 68
gnomon, 67
Gobi Desert, xiii, 14
goverment: K'ang-hsi's views of,
  xvi, xvii, 29–59, 109, 146–7,
  174; Mandate of Heaven,
  144–5; system and entities,
  xv–xvi
governor, office of, xv, 51–2
governor-general, office of, xvi
Grand Secretaries, xv, 32–3, 89,
  108
Great Learning, 69
"Great Plan" section, *Book of
  Histories,* 146, 170
Great Wall, 160
Great Way, 101–2
Grimaldi, Jesuit, 72, 76
gunpowder, 10–11

Han-chung area, 36
Han Dynasty, 70, 71, 144, 149,
  172
Han Dynasty tablets, 70
Hangchow, 52
Hanlin Academy, xvi, 44, 51, 125
Han-shu, 86
Heilungkiang, 15
Heir-Apparent crisis, 31, 111,
  128–39, 150
historiography, xix, xxii–xxiv,
  85–9, 174
History Bureau, 85
homosexuality, xxi, 125–7, 129
Honan province, 48, 50
Ho-t'u lo-shu, 74
Hou-ching, 149, 172
Hsiang Yü, 144, 172
Hsiao-ch'eng, Empress, 119,
  120, 121
Hsiao-k'ang, Empress, 108

Hsieh Wan-ch'eng, 101–2
hsien (counties), xvi, 109
Hsing-an area, 36
Hsiung Tz'u-li, 40, 125
Hsi-yüan Lu, 33
Hsüan-te, Ming Emperor, 88, 89
Huang Tsung-hsi, 108
Hui-tsung, Sung Emperor, 70
Hunan province, 36
Hung-wu, Ming Emperor, 89
hunting, xiv–xv, 8, 9–13, 16,
    22–3
*Hunting in the Ordos, the Hares
    Were Many* (K'ang-hsi), 5
Hupeh campaign, 30

Icangga, 35–6, 111
I Ching: see *Book of Changes*
impeachment, 41
"imperial bureaucracy," xv
incense associations, 85

Jao Modo, battle of, 21
Jartoux, Pierre, 72, 73
Jehol, palace in, xiv, 8, 9, 68, 99
Jesuits, xviii–xix, xxiv, 72–5,
    78, 79, 81, 82
justice, system of, xvii, 29–37, 41

Kansu province, 89
Kao Shih-ch'i, xxiv, 51, 95, 106
Kao-tsu, Han Emperor, 144, 149,
    172
Kao-tsung, Sung Emperor, 150
Keng Ching-chung, Prince,
    xvi–xvii, 31, 36, 37, 38, 43
Khalkas, 20, 21, 49
Kiangsi province, 56
Kiangsu province, 30, 49–50,
    52–3

Kuai, hexagram from *Book of
    Changes*, 57
Kung-kuang, Ming pretender,
    85
K'ung Shang-jen, xxiv, 69–70,
    71
K'ung Yü-ch'i, 69–70, 71
Ku Wen-hsing, xiii, xxii, 100;
    K'ang-hsi's letters to, 22,
    155–66
Kwangsi province, 36, 52, 53, 89,
    103
Kwangtung province, 48, 85, 160
Kweichow province, 53, 85

land tax, xvi, 53–5
Lao-tzu, 97
Lasi, guards officer, 20, 69
Legal Code, xvii, 30
licentiates, xvi
Li Kuang-ti, xxiv, 22, 40, 96,
    106, 134
*Lines in Praise of a Self-Chiming
    Clock* (K'ang-hsi), 63
Li Tzu-ch'eng, 144, 171
Liu Yin-shu, 42, 74
locust pests, 58
Lung-wu, Ming pretender, 85

magic square, 74
magistrate, office of, xvi, 109
Maigrot, Bishop, 79–80, 82
Manchuria, xiii, xiv, xx, 38
Manchus, 97, 99, 102, 104, 138;
    Banners, xx–xxi, 40, 41, 44;
    compared to Chinese, 41, 43–4;
    factionalism of nobles, xx–xxi,
    126, 128–39; hunting prowess,
    11, 12; officials, xv, xxi, 41;
    overthrow of Ming by, xiv,

Manchus (*continued*)
  xvii, 85; *see also* Ch'ing
  Dynasty
Mandate of Heaven, 144–6, 172
massage, 97
mathematics, 72, 73–5, 85
Mau, guards officer, 20, 127
medicine, xx, 95–101; doctors,
  xviii, 98–9, 100; drugs, 95–7,
  99; smallpox inoculation, 18;
  specialization, xx, 99; study
  of, 100–1; Western, 97, 98–9
meditation, 106–7
Memoirs of Hadrian (Yourcenar),
  xxii
memorials, palace, xxiii, 42,
  46, 47
metropolitan division, xv, xvi,
  109
Miao people, 34–5
military concerns, xiv, 12–22;
  camping, 14–15, 19; commanders' tenure and loyalty,
  42–3; discipline, 12, 13, 18,
  19–20, 30; officers' examinations, 18, 50; training, 12–13,
  18; transport and supply, 13,
  19; troop attitudes, 17–18;
  water supply, 14, 16; *see also*
  warfare
Ming Dynasty, 13, 30–1, 35,
  67, 70, 86–9, 144, 172; end
  of, xiv, xvii, 85, 87, 144, 171;
  eunuchs, 46, 87
Ming History, xix, 88–9
Mingju, 38, 57, 71, 132
missionaries, Christian, xix, 76,
  79–84; Jesuits, xviii–xix,
  72–5, 78, 79, 81, 82; preaching
  certificates for, 82–4

Molo, 38, 42
Mongolia, xiv
Mongols, xiv, 99, 125, 173; hunting prowess, 12; *see also*
  Khalkas
Mount T'ai, 69
murder cases, 33–4
music, Western, 73
musical instruments, 66, 72

Nanking, 85
Nan-shan-chi (Tai Ming-shih),
  85
Nan-yüan Palace, xiv, 8, 39
Neo-Confucianism, xviii
nepotism, 41, 50
Nerchinsk, Treaty of, 72
Ninghsia, 19, 21, 161, 162, 163,
  164
Nurhaci, K'ang-hsi's great-
  grandfather, xx; *see also*
  T'ai-tsu, Ch'ing Emperor

Oboi, Regent, xxi
officials, government, xv–xvi,
  108–9; retirement, 109–10
Ölöds, 21, 163
omens, K'ang-hsi's skepticism
  of, 52, 58–9, 150, 174
Ošan, General, 134, 135, 136

palace memorials, xxiii, 42, 46,
  47
palaces, imperial, xii, xiv
Pan Ku, 86
papal mission to China, xviii–
  xix, 75–9
Peking, 8; fall of Ming Dynasty,
  xiv, 87, 144, 171; government,
  xv; imperial palaces at, xii,

Peking (*continued*)
xiv; Manchu takeover of, xiv,
144, 171; religious temples
and sects, 84–5; uprising
during "San-fan War," 31–2
Peking Gazette, 88
Pereira, Thomas, xviii, 68, 72,
73, 76, 79, 81
P'i, hexagram from *Book of
Changes*, 110
piracy, controlling, 47–8
po-hsüeh hung-ju examination,
xix, 51
population increase, 53, 54
population statistics, xvi; on
religious sects, 84
preaching certificates, 82–4
prefectures (*fu*), xvi
prisoners-of-war, 34
Proust, Marcel, quoted, xxv
provinces, xv–xvi
provincial division, xv–xvi, 109
Public Works, Board of, xv, 16,
35
Puci, Duke, 128, 131
Punishments, Board of, xv, 30,
32, 34, 86

Records of Sunshine and Rain, 15
relaxation, 106–7
religion, 79–81, 84; sects controlled, 84–5
*Resting at Nanking on a Tour, I
Received a Greetings Memorial
from the Heir-Apparent, Reporting That He Had Just Finished Reading the* Four Books
(K'ang-hsi), 117
"Retreat," hexagram from *Book
of Changes*, 147

Revenue, Board of, xv, 14, 16, 38,
148, 172
Ricci, Matteo, 79, 81, 82
Rites, Board of, xv, 72
Rites, Chinese, and Westerners,
xviii–xix, 79–81, 82
river public works, 47, 73, 148
Russia: seen as threat, 82; warfare with, xiv, 34, 72

sacrifice, religious, 79
salt smuggling, 48–9
"San-fan War" (War of the Three
Feudatories), xvi–xvii, 31,
35–9, 53, 89, 148
Schall, Adam, 72
scholarship, xvi, 44, 50–1; *see
also* historiography
science, xviii, 15–16, 72–5, 85;
see also astronomy; medicine
Sekse, 14, 30
sexual vigor, 107
Seven Military Classics, 22
Shang Chih-hsin, xvi–xvii, 36,
37, 38, 43
Shang-ti (god), 79
Shansi province, xiii, 41, 49–50,
56, 160, 163
Shantung province, 35, 42, 48,
49, 160
Shao-hsing, xiii, 160
Shensi province, xiii, 41, 49, 159,
160, 163
Shih-chi, 86
Shih-huang, Ch'in Emperor, 71,
145
Shih I-te, 56, 109
Shih Lang, Admiral, 35, 108
Shih-tsu, Ch'ing Emperor, 128
shipbuilding, 72

Shun-chih, Ch'ing Emperor, xiv, 68, 107–8, 147, 171
smallpox inoculation, 18
Songgotu, xxi, 20, 39, 106, 126, 129, 131, 135–6
Son of Heaven, xii, 151
Soochow, 72, 126
Ssu-ma Ch'ien, 86
succession, question of, xxv, 128–39, 149–50, 173, 174
Sui Dynasty, 149, 172
Sung Dynasty, 70, 148, 149
Sung History, 86
supernatural forces, K'ang-hsi's skepticism of, 52, 58–9, 150, 174
surveying, 73
Szechwan province, 34, 53, 73, 86, 95

T'ai, hexagram from *Book of Changes*, 110
T'ai-ch'ang, Ming Emperor, 89
Tai Ming-shih, xix, 85–6
T'ai-tsu, Ch'ing Emperor, 128, 131, 144, 171, 173; *see also* Nurhaci
T'ai-tsu, Ming Emperor, 144, 172
T'ai-tsu, Sung Emperor, 149
T'ai-tsung, Ch'ing Emperor, 128, 144, 171; *see also* Abahai
T'ai-tsung, T'ang Emperor, 88, 149
Taiwan, occupation of, xiv, 29, 35
T'ang-ch'üan Palace, xiv, 8
T'ang Dynasty, 149
Taoists, 84, 101, 107
taxation, xvi, 53–5; assessment, 53, 54–5; collection, xvi, xvii, 53–4; unit (*ting*), xvii, 54

territorial expansion, xiv–xv
Thomas, Antoine, xviii, 67, 72, 79
Three Dynasties period, 145, 170, 174
Three Feudatories, xvi–xvii, 148, 172; *see also* "San-fan War"
T'ien-ch'i, Ming Emperor, 87, 88, 89
Tientsin, 47, 67
ting, xvii, 53–5
Tohoci, Peking garrison commander, xxi, 136
Tournon: *see* de Tournon
travels of K'ang-hsi, xiii–xiv, 7–23, 42, 43, 47, 69–72, 81, 110, 148, 157–66
treason, 30–1, 36–7
Tso-chuan, 22
Tung Chung-shu, 68
Tzu-chih t'ung-chien, 88

Uge, guards officer, 30, 126
Ula, xiii, 136, 160
Uli, General, 134, 135, 136
Uriang-hai people, 34
Uši, guards officer, 128, 129

valedictory edict of K'ang-hsi: early version, xxiv–xxv, 141–51, 173; final version, xxv, 167–75
Verbiest, Ferdinand, xviii, 12, 16, 72, 84
Veritable Records: Ch'ing, xxiii; Ming, 87, 88

Wang Chih, 11, 95, 98
Wang Hung-hsü, 126, 127, 132
Wang Tu-chao, 51, 52–4

Wan-li, Ming Emperor, 88, 89
War, Board of, xv, 32, 38
warfare, xiv–xv, xvi–xvii, 16–22;
    civilian victims of, 17, 31–2;
    see also military concerns
War of the Three Feudatories
    ("San-fan War"), xvi–xvii,
    31, 35–9, 53, 89, 148
water supply and quality, 14, 16
"way of the ruler," 143–4
weapons, 10–11
weather forecasting, 15, 57
Wei Chung-hsien, 87
Wei Hsiang-shu, 39, 96
Wen-ti, Sui Emperor, 149, 172
Westerners in China, xxiv,
    72–84; merchants, 82; mis-
    sionaries, xix, 76, 79–84 (*see
    also* Jesuits); papal mission of
    de Tournon, xviii–xix, 75–9,
    82; problems predicted by
    K'ang-hsi, 82; restrictions on,
    82–4; and science, xviii, 72–5,
    98–9; and technology, 67–8,
    72–3
"White Lotus" society, 85
Wu San-kuei, Prince, xvi–xvii,
    21, 31, 34, 35, 36, 37, 38,
    42–3, 85
Wu-t'ai-shan shrines, 69, 104–5
Wu-ti, Han Emperor, 139
Wu-ti, Liang Emperor, 149, 172

Yellow Emperor, 100, 107, 145
Yin and Yang, xviii, 15, 44; Yin
    nature of eunuchs, 45
Yin-chen, Fourth Son of K'ang-
    hsi (Prince Yung), 120, 125,
    173; *see also* Yung-cheng,
    Ch'ing Emperor

Yin-ch'i, Fifth Son of K'ang-hsi,
    120, 124
Yin-chih, Third Son of K'ang-
    hsi, 11, 73, 120, 124, 125,
    129–30
Yin-jeng, Second Son of K'ang-
    hsi, xx, xxi, 80, 106, 120,
    124–6, 128–34, 136–7, 139;
    demonic possession feared,
    129–30, 132, 134; in Heir-
    Apparent crisis, 111, 128–39;
    suspected of homosexuality,
    xxi, 125–7, 129
Yin-ssu, Eighth Son of K'ang-
    hsi, 120, 130, 131, 132, 133, 137
Yin-t'ang, Ninth Son of K'ang-
    hsi, 121, 131
Yin-t'i, First Son of K'ang-hsi,
    11, 73, 120, 124, 125, 130–1,
    132, 137
Yin-t'i, Fourteenth Son of K'ang-
    hsi, 121, 131
Yourcenar, Marguerite, xxii
Yü, Emperor, 147, 171
Yüan Dynasty, 124, 144, 172
Yüan History, 86
Yü Ch'eng-lung, 41, 47
Yung, Prince (Yin-chen), 120,
    125, 173; *see also* Yung-cheng,
    Ch'ing Emperor
Yung-cheng, Ch'ing Emperor,
    xxiii, 173, 175; as Yin-chen,
    120, 125
Yung-hsing, siege of, 39
Yung-lo, Ming Emperor, 89
Yunnan-fu, fall of, 37
Yunnan province, 34, 36, 38, 53, 85

Zungars, warfare with, xiv–xv;
    see also Galdan

A NOTE ABOUT THE TYPE

The text of this book was set in a film version of Palatino, a type face designed by the noted German typographer Hermann Zapf. Named after Giovanbattista Palatino, a writing master of Renaissance Italy, Palatino was the first of Zapf's type faces to be introduced to America. The first designs for the face were made in 1948, and the fonts for the complete face were issued between 1950 and 1952. Like all Zapf-designed type faces, Palatino is beautifully balanced and exceedingly readable.

The book was composed by Black Dot, Inc., Crystal Lake, Illinois; printed and bound by The Book Press, Brattleboro, Vermont.

The map of China is by David Lindroth.

The book was designed by Earl Tidwell.

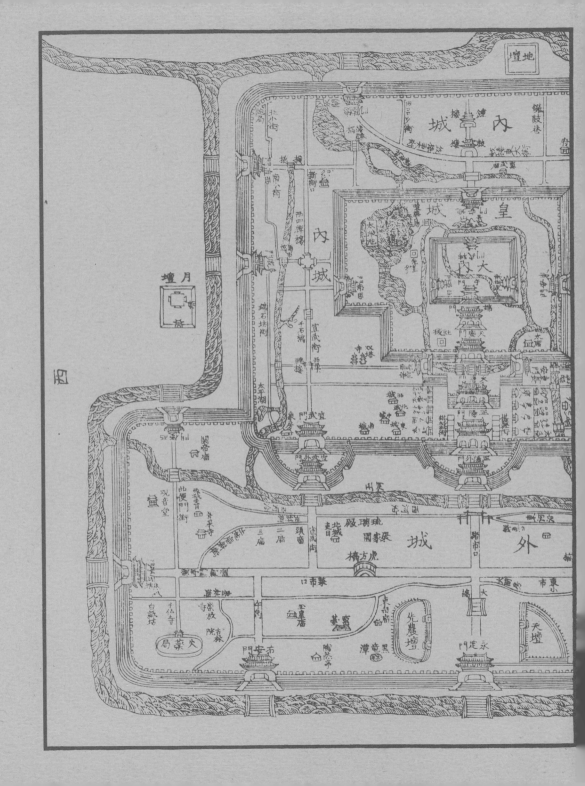